Controversies in Interreligious Dialogue and the Theology of Religions

D0873647

The Controversies in Contextual Theology Series
Series Editor: Lisa Isherwood, University of Winchester

Controversies in Interreligious Dialogue and the Theology of Religions

Paul Hedges

scm press

© Paul Hedges 2010

Published in 2010 by SCM Press
Editorial office
13–17 Long Lane,
London, EC1A 9PN, UK

SCM Press is an imprint of Hymns Ancient and Modern Ltd
(a registered charity)
13A Hellesdon Park Road
Norwich, NR6 5DR, UK
www.scm-canterburypress.co.uk

British Library Cataloguing in Publication data

A catalogue record for this book is available
from the British Library

978-0-334-04211-2

Originated by The Manila Typesetting Company
Printed and bound by
CPI Antony Rowe, Chippenham SN14 6LH

Contents

Acknowledgements and Dedications

There are almost too many people to thank for their contributions to this book, and my apologies to those who are forgotten or overlooked, it is not because your support has not been valued.

First, I would like to thank those people involved in bringing this book to publication. These include: Lisa Isherwood for asking me to contribute a volume to the 'Controversies' series (she asked me at first if there were any controversies in this field, I hope this text will convince her and others that not only are there controversies, but that they are very serious ones); SCM's commissioning editor, Natalie Watson, for her support, and above all patience, on this and other projects; the anonymous reviewers she passed my first draft chapter and outline to (the book has changed dramatically since then, but I hope in ways pleasing to all concerned); and the editing staff at SCM involved in this project.

Second, I would like to acknowledge Helene Egnell, for first raising my interest in writing Chapter 5 and for advice in shaping it, and also to my fellow 'malestream' theologians of religions whose provocative dismissal that the feminist angle had anything novel to contribute helped spark my interest in pursuing this (they will, of course, remain nameless). Also, to the various scholars who read my first draft of this chapter, both for advice and support and enabling me to write the chapter in the way I did. They include Helene, as well as Jeannine Hill Fletcher, Sigríður Guðmarsdóttir, Rose Drew, and Sara Singha.

Finally, to various individuals who have either helped shape me theologically and/or personally. My journey to writing this book has been inspired, in sympathy and conflict, with a range of theological voices too numerous to mention, as well as personal and family contacts. To all these people I acknowledge their support and, although almost clichéd to say so, they deserve the credit for what is good in this book, and I bear the blame for any remaining errors, inaccuracies and misjudgements. In particular I would like to dedicate this work to a number of these (who will hopefully know who they are): AR, PSL, JG, PB and ZZ.

Introduction

By their very nature the theology of religions and interreligious dialogue are embedded within controversy. The relationship between one religious tradition and another can never be easy, especially as issues of politics and culture (for example colonialism, imperialism, civilization, hegemony, gender) are bound up within all religions as part and parcel of their very being. Moreover, especially for Christianity, a history of warfare, crusades, persecution and colonialism provides the backdrop against which it needs to position itself in relation to the religious Other. All these are controversial issues, and many works address them. While fully acknowledging the importance of such issues, and their inevitability in any serious theology of religions or interreligious dialogue, I will focus primarily upon more theoretical and theological issues. For some, this may seem to avoid where the real controversy lies.[1] However, as Jeannine Hill Fletcher has argued, theory has 'material consequences'.[2] These consequences affect the way we see and regard the religious Other, and I will seek to show there can be real ethical issues at stake. The primary issue to be addressed is the impasse between, what may be variously termed, liberal and post-liberal, modern and post-modern, pluralist and particularist stances.[3] I

---

1 For instance, Gavin D'Costa has convincingly argued that in many supposedly 'religious' conflicts we find 'political' motives (*Christianity and World Religions: Disputed Questions in the Theology of Religions*, Chichester: Wiley-Blackwell, 2009, pp. 87–91), an argument made by many others.

2 Fletcher, Jeannine Hill, 2005, *Monopoly on Salvation: A Feminist Approach to Religious Pluralism*, London and New York: Continuum.

3 I will argue for nuanced usage of the terms 'exclusivisms', 'inclusivisms', 'pluralisms' and 'particularities' in Chapter 1. However, for those unfamiliar with

will seek, in exploring this, to show that we are drawn by the Christian heritage to a 'radical openness' to religious Others. This may be said, in some senses, to represent a pluralist stance; however, it is not a simple re-statement of a classical pluralist position, rather, through negotiating the impasse between pluralist and particularist camps, the need to respect both the plurality and particularity of religions will be argued. Indeed, I hope that I will articulate a 'pluralism' that many who may currently find themselves aligned with what are termed 'exclusivist', 'inclusivist' or other attitudes may find themselves in accord with. Fundamental to this will be a reconsideration of the notion of both 'religion' and 'religious identity' which makes traditional formulations of pluralist and particularist stand-points untenable. Moreover, I argue that the radical openness I associate with pluralisms is called for and necessitated by Christian tradition and scripture. It may even then be suggested that the approach I argue for, of radical openness, represents a biblical pluralist stance.

Positioning myself

I should begin by identifying myself and my agenda, as is the trend these days.[4] This book is written as an explicitly Christian theological work (although it is hoped those of other religions can learn from it). More particularly, it is written from, and to some extent for, a Western Christian audience, which reflects my own context. However, it does this in open conversation with a global theological context, and may be described as a work of Intercultural Theology (see Chapter 1). My own background is as a British Anglican (Episcopalian) theologian;

---

the terminology they may roughly be stated here as: the belief that Christianity alone is true and all others false (exclusivisms); the belief that Christianity is true but other religions may lead to it (inclusivisms); the belief that all religions may be true (pluralisms); the taking of a tradition-specific post-modern approach from a single tradition that regards all religions as integral wholes (particularities). These oversimplify the categories, but a fuller account is given in Chapter 1.

4 A rationale for identifying theological stances in academic work is found in Flood, Gavin, 1999, *Beyond Phenomenology: Rethinking the Study of Religion*, London: Cassell.

however, the work is decidedly ecumenical in tone and intention. Despite some contemporary moves towards strictly denominationally confessional theologies, I believe that our current situation demands and entails an ecumenical approach. Indeed, at places within the book I explicitly bring the ecumenical context into play. Theologically I have said something of my own position above. However, professionally I am both a theologian and a scholar of religious studies, which may well be reflected in this text. As regards the former, my interests are in modern and contemporary theologies as well as Christianity in its interreligious encounter, especially in the Asian context, although I also take an active interest in the Abrahamic problematic. I may also note that while I would not label myself as a liberation theologian, I have become aware that quite a few themes that could be described as 'liberationist' are evident in this work; however, I believe that this is something inherent in any responsible contemporary theology. Finally, my training is very much within the 'liberal' tradition; however, while deeply sympathetic to the liberal endeavour, I do not see a strict dividing line between 'liberal', 'post-liberal', 'conservative' and other theologies, and am critical of aspects of the 'liberal heritage'. Moreover, in contrast to some recent theologies that seek to disparage the whole liberal/Enlightenment movement as antithetical to Christianity, or a false turn in theology, I believe that we must, as David Tracy argues, move through it and not ignore it, while recognizing that it is part of the continuing and developing Christian heritage and so something all theologians should actively and seriously be in conversation with. As to the latter, I have interests in the history of religious encounter, especially between Christianity and other religions, as well as in methodological issues in defining and studying 'religion', and have a focus on the religions of South and East Asia.

Some key terms

It will be useful to explain my usage of some key terms:

First, 'religion', which is a central focus in this text. Readers should be aware that this is a deeply contested term, some scholars of religion even believing it should be done away with as a modernist myth (see Chapter 2). Its use should be read in the light of the definition and critique of it offered herein.

Second, 'Third World', which is another problematic term as the social and political context that gave rise to it has changed.[5] However, as used here it is primarily used to mean the non-Western world, which is the sense it has as a theological term in relation to EATWOT, the Ecumenical Association of Third World Theologians, which includes countries which are both deeply poor and non-industrialized (such as many African nations), as well as rich, industrialized nations (such as Japan), and some which stand between them (India may be an example of a country with depths of poverty, but also a rapidly growing industrial and economic base which makes it quite a 'rich' country). I may also occasionally use it in its general understanding of poor and non-industrialized countries, which should be clear in context. This is partly due to the problems of alternative terms, for instance: the distinction of the Global South and North ignores the fact that some poor countries are in the North; underdeveloped, or developing, has patronizing connotations and also suggests a Westernized industrial basis as a norm.

Third, 'globalization' is another recurring theme. There are many implications to this term; however, it is used herein with minimal connotations to refer simply to our increasingly interconnected world, in terms of cultures, media, etc., but space does not permit us to explore the various and contested ways the term is used and understood.[6]

---

5 See Parratt, John, 2004, 'Introduction', in Parratt, John (ed.), *An Introduction to Third World Theologies*, Cambridge: Cambridge University Press, pp. 1–15, p. 12.

6 The term 'globalization' and the factors within it are complex and disputed, I therefore refer the reader to the comprehensive discussion in Schreiter, Robert J., 2004, *The New Catholicity: Theology between the Global and the Local*, Maryknoll, NY: Orbis, pp. 1–27, the discussion in Boff, Leonardo, *Global Civilization: Challenges to Society and Christianity*, trans. Alexandre Guilherme, London: Equinox, pp. 21–9 and 83–93, and the discussion on the relation of local and global cultures in Featherstone, Mike, 1995, *Undoing Culture: Globalization, Postmodernism and Identity*, London: Sage Publications, pp. 86–101. Also useful to refer to are Banchoff, Thomas (ed.), 2008, *Religious Pluralism, Globalization*

Fourth, I use the term 'religious Others' with a capital 'O'. This is to reflect what I think should be a term of respect and recognition of their difference, which is necessitated by Christian hospitality (see Chapter 6).

Finally, I have throughout used traditional Christian terms in relation to other religions, which may, at times, seem to imply a distortion. For instance, as traditionally understood, terms such as 'God' and 'salvation' do not directly equate to the standpoints of many other religions. However, this is deliberately done to keep the work focused within the Christian theological tradition. We do address issues around this at various places.

Mapping the text

Finally, I will outline the structure of the book. As a text in SCM's 'Controversies in Contextual Theology' series, the book is intended both to be capable of use as a guide for those coming to the area, as well as a work that takes the debate forward and is something of a manifesto statement. As an introduction, it avoids simply working through the main positions and historical debates as recent good introductions already do this.[7] Instead, it takes the main impasse in the current debate and uses this as a focus to work through a number of live debates and controversies, as well as suggesting a way forward.

Chapter 1 begins by outlining the debate, discussing the nature of the theology of religions, but most particularly it discusses the basis of Christian theology and Christian identity. This will provide a basis for future discussions in the book. In the light of this it also discusses Intercultural Theology, which is the principal theological style of this work,

---

and World Politics, Oxford: Oxford University Press, and Held, David and McGrew, Anthony (eds), 2007, *Globalization Theory: Approaches and Controversies*, Cambridge: Polity Press.

7 For the most thorough and contemporary introduction to the field, see Hedges, Paul and Race, Alan (eds), 2008, *SCM Core Text Christian Approaches to Other Faiths*, London: SCM, and its accompanying reader, Hedges, Paul and Race, Alan (eds), 2009, *SCM Reader: Christian Approaches to Other Faiths*, London: SCM.

and which I argue is central for all theology today. This chapter intro-duces and argues for a nuanced application of the typological framework (exclusivisms–inclusivisms–pluralisms–particularities), as well as address-ing Comparative Theology, both of which, it is argued, are components and complements in the larger arena of the theology of religions, rather than being rivals or alternatives, as some suggest. I suggest that the typological terms can be usefully understood from the perspective of the motif terms: radical discontinuity, radical fulfilment, radical openness, and radical difference.

Chapter 2 turns to interreligious dialogue, which I suggest should not be seen in contrast to the theology of religions, rather both are different, but related, aspects of encounter with other religions. As well as discuss-ing the nature of, and some key controversies around, dialogue, such as its relation with mission, and power implications, a main focus of this chapter is on the term 'religion', which I will show is central to under-standing what dialogue may be about. Entering into debates in con-temporary religious studies scholarship, I argue that we cannot view 'religion' as a monolithic entity, but must see it as a fluid and cultural en-tity. Moreover, against its radical critics, I suggest it remains a useful and coherent term, especially in historical perspective. This ties in with our discussion of Christian identity in Chapter 1, as the nature of any essen-tialist religious identity is questioned by the nature of 'religion'. Also dis-cussed here are Scriptural Reasoning and multiple religious belonging.

Chapters 3, 4 and 5 look at three different contemporary theological styles, or movements, in the theology of religions, and to some extent interreligious dialogue, which are pluralisms, particularities and feminist approaches to religious Others. As one aspect of the impasse we are con-sidering can be said to lie between pluralist and particularist stances it is useful to address both of these, which are brought into conversation in Chapter 6. The relation of feminist theology to the debate is also im-portant so that is also considered, while specific debates also surround it. To consider each chapter alone, Chapter 3 introduces the pluralist hypothesis and subjects it to critical assessment. In particular, John Hick's pluralist hypothesis is briefly laid out, and the critique of it by other pluralist theories is considered. Philosophical challenges are also assessed. It is argued that, although far from proven, a pluralist stance is not referentially incoherent as some have charged. Finally, what may be seen as the most important critique is laid out, which is that it is not a Christian standpoint, in relation to which I argue that the radical openness pluralisms entail is actually implicit in the Jesus of the Gospels and in Christian belief. However, traditional forms of pluralisms suffer from problems raised in the critique of religion offered in Chapter 2, and also in relation to the notions of Christian identity discussed in Chapter 1. An outline and critique of the particularist stance is offered in Chapter 4. It discusses the main features of this popular post-liberal approach, and while suggesting we can learn from it, I nevertheless argue that it is fundamentally flawed. Chapter 5 asks what, if anything, is distinctive about a feminist theology of religions. It is argued that while no absolute differences exist between the way feminist (or female), and 'masculinist' (or male), theologies can be constructed, there are, nevertheless, a number of different emphases found in feminist approaches which contrast with mainstream (Western) theological norms, especially in the multiple interconnection of interstices between approaches. It should be noted that rather than seeking to isolate feminist theology as a discrete area that can be boxed off in one chapter, aspects of the feminist critique which are useful are discussed throughout the book. Moreover, as part of my argument in Chapter 1 I suggest the term 'contextual theology' is not useful; therefore, when encountered I do not normally explicitly label certain approaches as feminist, but include them as part of the general debate among varying theological styles.

Chapter 6 seeks to move beyond the impasse having assessed the various disputes, controversies and viewpoints outlined in the previous chapters. Although highly critical of the radical difference found in particularist approaches, I nevertheless believe that it holds insights which are sometimes neglected within other models, and seek to see what we can learn when taken alongside the radical openness of a pluralist stance. I suggest that we should espouse what I term a position of 'mutual fulfilment'. This is similar to positions adopted by others and walks a middle line between recognizing radical openness and the particularity of religions. However, by embracing the notions of theological/Christian identity as a contextually located notion, especially in the light of Intercultural Theology, and the critique of modernist concepts of 'religion' it advocates a stance that is both biblically and traditionally centred, while being theoretically nuanced and embracing the radical openness to the religious Other towards which, I firmly believe, Christians are called. We also discuss Comparative Theology and the notion of Interreligious Theology as ways to move forward.

Finally, Chapter 7 looks at some global ethical issues in the light of the discussion offered in the previous chapters. It seeks to show that the theoretical/theological stance we take is not simply neutral, but has very real consequences, and argues that the approach of radical openness, mediated between the poles of universalizing and particularizing tendencies is the most positive stance to deal with these.

Finally, it should be noted that I have tried to address a broad global dialogue, for instance discussing encounters with African religions, although I recognize that there may be a bias towards the religious encounters which reflect my primary interests. This is not intended as a bias towards their importance, but simply reflects the areas I know most about.

1

Negotiating Christian Identity
Exploring the Theology of Religions

Outline

We begin by setting out what many regard as the fundamental issue in the theology of religions today, the impasse between liberal and post-liberal approaches. This contrasts understandings of other religions under the tropes of, respectively, 'similarity' or 'difference'. In other terms, it explores the impasse between 'pluralisms' and 'particularities' (I will shortly outline the major terms in the area for those unfamiliar with them), or what I will term the Christian theological approaches to other religions of 'radical openness' and 'radical difference'. Negotiating a way beyond this impasse is the work of the whole book, but it begins here by discussing the nature of the theology of religions. This requires discussing theology more broadly, especially the basis of Christian theology and identity, as this is important in how we approach the theology of religions. We conclude by considering two theological schools, or styles, Intercultural Theology and Comparative Theology which, I suggest, are important for all contemporary theological thinking, and are intimately related to the theology of religions.[1]

The contemporary impasse

A number of recent works, many by highly respected scholars, suggest we have reached an impasse in understanding Christianity's encounter

---

1 A comparable case is argued in O'Leary, Joseph Stephen, 1996, *Religious Pluralism and Christian Truth*, Edinburgh: Edinburgh University Press, pp. x–xi.

with other religious traditions: the American Comparative Theologian James Fredericks believes the issue lies within pluralistic theologies; the German Anglican (formerly Roman Catholic) theologian Perry Schmidt-Leukel cites Klaus von Stosch's reference to an insoluble '*Grunddilemma*' related to Comparative Theology; the American theologian Hugh Nicholson suggests Kathryn Tanner's investigation of an impasse on Christian relations to culture applies to the theology of religions; and the British Roman Catholic Michael Barnes speaks of a 'current deadlock' in the area.[2] However, the nature of the impasse has been most clearly defined by the American Roman Catholic theologian Jeannine Hill Fletcher, who sees it as a division between liberals and post-liberals, or pluralist and particularist standpoints. Fletcher has suggested that the impasse is that between similarity and difference; pluralisms stress the commonality of all religions, and particularities their utter difference, or alterity. She believes that, within their own terms, we have no way of really encountering the religious Other or bridging the chasm that divides these views.[3] I agree that this impasse is the central controversy facing Christian versions of the theology of religions and interreligious dialogue today, and so seeking to resolve it will be the main thrust of this book, though along the way we will meet and discuss a number of other live debates. However, it may not be at once obvious why this debate is central, and so we will begin by sketching out some reasons for our focus.

First, it may seem the central question is between exclusivist and more open approaches to other religions. That is to say, the question is whether

---

2 See: Fredericks, James, 1999, *Faith Among Faiths: Christian Theology and Non-Christian Religions*, New York: Paulist Press, p. 8; Schmidt-Leukel, Perry, 2009, *Transformation by Integration: How Inter-faith Encounter Changes Christianity*, London: SCM, pp. 90–1, who cites Stosch, Klaus von, 2002, 'Komparative Theologie – ein Ausweg aus dem Grunddilemma jeder Theologie der Religionen?', *Zeitschrift für Katholische Theologie* 124, pp. 294–311, p. 294; Nicholson, Hugh, 2007, 'Comparative Theology After Liberalism', *Modern Theology* 23:2, pp. 229–51, pp. 241–2; and Barnes, Michael, 2002, *Theology and the Dialogue of Religions*, Cambridge: Cambridge University Press, p. 13.

3 Fletcher, Jeannine Hill, 2005, *Monopoly on Salvation: A Feminist Approach to Religious Pluralism*, London and New York: Continuum, Chapter 3, esp. pp. 63ff.

those outside Christianity can be saved at all, or even whether they can be approached with any degree of openness. Certainly, this debate has dominated what we now call the theology of religions and interreligious dialogue from its beginnings in the nineteenth century until well into the twentieth century.[4] However, I would suggest that this is no longer a real issue for at least six reasons (some of these will be explored further in due course):

1. All major churches in their institutional statements or interreligious activities (Roman Catholics, Orthodox, Anglicans, Lutheran, Methodists and others) have adopted a more open, generally inclusivist, approach, and as such the portrayal of other religions as demonic or utterly false (exclusivisms) has become a fringe belief.

2. Although many ordinary Christians are exclusivist, this is due, partly, to a misunderstanding or lack of awareness as to what their church teaches, combined with the fact that, for many, they have never really considered the issue. It is also not clear that this is the majority Christian point of view (see further on this below).

3. In an increasingly globalized world, with multireligious communities becoming more usual, it will become increasingly clear to Christians that exclusivisms are not a viable Christian option. Indeed, one reason for a growing appreciation of other religions among Christians over the last couple of centuries has been the fact that Christian missionaries, who left to bring 'light' to the

---

4 Barnes cites Jacques Dupuis' opinion that the theology of religions began 'as a "distinct theological *subject*"' in the 1970s (*Theology*, p. 7, citing Dupuis, Jacques, 1997, *Towards a Christian Theology of Religious Pluralism*, Maryknoll, NY: Orbis, pp. 2–3). This is certainly true of the Roman Catholic context, while as a distinct area it is a late arrival to theology, however, the issue becomes a serious area for discussion in the mainstream of Anglo-American theology from the nineteenth century, although its antecedents are much earlier, and traces from there a direct line to our present position.

'darkness' of non-Christian lands, ended up finding they had to respect and appreciate these other religions – a factor that counters the commonly assumed, or argued, position that religious tolerance was due primarily, or solely, to a growing liberal tolerance in society.[5]

4   Even among Christian groups where an exclusivist stance is considered normative, for instance Evangelicals, there is a shift towards either an inclusivist stance, a particularist stance, or else the term 'universalist' is brought into play, so we have 'exclusivist universalists' who, while arguing that all truth resides within Christianity, reject the traditional option of seeing all others condemned to hell, and instead argue that God can and will, because of his mercy, save all. Hence, the traditional 'hard-line' exclusivism is made into something that resembles a more inclusivist position.[6]

5   Related to this is Christian ecumenism, the opening of links between branches of Christianity. In the past, those outside one's own church were as much damned as those of other religions. Once it is accepted that there are various versions of Christian truth, and so not just one correct way of believing or being Christian (and therefore of being saved), a theological door is opened to other religions. In particular, when ecumenism extends to those who reject many traditional statements of faith, such as non-Chalcedon churches (I will discuss this below) or Quakers,

---

5 On this see Hedges, Paul, 2001, *Preparation and Fulfilment: A History and Study of Fulfilment Theology in Modern British Thought*, Bern: Peter Lang, especially the section on Monier Monier-Williams, and Chapters 4 and 7. The viewpoint that a liberalism in society is the cause is argued by D'Costa, Gavin, 2009, *Christianity and World Religions: Disputed Questions in the Theology of Religions*, Chichester: Wiley-Blackwell, Part II.

6 An example of this in popular Christian thinking of an evangelical inclination is the best-selling recent novel, *The Shack*, which seems to endorse the view that all will in due course be saved by an encounter with God's love (Young, Wm Paul, 2008, London: Hodder and Stoughton).

then a real theological door is opened to seeing truth and value further afield.[7]

6　Finally, I would suggest that exclusivisms are simply theologically untenable, flying in the face of basic Christian beliefs and values, and not being grounded in the words or attitude we see exemplified in Jesus. Indeed, we must understand that the kind of radical openness to other religious traditions I would argue for is not about watering down Christian commitment or accommodating the values of the world, but is inherent, even demanded, by a strong commitment to the Christian tradition itself (this is argued throughout, but see especially Chapter 3).

Second, some may say the argument is primarily one within the theology of religions not interreligious dialogue, and so centring it in a book on both of these skews the text. In reply, I would suggest that this implies a very narrow understanding of what the theology of religions is, a point addressed below; here, we may note that the two should be seen as intimately interrelated, the theology of religions is the *theoria* that informs the *praxis* of interreligious dialogue, while interreligious dialogue is the *praxis* that informs the *theoria* of the theology of religions. While they can be practised alone, one without the other is to some extent meaningless, even impossible – a point that should become clear as we proceed. With that said, this impasse, while primarily theological, affects the way we engage in dialogue; if we are informed by a particular thought world of what other religions are it will affect how we seek to engage them.

Third, my focus on theory may seem to neglect what, for many, is the most important aspect of interreligious encounter which is action, the involvement either in joint activism in such areas as ecology and social justice, or the interpersonal communication that is so essential to building

---

7　This connection is made in Panikkar, Raimon, 2002, 'On Christian Identity: Who is a Christian?', in Cornille, Catherine (ed.), *Many Mansions? Multiple Religious Belonging and Christian Identity*, Maryknoll, NY: Orbis, pp. 121–44, p. 125. Wesley Ariarajah has also discussed the relation of ecumenism to relations with other religions.

cohesion and understanding between communities and individuals. I accept this charge in part, but with the provision that different tasks are necessary in the broader framework of interreligious encounter – *praxis* and *theoria* should inform each other. If this work emphasizes one, it is not to exclude the latter. We will, though, not neglect ethical concerns (see especially Chapter 7).

Fourth, the impasse is not just in the theology of religions, but, arguably, the major contemporary division in (at least, academic) theology. On the one hand there are modernists or liberals, on the other postliberals (related to but not directly comparable to post-modernists, many of whom are seen as 'liberals').[8] The split is not a tidy or neat one as people will draw it in different places. Others may transcend these general boundaries. However, I hope that while only offering a sketch with broad brush strokes the distinction I offer here will at least be recognized in the following rough portrait. Liberal theologians believe theology is in a new era after the Enlightenment, which is seen as a positive influence which has allowed us to shake off the shackles of tradition and authoritarian dogma. In this situation all old doctrines and organizations are questionable and must be judged using the methods of historical criticism, contemporary understanding, reason and morality. Examples of liberal theologians include John Hick, Paul Badham, Karl Rahner, Rosemary Radford Ruether, Paul Tillich, Jacques Dupuis, etc. Post-liberal theologians believe theology must reject the Enlightenment

---

8 On such issues see: Vanhoozer, Kevin (ed.), 2003, *The Cambridge Companion to Postmodern Theology*, Cambridge: Cambridge University Press; Griffin, David Ray, Beardslee, William A., Holland, Joe, 1989, *Varieties of Postmodern Theology*, New York: SUNY Press; Hyman, Gavin, 2001, *The Predicament of Postmodern Theology: Radical Orthodoxy or Nihilist Textualism*, London: Westminster John Knox Press; and Hedges, Paul, 2010 (forthcoming), 'Is John Milbank's Radical Orthodoxy a Form of Liberal Theology? A Rhetorical Counter', *Heythrop Journal* 15:5. pp. 795–818. I might suggest that we could see the contrast exemplified by Modernist Theology and Radical Orthodoxy: see, respectively, Badham, Paul, 1998, *The Contemporary Challenge of Modernist Theology*, Cardiff: University of Wales Press, and Milbank, John, Pickstock, Catherine and Ward, Graham (eds), 2000, *Radical Orthodoxy: A New Theology*, London: Routledge.

heritage and 'free' itself from the shackles of historical criticism to look upon its own internal integrity as the source of its self-understanding. Christianity is seen as a narrative that must be accepted upon its own terms, therefore doctrines formed within this context are considered non-negotiable. Examples of post-liberal theologians include George Lindbeck, John Milbank, Gavin D'Costa, Alister McGrath, Stanley Hauerwas, Kevin Vanhoozer, etc. Within the theology of religions, liberal theology would be seen as marked by generous 'inclusivist' and 'pluralist' approaches, while post-liberal theology takes a 'particularist' approach.[9] Liberal theology suggests Christianity has much in common with other religions, and can learn and adapt ideas from them. Post-liberal theology would suggest that Christianity and other religions are divergent paradigms and that little can be learned from them – the Christian narrative has its own internal integrity, other religions have theirs, so mixing would be illegitimate syncretism, even impossible. These brief portraits are clearly too crude to do justice to the individual expressions that exist, and bring together a number of different, even conflicting, stances among a range of traditions on each side. Nevertheless, I believe it is a picture that mirrors an actual situation; for those who know the situation it can stand as a rough map into which they can envisage the subtleties and contours, while it will provide a guide for those unfamiliar with the territory.

The theology of religions

What is the theology of religions?

At one level, this is a sub-branch of the larger realm of Christian systematic theology which deals with the superstructure of Christian faith

---

9 On the particularist approach as a post-modern theological style, see Hedges, Paul, 2008, 'Particularities: Tradition-Specific Post-modern Perspectives', in Hedges, Paul and Race, Alan (eds), *SCM Core Text Christian Approaches to Other Faiths*, London: SCM, pp. 112–35, pp. 112–17.

in terms of doctrine and belief. The relation to other religions is part of this. However, just as one may specialize in any other area of theology, one can also practise the theology of religions without a grand systematic theology. At its most basic level, it involves constructing an interpretation of how Christianity relates to other religions, what the nature of these other religions is, and what may happen to followers of other religions soteriologically (to do with salvation). This may involve an exploration of other religions, or it may happen from what are seen as internal Christian tenets. The latter, or 'traditional', approach (traditional in the West, elsewhere Christians have lived alongside religious diversity) must be called into question, for reasons discussed below. In terms of discussing religious Others, the theology of religions is sometimes seen simply as related to the typological framework and the soteriology of religious Others, but this is far too limiting a definition. It would be like claiming that the philosophy of religion is limited solely to arguing for or against the existence of God. Two issues in particular need to be addressed. First, the enterprise known as Comparative Theology is seen by some as an alternative to the theology of religions. While discussed below, it is important to note here that this 'tradition' is part of the broader work of relating Christianity to other religions, so it is, like the typology, part of the larger body of the theology of religions.[10] Second, the theology of religions is not, as sometimes seen, a fringe interest within Christian theology, but something central to its very essence. While many theologians consciously seek to work within the context of their own tradition alone (true of post-liberals, evangelicals, and also many liberals), various factors make this untenable. These factors include: the intercultural nature of Christian theology; a nuanced understanding of Christian identity;

---

10 Two recent works are excellent examples of the theology of religions debating much larger concerns than soteriology and the typology, one 'liberal' the other 'post-liberal'. They are, respectively, Schmidt-Leukel, *Transformation* and D'Costa, *Christianity*. The former addresses syncretism, multiple religious belonging and other matters, the latter addresses the nature of 'religion', and religions within the public square.

and, the growing awareness of globalization in our pluralist world.[11] These are all issues to be discussed below.

Typological terms

The typology consists of a framework of options that describe, or frame, the debates. It consists of the 'classical typology' of exclusivisms, inclusvisms and pluralisms and, increasingly, the category of particularities.[12] Since being introduced by Alan Race the classical typology has had both its supporters and detractors; indeed, increasingly it seems fashionable in theology to disavow it. However, it remains very widely used even by detractors (which perhaps demonstrates its usefulness and applicability). I would argue that when used and understood appropriately it is a useful tool in the theology of religions. Before going on to describe the typology, and my understanding of it, it is useful to address some common criticisms. As there are a number of recent

---

11 The term 'globalization' and the factors within it are complex and disputed. I therefore refer the reader to the comprehensive discussion in Schreiter, Robert J., 2004, *The New Catholicity: Theology between the Global and the Local*, Maryknoll, NY: Orbis, pp. 1–27, the discussion in Boff, Leonardo, 2005, *Global Civilization: Challenges to Society and Christianity*, trans. Alexandre Guilherme, London: Equinox, pp. 21–9 and pp. 83–93, and the discussion on the relation of local and global cultures in Featherstone, Mike, 1995, *Undoing Culture: Globalization, Postmodernism and Identity*, London: Sage Publications, pp. 86–101. Also useful to refer to are Banchoff, Thomas (ed.), 2008, *Religious Pluralism, Globalization and World Politics*, Oxford: Oxford University Press, Held, David and McGrew, Anthony (eds), 2007, *Globalization Theory: Approaches and Controversies*, Cambridge: Polity Press.

12 For an overview of recent debates see Hedges, Paul, 2008, 'A Reflection on Typologies: Negotiating a Fast-Moving Discussion', in Hedges and Race (eds), *SCM Core Text Christian Approaches*, pp. 17–33. The fourfold usage was, I believe, first found in two works produced independently and both published in 2002: Knitter, Paul F., 2002, *Introducing Theologies of Religions*, Maryknoll, NY: Orbis; and Hedges, Paul, 2002, 'The Inter-Relationship of Religions: A Critical Examination of the Concept of Particularity', *World Faiths Encounter*, July, pp. 3–13. Knitter and Hedges, though, differ in where they draw the boundaries of the fourth category, a matter raised below.

defences of the typology, I will just outline some significant arguments and responses to them:[13]

1   It oversimplifies the possibilities.
2   Not everyone fits neatly inside the categories.
3   The terms are polemical.
4   They do not represent an accurate classification.

These arguments are not decisive against the typology and can be met by the following points:

1   The typology does not claim to say everything that can be said, but to offer some broad parameters. It is, moreover, particularly notable that those who reject the typology either create their own threefold schema, which tends to be remarkably similar, or else often use it because it provides much clarity for framing the discussion.

2   Race's original exposition of the typology readily admitted the way people didn't neatly fit the categories. As such this critique is more aimed against simplistic misunderstandings or solidified reifications of the typology than the typology itself.

3   Each term can have both positive and negative connotations, while many exclusivists happily accept the term. Also, the terms do clearly have a descriptive usage aside from any supposed rhetorical function.

4   One major critique is that by framing the discussion in soteriological form it misdirects our attention and creates a set of terms that best suit a Christian perspective that may not fit other religions. (Another critique of this type, that pluralism is actually

---

13 For two notable recent defences of the typology, see Hedges, 'Reflection' and Schmidt-Leukel, Perry, 2005, 'Exclusivism, Inclusivism, Pluralism: The Tripolar Typology – Clarified and Reaffirmed', in Knitter, Paul F. (ed.), *The Myth of Religious Superiority: A Multifaith Exploration*, Maryknoll, NY: Orbis, pp. 13–27. The following is largely a summary of the arguments found in these two works.

a form of inclusivism or pluralism, is addressed in Chapter 3.) However, the typology was intended to describe, and clarify, a range of Christian perspectives that did explain the relation to other religions in a soteriological way. As such, the critique by shooting the messenger is missing its target. However, Schmidt-Leukel has argued that salvation is, at least from the Christian standpoint, the bottom line and so makes a suitable place to ground a discussion. I think he has a good point, that this question must, at some level, be addressed. However, I recognize that for others it does not form a useful grounding for dialogue, and may stifle the discussion or not reflect the 'personal and social' level.[14]

Taking the above into consideration, to suggest that the typology can be a viable tool requires that it is appropriately understood and employed. Therefore against Schmidt-Leukel's proposal of it as a logically compressive philosophical category based on soteriological options,[15] I would argue that:

> the typology should be seen as descriptive (it tells us what positions have been taken, not what the positions should be), heuristic (it gives guidelines to help understand the complexity of ideas and their relationships), multivalent (each category is not a single approach, but a spectrum of related approaches), and permeable (people may express ideas that spill over several of the categories), rather than as prescriptive, normative, defining, and closed.[16]

In short, the typology is a tool to help us make sense of the range of options that have been presented. The main danger comes when we reify (caricature?) the typology, and suggest that the terms either tell us

---

14 See, for instance, King, Ursula, 1998, 'Feminism: The Missing Dimension in the Dialogue of Religions', in May, John D'Arcy (ed.), *Pluralism and the Religions: The Theological and Political Dimensions*, London, Cassell, pp. 40–55, p. 46.

15 See Schmidt-Leukel, 'Exclusivism', and Hedges, 'Reflection', pp. 23–4.

16 Hedges, 'Reflection', p. 27.

all we need to know about any one person's theology (as we will see there are many types of inclusivist, exclusivist, etc. – hence the use of inclusivisms, exclusivisms, etc.), or else see it as something to direct the encounter with those of other religions. Moreover, I think it can be usefully deployed to describe tendencies. This is how Fletcher employs it discussing the recent Roman Catholic document *Dominus Iesus*, which although she notes it propounds an inclusivist theology, nevertheless has an exclusivist air: 'For example, when the Congregation for the Doctrine of the Faith issued the document *Dominus Iesus*, the argument was not exclusivistic, but the tone of the document often tended to be.'[17] It should also be mentioned that, as a descriptive tool, it is justifiable to add a new category, 'particularities', as this represents a theological style that has mainly developed since the classical typology was first proposed.

I will therefore now offer a definition of each of the terms within the typology: exclusivisms, inclusivisms, pluralisms and particularities. We should note that while different people define these terms in different ways, however, even where different terms are used (for example Knitter terms them, respectively, 'the replacement model', 'the fulfilment model', 'the mutuality model', 'the acceptance model') the definitions tend to be very similar.[18]

Exclusivisms: Stated most plainly, exclusivisms are the range of beliefs that say only Christianity leads to salvation and that, generally, anyone who adheres to a different religion must therefore be going to damnation. It is a simple 'in' or 'out' option, the logic and internal coherence of

---

17 Fletcher, *Monopoly*, p. 54.

18 See Knitter, *Introducing*. Knitter does, though, include Comparative Theology in his acceptance model alongside what I term particularities, a position I consider unsuitable as its advocates tend to take a stance very different from most particularists. Moreover, as will be noted below, the stance of most proponents of Comparative Theology tends to be either pluralist or inclusivist inclined, with a particularist-style approach being deeply problematic for it. It should also be noted that D'Costa has recently redefined 'exclusivism' to make his own recent inclusivist-particularist theology fit this label. However, the rhetorical nature of his own self-labelling alongside the fact that his theology is inclusivist according to most other characterizations, as well as essentially particularist in character, should not lead us to modify the mainstream usage (see D'Costa, *Christian*, Chapter 1).

which has been set forth by a number of proponents.[19] It is not a mono-lithic entity, however, and variations exist within it. Principally, these exist between two options which we can term '*extra ecclesia nulla salus*' and 'by no other name'. The former is a classical statement that 'outside the Church there is no salvation', propagated by the Roman Catholic Church at various times, though far from universally. Essentially, it sees the boundaries of exclusivity as being set by institutional belonging to the right church (not that all within it are saved of course). The latter is a more Protestant version, which sees salvation as coming through acceptance of Jesus as a personal saviour – entry therefore being by belief rather than belonging (though, for many, such belief constitutes *the* Church). For some, this would require a full adherence to what is seen as the principal tenets of Christian orthodoxy, generally as laid down as Chalcedon orthodoxy.[20] In some traditions an experiential dimension, the sense of being saved, is deemed necessary, indeed, some Pentecostal traditions suggest that without proof of charismatic gifts (primarily speaking in tongues) one is outside the borders of salvation.[21]

Another variation concerns the nature of other religions. For some, they are Satanic perversions, perverse systems of deceit to keep people from true faith – indeed, some have even suggested that the reason why similarities to Christianity exist is because the Devil has made approximations to Christianity to make it harder to convert people. For others, they are simply systems of human folly, imaginations of the mind. As

---

19 One of the best recent expositions of this is Strange, Daniel, 2008, 'Exclusivisms: "Indeed Their Rock is Not like Our Rock"', in Hedges and Race (eds), *SCM Core Text Christian Approaches*, pp. 36–62. See also his selected readings in 2009, 'Exclusivisms', Hedges, Paul and Race, Alan (eds), *SCM Reader: Christian Approaches to Other Faiths*, London: SCM, pp. 5–21.

20 But for many Protestants today defined primarily through the 'fundamentals', that is belief in the Virgin Birth, miracles, substitution atonement, etc.

21 However, some Pentecostals adopt a more inclusivist approach; see for instance, Yong, Amos, 2005, 'A P(new)matological Paradigm for Christian Mission in a Religiously Plural World', *Missiology: An International Review* 33.2, pp. 175–91; this is reproduced in Cheetham, David, 2009, 'Exclusivisms', in Hedge and Race (eds), *SCM Reader: Christian Approaches to Other Faiths*, pp. 22–40, pp. 33–40.

such, they may be depraved systems because of man's innate sinfulness; such a position we may say characterizes Karl Barth's Neo-orthodox discourse, who sees all religion as humanity's flight from God for its own self-serving.[22] For others, humanity is seeking God, but cannot find him, and so we may find things which are noble and worthy within other religions. Barth, though, never spent much time considering the relationship of Christianity to other religions, and so it was the Dutch missiologist Hendrik Kraemer who took the Neo-orthodox worldview into the context of the Christian theology of religions, outlining what he termed 'discontinuity'. This, of course, was very much a reaction to the term 'fulfilment' (see inclusivisms below). Rather than seeing links between 'religions', Kraemer believed that a vast gulf ('discontinuity') separated 'revelation' and other religious traditions.[23]

Some exclusivist thinking propounds what is termed 'universalism'. This term refers to the notion that there will be a universal salvation, that is that all people will finally be saved. Although this may seem anathema to the tenets of exclusivism (indeed, many exclusivist-style thinkers would insist it is), it is claimed that although salvation only comes from God through Jesus, because of God's great mercy all will be saved and so, on the Day of Judgement, all will be given a choice to repent and it is hoped that all shall.[24]

Three points are useful to conclude. First, it is hopefully clear why the term 'exclusivisms' rather than 'exclusivism' is used as the generic marker, because a vast number of forms of this type exist. Second, although many (including ordinary Christian believers) feel that this is

22 On Barth see Strange, 2008, 'Exclusivisms', pp. 43–4.

23 See Kraemer, Hendrick, 1947 [1937], *The Christian Message in a Non-Christian World*, London: Edinburgh House Press, and for a discussion, see Hedges, *Preparation*, pp. 369–74. In later years, though, Kraemer came to see the need for dialogue (1960, *World Cultures and World Religions: The Coming Dialogue*, London: Lutterworth Press).

24 See Cheetham, David, 2008, 'Inclusivisms: Honouring Faithfulness and Openness', in Hedges and Race (eds), *SCM Core Text Christian Aproaches*, pp. 63–84, pp. 63 and 75–6. See also, Cameron, Nigel M. de S. (ed.), 1992, *Universalism and the Doctrine of Hell*, Carlisle: Paternoster Press and Grand Rapids, MI: Baker Book House.

the traditional/normative/most committed Christian approach to other religions, it is far from being the mainstay of Christian thought, with other approaches being exhibited from biblical times onwards (see below). Third, although many see it as a normative or authentic Christian approach, my own interpretation is that exclusivisms are the most 'un-Christian' (see Chapter 3).

Inclusivisms: According to Race, inclusivisms are a 'yes' and 'no' to other religions.[25] The most basic definition is that inclusivisms hold only one religion as ultimately true, and therefore leading to salvation, but other religions lead people towards this true religion. Usefully, Knitter characterizes the inclusivist approach as the fulfilment paradigm. That is to say, other religions are 'fulfilled' (find their completion and perfection) in Christianity; there is even a form of inclusivism explicitly called 'fulfilment theology'. The Bible, especially the New Testament, forms the bedrock of inclusivisms. For instance, Jesus' response to the centurion who has faith in him, 'I tell you not even in Israel have I found faith such as this' (Luke 7.9, see also Matt. 8.10), is seen as indicative that religious truth is not closed within confessional or traditionally drawn religious boundaries. Again, Saint Paul's preaching on the Areopagus in Athens where he argues that the altar to 'an unknown God' is a sign that the religion of the Greeks pointed towards Christianity, so he can suggest that they unknowingly acknowledge Jesus already (Acts 17.23). Of great importance has been the prologue of John's Gospel which tells us 'That was the true Light, which lights *all* men', interpreted as meaning that Jesus, as the Logos, is already inside, and hence capable of directing *all* people (John 1.4–9). Moreover, throughout Christian history we find inclusivisms being propounded by such figures as Justin Martyr, Augustine of Hippo, Thomas Aquinas, Martin Luther, Matteo Ricci, Charles Wesley, and others.[26] As such, claims that exclusivisms are somehow the mainstream Christian approach are wildly exaggerated.

---

25 Race, Alan, 1983, *Christians and Religious Pluralism*, London: SCM, p. 38.

26 On biblical and historical precedents, see Cheetham, 2008, 'Inclusivisms', pp. 64–9.

As with exclusivisms, inclusivisms also come in a whole range of forms. Here a few brief examples will suffice.[27] During the nineteenth century, as knowledge of other religions was starting to spread across the Christian West and missionaries went out to convert, it became apparent that what were seen as common features could be found among different religions. What could account for this? Two main nineteenth-century trends existed, one a paradigm of decay, the other a paradigm of growth. For biblical literalists, God had originally revealed himself to mankind in Adam and so a primitive revelation existed which would have been known to the people at the time of the building of the Tower of Babel. In this well-known biblical story (Gen. 11), humanity tries to build a tower up to heaven and God destroys it, scattering the people and dividing them by nation and language. Apart from explaining human diversity, the story was also employed to explain how what were seen as great truths and moral insights could exist in the religions of a fallen and sinful human race: all good elements were remnants of the original revelation. This marked the paradigm of decline. For others, however, the good in other religions could not simply be explained in this way, and some propounded a Logos Theology. Following John's Gospel and the Church Fathers, they taught that God has always and everywhere been active in witness to people. This was the paradigm of growth. Alongside this, fulfilment theology could also be seen to operate in several ways. According to John Nicol Farquhar, fulfilment theology's most famous proponent, the good elements of Hinduism would lead somebody, if correctly understood, to Christianity. Thus, for instance, he proposed that avatars showed that people longed for a God made incarnate that

---

27 For a longer introduction to inclusivisms see Cheetham, 2008, 'Inclusivisms'. For more detailed readings on the issues: on fulfilment theology generally see Hedges, *Preparation*, especially pp. 15–43; on the paradigms of growth and decay and Logos Theology, see Hedges, *Preparation*, pp. 35–7 (further references to Logos Theology appear throughout), and specifically on Logos Theology, see Cheetham, 'Inclusivisms', pp. 66ff.; on Farquhar, sometimes mistakenly seen as the 'founder' of fulfilment theology, see Hedges, *Preparation*, Chapter 7; on Rahner see Cheetham, 2008, 'Inclusivisms', pp. 69–74, and Kilby, Karen, 2007 [1997], *The SPCK Introduction to Karl Rahner*, London: SPCK, pp. 30–7.

they could relate to, the idols and numerous shrines showed people longed for a God who would always be close and intimate to them, while various rituals showed the innate human consciousness of sin and the need for purification. All this, Farquhar argued, was found in its most perfect form in Christianity, hence a Hindu who truly understood his or her faith, he believed, would become a Christian. Such a change, however, for him needed their commitment to Hinduism to come to an end, a process that can be seen as the death of Hinduism, so that a new Christian faith can be reborn. Here we are bordering on exclusivist territory, for nothing in the old faith in and of itself leads somebody into Christianity. By way of contrast, perhaps the best known inclusivist theologian of the late twentieth century, Karl Rahner, believes that it is the very structure of the other religion itself which leads the person to the position of salvation. That is, by being a good Hindu, Muslim, Sikh, etc., someone can die in that faith having advanced themselves sufficiently to be, it may be said, worthy of salvation; indeed, while he sees a post-mortem encounter with Christ as necessary, this seems almost a formality. His theology has given rise to the term 'anonymous Christians'. We can therefore see a great gulf between different types of inclusivist-style thinking. Both Farquhar and Rahner see non-Christian religions as leading towards Christianity and Jesus, but the understanding of the salvific potency of these other religions varies greatly.

To end this description several points are in order. First, inclusivisms can now be described as the mainstream Christian option, all major denominations (Roman Catholic Church, the Orthodox Churches, the Anglican Church, the Lutheran Church, and many Calvinist Churches) either endorse or issue statements suggesting it (although their approach to particular groups may vary greatly).[28] Second, I find it problematic to define inclusivisms in strictly soteriological terms because of the type

---

28 See Hick, John, 2005, 'The Next Step Beyond Dialogue', in Knitter, Paul F. (ed.), *The Myth of Religious Superiority: A Multifaith Exploration*, Maryknoll, NY: Orbis, pp. 3-12, p. 7. On current Lutheran thought, see Peters, Ted, 2007, 'Re-framing the Question: How Can We Construct a Theology of Religions?', *Dialog: A Journal of Theology* 46:4, pp. 322-34.

of disparity between Farquhar and Rahner; both believe Hinduism can lead to Christianity, yet, for Rahner, this is built into the essence of Hinduism, for Farquhar it is not, so we may say for Rahner other religions have salvific potency, for Farquhar they do not. Perhaps, Farquhar adopts an exclusivist form of fulfilment theology. It is, perhaps, though, better to leave this as one of our permeable membranes between the categories. Third, one problem that may have occurred to the reader is the rather patronizing stance of inclusivisms, which places other religions in a good position (in contrast with exclusivisms) yet at the same time placing them in a much inferior position in relation to one's own religion. This is increasingly recognized as a problem in engaging with other religions (leading many to the particularist stance, see below). Fourth, while it is difficult for institutional churches to take the step, many theologians find themselves on a tricky border between the inclusivist stance and the pluralist stance, seeing their Christian faith and the guidance of the Holy Spirit leading this way.

Pluralisms: Of all the approaches, pluralisms see the least barriers between religions. Simply stated, pluralisms are the range of approaches that suggest there is more than one legitimate way to what can broadly be termed 'salvation'. It is a much more recent option than either the exclusivist or inclusivist approach, yet it too may look to both Bible and tradition for support.[29] As a major option, though, it developed in the twentieth century, but finding a significant place in Christian theology only into the second half of that century. As with the other options, it exists in a variety of forms, and this is usefully explored, in one aspect, by Schmidt-Leukel's comprehensive breakdown of the paths that can be seen leading into pluralistic options: interfaith dialogue; comparative religion; systematic theology and the philosophy of religions; 'perennial philosophy'; ecumenism and missiology; liberation theologies; interreligious feminisms.[30] As this suggests, Christian thinkers have embraced

---

29 See Schmidt-Leukel, Perry, 2008, 'Pluralisms: How to Appreciate Religious Diversity Theologically', in Hedges and Race (eds), *SCM Core Text Christian Approaches*, pp. 85–110, pp. 88–9. See also Chapter 3.

30 Schmidt-Leukel, 'Pluralisms', pp. 89–92.

pluralisms for a variety of reasons, resulting in a variety of different understandings.

As Chapter 3 explores the pluralist hypothesis, I will not expound upon issues here, but will conclude with a few notable points. First, pluralisms did not come into existence principally as a 'soft' option for not very committed Christians; the main pluralist thinkers either came to it from strong exclusivisms, or else are Christian theologians, priests and devotees, who take their faith very seriously. Pluralisms have therefore been forged as lived Christian theologies in response to tradition, the Bible and Jesus' teaching; we must therefore take pluralisms as a form of serious and committed Christian theology. Second, while some pluralisms challenge fundamental tenets of what many see as basic Christianity they do this in an attempt to present a viable Christian approach. Third, when most people refer to 'pluralism' they are thinking of John Hick's exposition, which is not the only form (I develop this point further in Chapter 3).

Particularities: This final option has only recently entered the arena, and is harder to offer a simple description for than the others. Nevertheless, if we try, it can be spoken of as indeterminacy in relation to other religions, alongside a commitment to speaking from, for and of one tradition.[31] While, like pluralisms, we dedicate a later chapter to particularities, we must still try to provide some description here. To this end I offer the following six-point definition:

1) each faith is unique, alterity[32] is stressed over similarity, as seemingly common elements in religious experience or doctrine are

---

31 The sense of indeterminacy is seen as defining by Knitter (*Introducing*, p. 218), while Gavin D'Costa has defined his own approach as tradition-specific (see 2000, *The Meeting of Religions and the Trinity*, Edinburgh: T. & T. Clark).

32 'A word frequently used in post-modern discourse, which may simply be read as difference – though various post-modern writers might give various sublayers of meaning to it' (Hedges, Paul, 2008, 'Particularities: Tradition-Specific Post-modern Perspectives', in Hedges and Race (eds), *SCM Core Text Christian Approaches*, pp. 112–35, p. 132 fn. 5).

regarded as superficial; 2) it is only possible to speak from a specific tradition, there can be no pluralistic interpretation; 3) the Holy Spirit may be at work in other faiths, requiring them to be regarded with respect and dignity; 4) no salvific potency resides in other faiths, though they are somehow involved in God's plans for humanity but in ways we cannot know; 5) particularity is based in a post-modern and post-liberal worldview; 6) the orthodox doctrines of Trinity and Christ are grounding points from which to approach other faiths.[33]

These six points are fundamental to most, if not all, particularist positions. We may briefly unpack each one:

1 Against Hick's pluralism, particularities deny the possibility that there can be a common core to all religions.

2 This is taken further, in the belief that you can only speak from within your own tradition. Theology can only be tradition-specific; different religions represent closed and incommensurate cultural islands.

3 Having said this, many particularists think God may be at work in other religions, but unlike inclusivists who tend to claim that they know where the Spirit operates in other religions, they leave this as maybe, somehow, and unknown (some, though, are more exclusivistic).

4 Being based in a Christian context, they believe that tradition tells them that salvation is only possible through their path, yet they feel that respect for other religions is necessary: they may hold value in God's plans, but we cannot know how. It engages other religions in indeterminacy and without pigeonholing, saying 'you are fulfilled by my faith' or 'your faith is equal to mine'.

5 The particularist approach comes primarily from the post-liberal theological tradition, and, in its contemporary formulation,

---

33 Hedges, 'Particularities', pp. 112–13.

George Lindbeck can be seen as the first main proponent. Post-modern philosophical currents include respect for the Other, the belief that knowledge (or claims to knowledge) involve acts of power against the Other, the motif of indeterminacy. In this regard, pluralisms (and to some extent inclusivisms) are seen as bound up with a liberal theology that is based in a modernist Enlightenment worldview, which delights in meta-narratives (the construction of grand overarching theories to explain everything) – Hick's pluralism is often cited as a prime example. Against this, particularity is seen as a turn to local stories, or *petite narratives*, which speak only from and within one tradition with no grander claims.

6   Seeing itself as true to the Christian tradition, particularists adopt what they would term an orthodox theological position, with Christ and the Trinity centred. Particularists have claimed that the Trinity allows greater fidelity to their tradition and greater openness and respect for others.

To conclude with some key points. First, despite the growing appeal of particularities, related to the rise of post-liberal style theologies, they hold some fundamental weaknesses, even gross errors of approach (see Chapter 4). Second, another reason, it seems, for its increased popularity is the problematic we noted with inclusivism, of its apparent disrespect for other religions, whereas particularities claim the high moral ground of absolute respect for the religious Other, claiming to be more respectful than pluralisms too. As such, especially in documents and statements on other religions, theologians and churches wish to distance themselves from an old-style inclusivist stance and, instead, to advocate a particularist indeterminacy. However, its talk of respect underlies a deeper disrespect and sidelining of other religions (see Chapter 4).[34]

Summation: I have suggested that these four standpoints can best be understood heuristically, and representing styles of approach.

---

34 I discuss this specific point in Hedges, 'Particularities', pp. 127–30.

I would also suggest that each is marked by a different motif, exclusivist approaches typify 'discontinuity', inclusivist approaches typify 'fulfilment', pluralist approaches typify 'openness', and particularist approaches typify 'difference'.[35] Indeed, we may say they represent *radical discontinuity*, *radical fulfilment*, *radical openness* and *radical difference*. I have suggested above, and as will become clear below, that radical discontinuity to other faiths is untenable. Radical fulfilment, whereby the whole of the 'other' is absorbed into the known, has become increasingly seen as problematic (an issue we can't fully develop here).[36] We therefore find an impasse between the options of 'radical openness' (seen by many as requiring letting go of Christian integrity) and 'radical difference' (which we will see is an untenable conception). However, before we can suggest a resolution of this impasse, to which work most of the remainder of this book is devoted, we need to consider a number of themes.

Theology and theologies

To understand the impasse we must consider a key term: 'theology'. If the primary impasse we are considering is theological in nature then we must consider, even if not resolve, the tension within theological systems. A good place to begin would be the grounding of a theology of religions. To this end, I will consider some foundations for theology within this

---

35 It will be noted that my terms 'discontinuity' and 'fulfilment' stem from the traditional language of exclusivist and inclusivist stances. Discontinuity is Kraemer's term, and fulfilment theology is the term associated with Farquhar and others. My terminology may also, therefore, overcome the problem that some see with the classical typology of having polemical terminology.

36 On this, see D'Costa, *Christianity*, pp. 19–25, also Hedges, *Preparation*, pp. 374–92. In brief, though, it is increasingly recognized that one thought world cannot fulfil, encapsulate and represent another without distortion and misrepresentation. I would suggest that the problems seen as inherent in inclusivisms have led to many wishing to align themselves with what is seen as the less patronizing and imperialist particularist approach.

context, which will lead us on to consider Christian identity. After that, I will consider some particular theological styles that helpfully address the issues we are dealing with.

What is the basis of Christian theology?

Let us take three works as examples of what is taken to be the essential core of Christian theology, with specific reference to the theology of religions. The first two are Timothy Tennent's *Christianity at the Religious Roundtable: Evangelicalism in Conversation with Hinduism, Buddhism, and Islam*, and D'Costa's *Christianity and World Religions: Disputed Questions in the Theology of Religions*.[37] Tennent is an American Evangelical theologian, while D'Costa is a British-based Roman Catholic of a post-liberal stamp; as such the two are from quite different branches of the Church. According to Tennent, despite reading many books on interreligious dialogue he has 'enjoyed precious few of them', the reason being that they do not present the Christianity 'average Christians' or 'the apostles' would recognize; indeed some he suggests have 'abandoned the historic faith'.[38] Meanwhile D'Costa sets out four tenets he thinks essential for anything to be called a Christian theology of religions: 'salvation comes from [1] the triune God [2] through faith in Christ and [3] his church, [4] through the power of the Spirit', which form what he calls theology's 'controlling beliefs' which he thinks must be tradition-specific.[39] Our third work is Rowan Williams' 'The Finality of Christ'; he is the Anglican Archbishop of Canterbury, a world-renowned theologian with post-liberal tendencies.[40] Williams seeks to cast Jesus as the 'Meaning of meaning' within a Christian narrative and asks: 'What is it that

---

37 Tennent, Timothy C., 2002, *Christianity at the Religious Roundtable: Evangelicalism in Conversation with Hinduism, Buddhism and Islam*, Grand Rapids, MI: Baker Academic, and D'Costa, *Christianity*.

38 Tennent, *Christianity*, pp. 9–10.

39 D'Costa, *Christianity*, p. 37, and pp. 3–4.

40 Williams, Rowan, 2000, 'The Finality of Christ' in *On Christian Theology*, Oxford: Blackwell, pp. 93–106.

makes religious meanings self-enclosed, self-referential, self-justifying?'[41]
This brief synopsis certainly does not do full justice to all the subtleties
and nuances of these writers, especially Williams whose exposition is in
many ways the most sophisticated of them all, and whose thought we
will use to draw us on further (beyond even his own standpoint). Now,
despite much disagreement between these figures in theological style,
I think each would concur with what is said by the others in the comments cited above (although Williams, and even more so Tennent, would
undoubtedly differ from D'Costa as to what is meant by 'the Church').
However, the danger with their approach is that it can highlight one interpretation of being Christian or one interpretation of Christianity: the
historical faith (Tennent) as a set of fixed propositions (D'Costa) and
as a self-enclosed and self-justifying whole (Williams). As such, their
standpoint could be seen to accord with a traditional statement of Christian self-belief and identity summed up in what is called the Vincentian
Canon, that Christian belief is 'that which has been believed everywhere,
always, and by all people [*quod ubique, quod semper, quod ab omnibus
creditum est*].'[42] Yet, Christian theology is not simply about accepting a
unitary and undisputed tradition. Indeed, the problem with the Vincentian Canon approach is that, as is colloquially said, 'it just ain't so'. Rather,
Christianity and Christian theology is about the creation and recreation
of identity, and the basic elements and their constitution reflect not some
pure essential Christianity but rather the theological identity claimed.[43]

41 Williams, 'Finality', p. 93 (citing Corenelius Ernst, 1979, *Multiple Echo.
Explorations in Theology*, ed. Fergus Kerr and Timothy Radcliffe, London), and
pp. 97–8.

42 Vincent of Lérins, 2009 [434], *Commonitorium II*, cited in McGrath,
Alister (ed.), *The Christian Theology Reader*, 3rd edn, Oxford: Blackwell, p. 90.

43 See: Tanner, Kathryn, 1997, *Theories of Culture: A New Agenda for The-
ology*, Minneapolis, MN: Fortress Press, p. 124; Panikkar, 'Christian'; Jeanrond,
Werner G., 2002, 'Belonging or Identity? Christian Faith in a Multi-Religious
World', in Cornille (ed.), *Many*, pp. 106–20, pp. 115–19; and Gruber, Judith, 2009,
'Christian Identities: An Imaginative and Innovative Quest for Heterogeneous
Unity', *ESharp*, 14, pp. 23–8, available from, http://www.gla.ac.uk/departments/
esharp/issues/issue14winter2009imaginationandinnovation/, accessed 25 May 2010.

On the construction of theological identities[44]

We turn back to Williams for our starting point, whose exposition deals with the problems of seeing religions as closed units of identity (on this see Chapters 2, 5 and 6). He speaks of the Jewish context of early Christianity as 'an episode in the political life of a religious people . . . whose corporate life involves some shared myths, texts and rituals, not necessarily consistent or systematized, but loosely intermeshed, sometimes in conflict', while the early Jesus movement called for a 'more intense unity or consistency'; yet, and here he invokes the American feminist theologian Rosemary Radford Ruether, 'there is nothing formally unique' about this.[45] What Williams means is that Jewish and Christian identities of this period were bound together, and that Christian identity emerged from this context. Indeed, both Rabbinic Judaism and Christianity emerge as twin sisters from the death throes of their mother, Second Temple Judaism. The story we therefore find is of the emergence of Christianity out of its Jewish heritage to claim a separate identity.[46] However, this is not a simple story, and here we can only sketch an outline.[47]

For nearly 2,000 years, Jesus' Jewish identity has been lost, with Christians identifying him as the first Christian, with his disciples as members

---

44 While the term 'identity' may be a modern construct it is useful. This is suggested by Judith Lieu in her analysis of early Christian identity (2006, *Christian Identity in the Jewish and Graeco-Roman World*, Oxford: Oxford University Press, pp. 11–17), while John Tomlinson suggests that, in a cultural sense, we have an '*essentially* modern "organizational" category', but that: 'All historical cultures . . . have constructed meaning via localized practices of collective symbolization, although not constructing identity in institutionally regulated ways' (2007, 'Globalization and Cultural Analysis', in Held, David and McGrew, Anthony (eds), *Globalization Theory: Approaches and Controversies*, Cambridge: Polity Press, pp. 148–68, pp. 160 and 162.)

45 Williams, 'Finality', p. 96.

46 For more on this see Lieu, *Christian*, pp. 2ff., and Miller, Ron, 2008, 'Judaism: Siblings in Strife', in Hedges and Race (eds), *SCM Core Text Christian Approaches*, pp. 176–90, esp. pp. 176–81. Some of these early struggles are of course clearly documented in the Acts of the Apostles.

47 I therefore refer the reader to the works cited for an evidential basis to the claims made.

of a ready-made new 'religion'. Instead what we need to consider is a rather different story, and we should spend a little time unpacking this before considering some implications for theology. In this story we will see that Christianity does not just appear as a 'given' and ready-made system, but is produced in interaction with the cultures and religions that surround it and, moreover, is made through acts of political power, violence and oppression.

In considering the formation of early Christian identity, Judith Lieu starts with the question of when it became possible for Christians to clearly self-identify in a way that would make sense both to themselves and those around them:

> In about the middle of the second century CE, Polycarp, bishop of the church in Smyrna, seals his own death warrant by acknowledging that he is a Christian . . . Perhaps the most striking thing about this scene is the way that the terms 'Christian' (χριστιανός) and 'Christianity' (χριστιανισμός) are used without comment or explanation. At what point in the century or more since the death of Jesus and the earliest preaching of his followers did this become possible?[48]

At some point we see Christian identity forming; however, it is clear that this was neither uniform nor monolithic. We know that Jesus and his earliest followers were all Jewish: they observed the Passover and other Jewish festivals and engaged in debate with other Jewish authorities about how to interpret the Law. This knowledge gives us different options:

1   We may ask why Jesus' Jewishness was lost (his Jewishness is a fact which, according to Jaroslav Pelikan, was obvious in the first century, an embarrassment in the second, and obscure by the third[49]). Factors include: the Jewish rebellions, which led the

48 Lieu, *Christian*, p. 1.
49 Pelikan, Jaroslav, 1999, *Jesus Through the Centuries: His Place in the History of Culture*, New Haven, CT: Yale University Press.

emerging Christian community to try and distance itself from Jewish identity;[50] the decision to take the Israelite story to all; and, the increasingly Gentile constituency making Jewish concepts less familiar.

2   We must read the New Testament canon in its Jewish context. Mark's Gospel, for instance, suggests an adoptionist Christology, that is to say that Jesus was simply human and given a special commission by God with his baptism.[51] The words it begins with, 'The Gospel of Jesus Christ the Son of God' (Mark 1.1), must also be understood as they would have been by a first-century Jew. The term 'Son (or Daughter) of God' could apply to any or all Jewish people (as God's chosen people), even to any person (as part of God's creation), but had a tradition of being used to single out some particular people, such as kings and prophets (as those especially close to God in some way).[52] Hence, no divinity is claimed for Jesus in this Gospel, rather the Christian tradition has come to read this from within its early context of a Greco-Roman world where God-men were a familiar feature. (We address issues of Christology in Chapter 3.)

---

50 See Kwame, Bediako, 1992, *Theology and Identity: The Impact of Culture Upon Christian Thought in the Second Century and in Modern Africa*, Oxford: Regnum, p. 34, who references Simon Marcel, 1964, *Verus Israel, Etude sur les relations entre Chrétiens et Juifs dans l'empire romain (135–425 AD)*, Paris: E. de Boccard, pp. 87ff. Kwame, following Simon, sees the AD 70 and 135 as of crucial importance; however, the continued interaction and cross-penetration we know went on much longer. For a very judicious study of this, see Fredriksen, Paula, 2007, 'What "Parting of the Ways"?: Jews, Gentiles and the Ancient Mediterranean City', in Becker, Adam H. and Reed, Annette Yoshiko (eds), *The Ways that Never Parted: Jews and Christians in Late Antiquity and the Early Middle Ages*, Minneapolis, MN: Fortress Press, pp. 35–63.

51 See, Bart Ehrman, 1993, *The Orthodox Corruption of Scripture*, Oxford: Oxford University Press.

52 See, Ehrman, Bart D., 2004, *The New Testament: A Historical Introduction to the Early Christian Writings*, Oxford: Oxford University Press, p. 77, Box 5.5.

3   We must be aware of how Christianity became implicitly bound
     up in a history of anti-Semitism.[53] Whatever way we take this, it
     is important that we realize that 'Christianity' and 'Judaism' do
     not refer to two clearly distinct religions, or religious identities,
     rather they are intertwined and enmeshed traditions, with a per-
     meable border where each, especially in the early centuries AD,
     crossed into the other.

To continue our story, we find the creeds, the statements of required
Christian belief, being written in a particular context, and one which
emerges long after Christianity and Judaism appear to have become primarily separate religious streams. Their context is significantly related to
power struggles within the early church.[54] Indeed, historical investigation
of the origins of Christianity shows that the development of Christian
belief and theology is not a clear outworking of a set of universally agreed
beliefs against a backdrop of various heretical groups rising up to challenge this. Rather, a plurality of beliefs existed side by side, and those who
were considered orthodox by one generation could, after the creedal formulations of a later generation, become heretics. What has been described
as the archetypal heresy, Arianism, is a good case. Rather than being
founded by Arius, we simply find a priest refusing to accept what he deems
a novel and unwarranted innovation, Jesus' co-existence with God. Victory, as it is commonly seen, was accorded to those who sided with the
imperial might of Rome, for it was first Constantine and then later Roman
emperors who endorsed the winning side and enforced 'orthodoxy'.
    In this period, we see Christianity moving from a position of being an
'outsider' religion, marginal to the empire, to being one bound up and

---

53 The classic statement of Christianity's anti-Semitic problematic is Ruether,
Rosemary Radford, 1974, *Faith or Fratricide: The Theological Roots of Anti-
Semitism*, New York: Seabury Press. For a recent overview see Miller, 'Judaism',
pp. 176–83. See also the selections in Race, Alan, 2009, 'Judaism', in Hedges and
Race (eds), *SCM Reader: Christian Approaches*.

54 An excellent overview of these issues can be found in Woodhead, Linda,
2004, *An Introduction to Christianity*, Cambridge: Cambridge University Press,
pp. 33–51.

central to its very fabric, a move which parallels a growing exclusion and oppressive tendency in the Church; under Constantine and the patronage of other emperors the very nature of Christianity is transformed.[55] Tied to this is a fact most people conveniently overlook if they wish to see the decisions of Nicaea and Chalcedon as normative of Christian belief: Constantine was almost certainly not a Christian (something which has been very persuasively argued, although dismissed as not within the worldview they wish to inhabit by many traditionalist Christian scholars), and that even if he was his interest in enforcing orthodoxy was not purity of belief, but peace and stability within his empire. The belief system created and enforced by imperial Christianity, often referred to as Chalcedon orthodoxy, taken as a touchstone of correct belief by many, can be briefly stated as the idea that Jesus is both fully God and fully man, and ties him into divinity as the second member of the Trinity, alongside the Father and the Holy Spirit. However, there were, and still are, many Christians who do not accept the Council of Chalcedon as authoritative. Indeed, the record of the controversies tells us that the

---

55 See Kwok Pui-lan's discussion of how Christian exclusion and empire are related (Kwok, Pui-lan, 2007, 'Theology and Social Theory', in Kwok, Pui-lan, Rieger, Joerg, and Compier, Don H. (eds), *Empire and the Christian Tradition: New Readings of Classical Theologians*, Minneapolis, MN: Fortress Press, pp. 15–29, pp. 8–10. Wesley Ariarajah makes similar points (Ariarajah, Wesley S., 2005, 'Power, Politics and Plurality: The Struggles of the World Council of Churches to Deal with Religious Plurality', in Knitter, Paul F. (ed.), *The Myth of Religious Superiority: A Multifaith Exploration*, Maryknoll, NY: Orbis, pp. 176–93, p. 178). Another important work is Kee, Alistair, 1982, *Constantine Versus Christ: The Triumph of Ideology*, London: SCM, which while subject to some hostile criticism and summary dismissal, has never been adequately countered. For a recent theological meditation that powerfully addresses issues of power in empire and Church see also Rieger, Joerg, 2007, *Christ and Empire: From Paul to Postcolonial Times*, Minneapolis, MN: Fortress Press, esp. Chapter 2. While my references are mainly to scholars who may be termed 'liberal' or 'liberationist' by some, the imperial Christianity that emerged under Constantine, and the fact of changing doctrines are widely accepted even in quite conservative mainstream Church history, and was even recognized by such early Church Fathers as Gregory of Nazianzus (see Hall, Stuart G., 1991, *Doctrine and Practice in the Early Church*, London: SPCK, pp. 237–41, see also, related to discussions below, pp. 118–20).

beliefs we call 'orthodox' were not the most widespread in their day, but what seemed to be, in part at least, innovative and minority standpoints, but associated with those who knew how to use power.[56] Quite simply, the reification of Christianity as found in Tennent, D'Costa and Williams neglects the actuality of Christianity's historical construction over centuries. It is not a single tradition stretching back to Jesus and the disciples but a composite product of centuries, with what is taken as 'orthodox' belief being a production of many factors. We shall explore some of these below, though space does not allow elaboration (the references are given for those who wish to delve further into the issues I simply outline).

There are many and complex factors behind the eventual emergence of these creeds, as well as other beliefs and practices, and the acceptance or rejection of them by different churches. In part it was related to cultural systems; Christianity changed as it spread, syncretistically 'absorbing "Hellenistic, Germanic, Celtic, Syrian 'influences'"'.[57] This speaks of the multivalent nature of the early church. This has important implications for what we consider to be normative. In the centuries following the Council of Chalcedon, those Christians who had rejected its decisions were forced beyond the borders of the Roman Empire, they spread through Germany, parts of Africa, but also through Syria and beyond, reaching India and China. By the seventh century the numbers of non-Chalcedon Christians vastly outnumbered, in both geographical spread and population, the Chalcedonian Christians. Various factors, however, saw their decline, notably the spread of Islam. Meanwhile, the rise of European colonialism from the early modern period onwards, first Spanish and Portuguese then (primarily) British and Dutch, saw Chalcedonian Christianity spreading and

---

56 Two of the great heroes of 'orthodoxy', Athanasius and Cyril of Alexandria, used mob violence and intimidation to silence their enemies, and were bound up with power struggles in the Church (see Miles, Margaret M., 2005, *The Word Made Flesh: A History of Christian Thought*, pp. 90 and 107 (respectively)). On the creation and usage of the terms 'heresy' and 'orthodoxy' in relation to this context, see Ayres, Lewis, 2006, *Nicaea and its Legacy: An Approach to Fourth-Century Trinitarian Theology*, Oxford: Oxford University Press, pp. 78–84.

57 Schmidt-Leukel, *Transformation*, p. 85, quoting Schreiter, Robert, 1986, *Constructing Local Theologies*, Maryknoll, NY: Orbis, p. 151.

becoming dominant. As such, we can see that our perception of what is normative Christianity is not shaped by issues of truth or biblical belief, but rather by political power, especially the rise and fall of empires, that saw different versions of Christianity spread at different places in different times. Twelve hundred years ago a 'heretical' form of Christianity was the global norm, today, with a legacy of European colonialism (which has evolved into American dominance), another form of Christianity is the global norm. The Vincentian Canon approach is looking very shaky indeed!

We can only briefly note some of the changes and syncretisms of early Christianity. Entry into Germanic lands saw high levels of group solidarity help replace the anomie of early Christianity as an 'outsider' religion, thus shaping the Christianity of community and national unity which became typical. The belief in substitution atonement, that Christ died to appease a justly angry God, arose from the social context of Northern European feudalism, a view utterly at odds with the early Jewish and Hellenic concepts of cosmic battles between angels and devils, or the conquest of Hades, while different interpretations of the cross also arise. Again, Jesus' understanding as a deity used motifs from other Mystery Religions of the Roman Empire (including images of Orpheus and Mithras to represent Christ, seen in the earliest Christian art and the pastoral scene of Jesus' birth in the Gospel accounts), and Greek philosophy (for instance, the Neoplatonism that shaped Augustine's thought and the creeds). The Christianity that was formed as 'normative' in Christology by the fifth century was, from its earliest days, a syncretistic religion.[58]

---

58 On Germanization, see Schreiter, *New*, pp. 66–7. Other effects of this Germanization were the rise of Christmas to rival Easter, the differentiation of clergy and people (on this see also Kwok, 'Theology', p. 13), and the attitude of prayer with hands folded, a vassal before their Lord, replacing the older *orans* position (raised and open arms). On atonement, see Schreiter, *New*, p. 80. We discuss some further cases and issues in Chapters 2 and 6. For some aspects of Christianity's relation to the Mystery Religions of the early Christian era see Rahner, Hugo, 1963 [1957], *Greek Myths and Christian Mystery*, trans. Brian Battershaw, London: Burns and Oates, and Herman, A. L., 2004, *Influences: How Ancient Hinduism Dramatically Changed Early Christianity*, Stevens Point, WI: Cornerstone Press – the former is probably overly conservative, the latter overly enthusiastic about the extent of influences. On Neoplatonic influences as well as Mystery

As Fletcher has observed a 'cultural [or religious] purity is an oxymoron'.[59] There is no 'pure' Christianity unmixed with other cultural elements. Indeed, to claim a Christian identity is to do so in relation to other identities: 'Self-definition does not occur in a vacuum, but in a world already defined',[60] as such it will be shaped in the encounter. As the German-American Roman Catholic Intercultural Theologian Robert Schreiter has observed, contexts are always hybridized, and cultural or religious purity has only ever been an aspiration, never an actualized ideal of purity.[61] It may be objected that my arguments are not applicable to Christianity and that, perhaps, the monotheism inherited from Judaism, or the idealist Neoplatonism that shapes Christian orthodoxy, provides the basis for a distinct and unitary identity or for its practice of exclusion and defining 'orthodoxy' and 'heresy'.[62] Hence, some may believe that by surrounding early Christianity by claims of syncretism and political power play as the sources of its creation I have actually gone astray. It could be argued that I have produced one version of history when: 'Making history is a way of producing identity insofar as it produces a relation between what has supposedly occurred in the past and the present state of affairs.'[63] However, this applies as much to the traditional story as to that outlined here; if I have presented a particular reading,

Religions, see McGinn, Bernhard, 1991, *The Foundations of Mysticism: Origins to the Fifth Century*, London: SCM, Chapter 2.

59 Fletcher, Jeannine Hill, 2008, 'Religious Pluralism in an Era of Globalization: The Making of Modern Religious Identity', *Theological Studies*, 69, pp. 394–411, p. 405; she is quoting Appiah, Kwame Anthony, 2006, *Cosmopolitanism: Ethics in a World of Strangers*, New York, NY: Norton, p. 113.

60 Friedman, Jonathan, 1994, *Cultural Identity and Global Process*, London: Sage Publications, p. 117.

61 Schreiter, *New*, p. 27. The issues Schreiter, as a Catholic theologian, raises creates problems for defining a normative Catholic Christian identity, but is an issue which younger Catholic theologians are seeking to deal with (for instance, Gruber, Judith, 2009, 'Culture as a Theological Challenge', paper delivered at the European Society for Intercultural Theology and Interreligious Studies, Salzburg).

62 On questions around the Bible as an identity foundation over and against others, see Kwok, *Postcolonial*, pp. 11ff.

63 Friedman, *Cultural*, p. 118.

then so do Tennent, D'Costa and Williams. However, I would argue for the case outlined here as more compelling because other stories make claims for a purity of ideas or spiritual values which unnaturally divorces 'religion' from culture, politics and society, and neglects the forces that shaped Christianity (for more on this, see Chapter 2).[64] The categories of 'heresy' and 'orthodoxy' were not painted by those most inspired by the Holy Spirit, but by those who had the political power to tell the story. What is clear is only that we have no 'immediate access to an originary identity or "received" tradition'.[65] Let me, however, make one thing clear. I am not arguing that we must abandon the beliefs that are held dear by many, rather to recognize that they are just one telling of the Christian story. Moreover, the approach that defines the accounts of Tennent, D'Costa and Williams as 'orthodox' and others as 'unorthodox' is not unproblematic – given the various traditions represented by this trio we must realize that at certain points within their tradition's histories (and from some perspectives occupied by those allied to their positions today) each would have been classed by the two others as heretics or unbelievers!

To move our story to contemporary issues, the traditional expression of Chalcedon orthodoxy has been questioned in many contexts. In Latin America, liberation theologians have questioned the usefulness of a Trinity expressed as a mathematical puzzle, while Christians in India have suggested the Greek philosophical wording of the creeds needs a re-expression in the terms of Indian philosophy to make it come alive to them.[66] Should we reject such moves, or accept them as part of the continuing story of Christian identity-making in context? To reject them

---

64 On the importance of understanding Jesus and Paul in relation to empire, see Rieger, *Christ*, Chapter 1.

65 Bhabha, Homi, 1994, *The Location of Culture*, London: Routledge, p. 2.

66 See: on Latin America, Boff, Leonardo, 1988, *Trinity and Society*, trans. Paul Burns, Maryknoll, NY: Orbis, pp. 156ff.; on India, Collins, Paul M., 2007, *Christian Inculturation in India*, Aldershot: Ashgate, esp. pp. 77–89 on the Ashram movement. For some, the kind of cultural fusion suggested by the latter particularly implies not just inculturation but adaptation to another religious system; we address this in Chapter 2.

is, arguably, to be guilty of what has been called the 'sins of cultural and religious chauvinism'.[67]

Within this context, to claim Christian identity is not to automatically be part of a 'self-enclosed, self-referential, self-justifying' system of meanings united around things implied within the Vincentian Canon. We know that there was an 'orthodox' Jewish-Christian aspect to the early Jesus movement that knew nothing of Jesus' divinity or the Trinity. This is not to say that this is the only way to read the texts, nor that it leads us to accept one Christological formula, nor that we can go back to an 'original' Christian set of beliefs. Indeed, recent ecumenical movements between the churches mean we must rethink some of the issues around heresy and orthodoxy, with reconciliation being a key feature.[68] Yet, the problems raised do not mean we must let go of all tradition, but that our acceptance of it must be rethought in relation to power agendas, and it must also not be taken as normative in an absolute sense. Christianity as a system is always formed in cultural contexts, never as a single universal 'God-given'.

In light of the above, I would argue that we should realize that there are a variety of ways of being Christian, and that Christian identity is far from simple or monolithic. Moreover, the boundaries we typically draw up are not so firm as we often believe; for instance, in the early centuries we have texts that have what we would now identify as having both 'Jewish' and 'Christian' elements, such that a clear dividing line between these two 'religions' is not as simple as supposed. Rather we have a variety of Christian identities emerging and conflicting over the ensuing centuries. Where we stand and how we define Christian orthodoxy or normalcy will depend in part upon which of these identities we follow. However, this is the nature of identity: to be in relationship to other identities. It can never be isolated, so that a concern often

---

67 Berling, Judith, 1997, *A Pilgrim in Chinese Culture: Negotiating Religious and Cultural Diversity*, Eugene, OR: Wipf and Stock, p. 24.

68 See Lyman, Rebecca, 2007, 'Athanasius of Alexandria', in Kwok, Compier and Rieger (eds), *Empire*, pp. 63–78, p. 76.

expressed is 'the uncertain crossing and invasion of identity'.[69] This applies as much to Christian identity as any other. So what does this have to say for contemporary Christian identity? I would suggest at least five things:

1   The type of monolithic Christian identity expressed by most confessions is a selective remembering of a certain history which 'hide[s] the complex origins' of the tradition.[70]

2   In remembering, or rediscovering, Christian identity as multivalent we need not let go of the baggage of the inherited tradition; however, we must allow for a variety of expressions of Christian truth or being.

3   Christianity has always been created in interaction with other creeds, systems of belief and religious identities, and so we must allow ourselves to retell the Christian story again, and in the act to recreate it as we engage the contemporary globalized world situation and forge a sense of what Christian identity may be in this context.

4   Identity is far from simple and never, or even primarily, individual, it relates us both to our communities and to those we see as others, while it is often given as much as claimed. Moreover, identity theorists such as Homi Bhabha have shown how it is never single but always multiple; we cannot simply say we are 'Christians' because to be a Christian involves being a type of Christian in a particular place, and this is then mediated through other factors, such as whether you are male or female (of course, in some churches gender excludes you a priori from certain forms of church activity), while social and ethnic factors

---

69 Young, Robert J. C., 1995, *Colonial Desire: Hybridity in Theory, Culture and Race*, London: Routledge, p. 3. He is speaking of literature, but we may take it that the worry extends to other spheres; this relates to the relationship of 'religion' and 'culture' which cannot be clearly distinguished – a matter discussed in Chapter 2.

70 Lieu, *Christian*, pp. 63–4.

also play into this network.[71] This means that far from seeking a single 'pure' Christian identity we should embrace a hybrid identity against the 'totalizing' identity that Christianity sometimes enforces.[72]

5   We may still seek to develop some criteria for Christian identity.[73] Indeed, Schreiter suggests that although the gospel changes with cultures, the message remains the same but with an 'indeterminate character', and so it may be said that it is neither true to paint Christian identity as totally arbitrary and relative, nor as utterly unitary and monolithic.[74]

Theological styles and the theology of religions

Intercultural Theology

Before discussing Intercultural Theology directly, it will be useful first to address the question of 'contextual theology'. Theology, as we have argued above, is always a contextualized affair, however, the term 'contextual' theology is often used to distinguish it from 'proper' theology and this must be addressed. Often, Third World theologies (theologies of Asia, Africa, Latin America, etc.) are classed as 'contextual theologies'. For instance, most textbooks of theology (at least in the Western world)

---

71 See Chapters 2 and 5 for more on this. However, here we may note that Kathryn Tanner's work also disputes a 'substantialist' notion of Christian identity (Tanner, *Theories*, pp. 93–119).

72 Fletcher, 'Religious Pluralism', p. 408. Indeed, the notion of hybridity is useful because simply in translation we see words crossing barriers, and can have different meanings (for a discussion related to this see the discussion on Bakhtin and the hybridity of language in Young, *Colonial*, pp. 20–1).

73 Schreiter, *New*, pp. 81–3.

74 Schreiter, *New*, pp. 71 and 79. Gruber also wrestles with the problems of defining unity, which she sees as centred upon scripture ('Christian Identities').

class Third World theologies in the peripheral sphere of 'contextual theologies'.[75]

This bracketing of Third World theologies as contextual implies, for most 'mainstream' (Anglo-American and European) theologians, that they are an optional add-on if one is interested, but not really essential to doing 'proper' theology.[76] Indeed, some have even argued for ignoring, or the illegitimacy of, non-classical (that is non-Western) theologies![77] The arrogant, imperialist nature of such an attitude may, one thinks, hardly need to be pointed out or criticized; however, the normative pattern of Western theology has become so ingrained that it needs to be highlighted and challenged. Such a patronizing and short-sighted view

---

75 To give some statistics from three leading textbooks, Alistair McGrath's *The Christian Theology Reader*, Colin Gunton, et al.'s *The Practice of Theology*, and David Ford's *The Modern Theologians*. They all contain less than half a dozen contributions on Third World theologies. The first edition (later ones have done little to change this particular imbalance) of McGrath had around 300 texts, of which 57 are twentieth century, but only 4 from the Third World. In Gunton, Third World theologies are classed as 'local theologies'. Finally, in Ford, European and American theologies get 20 chapters, all Third World theologies (Latin American, African and Asian theologies) get 4 chapters, while other subjects (for example evangelical and feminist theologies) get 13 chapters; meaning we have 33 'Western perspectives', yet only 4 'Third World perspectives' (of which half are written by people born as Westerners, and half work in a Western university). Given that the vast majority of Christians now live in the Third World this is simply shocking.

76 See Parratt, John, 2004, 'Introduction', in Parratt, John (ed.), *An Introduction to Third World Theologies*, Cambridge: Cambridge University Press, pp. 1–15, pp. 1–2.

77 This is implied in Williams, Stephen, 1997, 'The Trinity and "Other Religions"', in Vanhoozer, Kevin (ed.), *The Trinity in a Pluralistic Age: Theological Essays on Culture and Religion*, Cambridge: Eerdmans, pp. 26–40, who although noticing some contacts, suggests that on the whole other faiths are inadequate to express what Christianity stands for (see esp. pp. 35–6). The same adherence to established Western norms is also found in Radical Orthodoxy, especially as expressed by John Milbank (see Milbank, John, Ward, Graham and Catherine Pickstock, 1999, 'Introduction: Suspending the material: the turn of radical orthodoxy', in Milbank, Ward and Pickstock (eds), *Radical*, pp. 1–20; for a discussion around this see Hedges, 'John').

ignores both the reality of Christianity (most Christians today live in the Third World); and, from an intercultural and interreligious standpoint, neglects the very real encounter with other religious traditions that is happening across the globe and, indeed, has gone on for centuries – the Mar Thomas Churches of India have long ago adapted to their context, while the Christians who have lived under areas of Islamic influence for centuries have a living tradition of engagement and dialogue.[78] It is simply scandalous that these encounters and experiences are not drawn upon more broadly.

Today, theology must engage our global context, and this means at least three things. For one it means accepting a theology that engages with other Christianities from around the globe. Second, engaging with other religious traditions and their identities; something which has often been the case for Third World theologies. Third, realizing that all theology is 'contextual'. We must not be bound to a regional imperialism that accepts a Constantinian version of Christianity based in worldly power and oppression, and which offends against the earliest Christian message; something represented throughout history in counter narratives based in humility and solidarity with the oppressed.[79]

Also, our contemporary situation may need us to be aware of many other styles and contexts of theology which may include feminist, liberation, queer, relational, ecological, etc. Some may see these as foundational, while others would suggest that the construction of an orthodox

---

78 See Griffiths, Sidney H., 2008, *The Church in the Shadow of the Mosque: Christians and Muslims in the World of Islam*, Princeton: Princeton University Press.

79 On the Constantinian reversal in Christianity see esp. Kee, *Christ*, and Woodhead, *Introduction*; counter movements would include the monastic movement that developed while the rest of the Church absorbed the wealth and prestige Constantine offered, parts of the Franciscan vision, some groups of the radical, non-magisterial reformation, and can be found expressed in parts of the liberation theology perspective today. There is, though, another side to the interpretation of the creeds in relation to empire; see Rieger, Joerg, 2007, 'Christian Theology and Empires', in Kwok, Compier and Rieger (eds), *Empire*, pp. 1–13, pp. 9–10. For an outline of some different views on this period, see Lyman, 'Athanasius', pp. 64–5.

Christian theology of religions cannot begin here. However, once we understand that a range of identities composes who we are, it is easier to see how, for some at least, they will come into theology (see Chapters 2 and 5). Certainly, an attention to such theologies helps to radically destabilize the supposition that we can readily begin with some preset fixed and solid Christian identity or theology; rather the message that comes through from contemporary 'contextual' theologies is that 'any religious tradition is false which forces its adherents to define their faith and practice solely in terms of past forms'.[80] Rather, we must give attention to theologians such as the African Methodist theologian Mercy Amba Oduyoye whose work 'points to a postcolonial trajectory for a future history of Christian theology that is dialogical, uses narratives genres, respects all cultures, and addresses gender dynamics in complex ways'.[81]

The merging of cultures and meeting of religions is unavoidable in a world marked by globalization. Indeed, any notion of our separation from other cultures is sundered by the 'conscious mixing of traditions and crossing of boundaries [that] highlights the ways in which the rest, now so obviously visible in the West, have always been part of the West'.[82] This would lead us to Intercultural Theology, which, in many ways, is the principal theological mode throughout this work.

Intercultural theology can be understood in a number of different ways. For some, it is simply an updated term for missiology – that avoids the pejorative term 'mission' while being attentive to inculturation (making indigenous forms of Christianity in new contexts). However, it can be used with another sense, and this is how I see it here,

---

80 Ingram, Paul, 1997, 'Reflections on Buddhist-Christian Dailogue and the Liberation of Women', *Buddhist-Christian Studies*, 17, pp. 49–60, p. 56, cited in Egnell, Helene, 2006, *Other Voices: A Study of Christian Feminist Approaches to Religious Plurality East and West*, Uppsala: Studia Missionalia Svecana, p. 310, where he discusses what he has learned from feminist theology, notably Rita Gross and Paula Cooey.

81 Kwok, Pui-lan, 2007, 'Mercy Amba Oduyoye', in Kwok, Compier and Rieger (eds), *Empire*, pp. 471–86, p. 485.

82 Featherstone, *Undoing*, p. 11. This anticipates themes developed further in Chapters 2 and 6.

which is to do with the global context of theology today, along with the contextual nature of all theology. Certainly, as British-based German missiologist Werner Ustorf demonstrates, the term originates in missiological circles, but its attentiveness to religious plurality and the contextualized nature of theology can, I believe, give it a wider sense.[83] One of the best expressions of this is found in the work of the German Protestant theologian Volker Küster: 'Inter-cultural theology explores the inter-confessional, inter-cultural and inter-religious dimensions of the Christian faith. An interdisciplinary approach and the use of multimedia are significant.'[84]

The important notion here is that, as Frans Wijsen argues, all theology is 'contextual'.[85] It is not the case that we have a normative Chalcedon Western Christianity, and other approaches are somehow 'contextual' in relation to this; rather plurality is normative as suggested by Schreiter:

> The universal [Western] theologies . . . were in fact *universalizing* theologies; that is to say, they extended the results of their own reflections beyond their own contexts to other settings, usually without an awareness of the rootedness of their theologies within their own contexts.[86]

Both Wijsen and Schreiter warn us to be aware that in the past theological reflection took place within one framework, but the contextual nature of this was not recognized, rather (in many cases) white, European men made decisions about what was universally true for all based upon

---

83 Schmidt-Leukel understands the term as an updated version of missiology. For a solid account of the term's origin, usage and potential see Ustorf, Werner, 2008, 'The Cultural Origins of "Intercultural Theology"', *Mission Studies* 25, pp. 229–51. For an excellent overview of the inculturation initiative in various churches see Collins, *Christian*, Chapters 1 and 2.

84 Küster, Volker, 2005, 'The Project of an Intercultural Theology', *Swedish Missiological Themes* 93:3, pp. 417–32, p. 429.

85 Wijsen, Frans, 2005, 'Intercultural Theology and the Mission of the Church', available at, http://www.sedos.org/english/wijsen.htm, accessed 24 July 2009.

86 Schreiter, *New*, p. 2.

their own experience and reflection. This, as noted above, in relation to contextual theology, has implications for our context because we cannot deride the reflection of other nations and peoples as inadequate in relation to our own local theology (because that is what it is). This means we cannot favour any one theological style, or local theology (which includes 'normative orthodox Western' forms), over and above all others. Rather, all theologies must be in relationship, the 'inter' of intercultural. However, it is not a call for a single 'world theology', we must be attentive to the local needs, the continuing need for contextuality. What this means is that although recognizing our own local context, we must also create theology as global and ecumenical beings. Of course, local identity is not as monolithic as it was with the growth of multiculturalism, meaning that, today, identity is not as easily mapped to locality as it has been in the past.[87] This certainly has the advantage of helping us be aware that monolithic notions of identity as a culturally pure concept are untenable.[88]

For our purposes we should consider the experience of non-Western Christians, especially in Asia and parts of Africa because they live within a religiously plural world where Christianity is not the norm. To some extent this could be said to apply also to Latin America, and increasingly it is true of Europe and America; however, here the context is different. In India, as noted above, some have called for a Trinitarian formulation based in indigenous philosophical motifs. The claim is that fourth-century Mediterranean Greco-Roman Neoplatonic formulations simply have no meaning to Indians. We are giving them a definition of Trinity from a thought form utterly antithetical to their own. If the use of the term *sat-cit-ananda* (being-consciousness-bliss) forms a concept of Trinity that speaks to the heart of many Indians then we should recognize that just as our terms derive from Greek philosophy, these derive from Indic philosophy, and that each is just a localized expression of

---

87 See Morley, David, 2000, *Home Territories: Media, Mobility and Identity*, London and New York: Routledge, p. 10.

88 See also Schreiter's discussion of integrated and globalized concepts of culture, which relate both to identity and religion (*New*, pp. 47–58).

Christian belief.[89] To decry this as unorthodox is to insist upon the 'Latin captivity of the Church', to use a well-known phrase.[90] The experience of Thomas Christians in India for around two millennia shows that a faithful Christian witness can exist expressed in Indian terms (the attempts to Westernize this that were imposed by early European colonizers is a shameful period of church history), although we may, rightly, criticize some aspects of it, for instance its adoption of caste regulations. At the same time, we should recognize that aspects of our Western tradition are equally open to critique from perspectives that come from other parts of the world (see especially Chapters 6 and 7). Moreover, specifically with respect to relations with other religions, we will find that those Christians who have lived for centuries in areas dominated by another religion will have insights and a history of encounter and engagement from which we can usefully learn.[91]

An Intercultural Theology is one that recognizes the context of theology and seeks to address it. It is not, though, to suggest we universalize these experiences. It makes little more sense to suggest that we, as Westerners, adopt an Indic notion of Trinity, as to suggest that Indians, Africans, or anyone else should adopt ours. We need to be aware that our formulation is not universal; however, theologies must be in conversation to see what we can learn. This will be, as Küster says, between denominations, between cultures and between religions. This, in turn, will require an intercultural hermeneutics to suggest the process of how we relate between cultures.[92] This is a tricky business, for culture itself is

---

89 The use of this classical Sanskrit term as an indigenous expression of the Trinity was found in Indian converts in the nineteenth century and has been used by many since then; see Hedges, *Preparation*, and Aleaz, K. P., 2008, 'Pluralisms: We are No Longer "Frogs in the Well"', in Hedges and Race (eds), *SCM Core Text Christian Approaches*, pp. 212–33, pp. 216–17 and 223–4.

90 Boyd, R. H. S., 1974, *The Latin Captivity of the Church: The Cultural Context of the Gospel*, Cambridge: Cambridge University Press.

91 On the experience of Christians who have lived under Muslim rule in the Middle East with an eye to this very question, see Griffiths, *Church*.

92 On this see Schreiter, *New*, pp. 28–45. Wijsen ('Intercultural') notes that an intercultural hermeneutics is in the early stages of development.

not easily defined and is always 'contested, temporal and emergent' in its expression.[93] I do not wish to get bound up with here with hermeneutical questions, rather my aim, seeking to strive beyond the impasse, is to show that an intercultural and interreligious theology is both viable and necessary.

As we have seen, Intercultural Theology leads us to understand that all theology is 'contextual', that is created and related to its context, but also it destroys the category of 'contextual theology'. It tells us there is not one normative theology surrounded by a host of 'contextual' theologies, rather every theology is universal, that is to say, it speaks from some part of the human situation, and by doing this of necessity can speak to and inform all other parts. This is not the false 'universalizing' that Wijsen spoke of, that claims its insights are the only ones that apply to all. No one theology is absolute. Yet this is not to slide into relativism. As the anthropologist Clifford James has observed:

> Interpretive social scientists have recently come to view good ethnographies as 'true fictions,' but usually at the cost of weakening the oxymoron, reducing it to the banal claim that all truths are constructed. The essays collected here keep the oxymoron sharp.[94]

My intention here, like Clifford's essayists, is to maintain the oxymoron of 'Partial Truths' (the subtitle to his chapter) as a theological proposition. To claim we posses the whole gospel in all its possible interpretations and understandings is not only arrogance, but also, perhaps, the proper use for the term 'heresy'. However, we need not, and must not, thereby say that our theology is only local; it has truths, universal truths, but these may (will) need to be translated if we are to reveal them to others. Moreover, we must also realize that it may not be the best or only

---

93 Clifford, James, 1986, 'Introduction: Partial Truths', in Clifford, James and Marcus, George E. (eds), *Writing Culture: The Poetics and Politics of Ethnography*, Berkeley: University of California Press, pp. 1–26, p. 19. We engage again with culture in Chapter 2.

94 Clifford, 'Introduction', p. 6.

way to express the truths we are seeking. To acknowledge what we have to learn of Christ and the gospel is the path of Christian humility (see Chapters 3 and 6).[95]

Comparative Theology

In using the term 'Comparative Theology' we are speaking about a particular recent trend or emphasis in interreligious theological thought, associated very much with the work of such figures as Francis Clooney and James Fredericks. The former, in particular, has defined a particular field of practice, which should not be confused with the comparative theology of the nineteenth century associated with such figures as Frederick Maurice.[96] However, even in the contemporary sense it is not a unified school or tradition.

Comparative Theology refers to a particular form of the theology of religions that seeks to engage in thinking about the Christian faith by comparison with, or in relation to, one or more other religious traditions. In Clooney's case this means Hinduism, and it entails considerable expertise in both the Christian and Hindu traditions, with a very specialist

---

95 I do not suggest my claims here are, in themselves, original. A similar argument is put forward by, for instance, Barnes (*Theology*). Where I would see the difference is that while many figures, Barnes being a good example, often seem to be advancing the kind of radical theological rethinking I am proposing, they often tend to step back from it, and either defend a confessional position as somehow inviolable or make their claims opaque in relation to what they think they should be saying. For instance, while at times Barnes' advocacy of Christian humility in relation to doctrine and other religions sometimes mirrors my own (for example pp. 245, 252) in others he is clearly writing carefully around Roman Catholic standpoints that control what he says (for example pp. 241–2, 250) and, as such, his work fails to really challenge the imperialist theological hegemony of the West.

96 On Comparative Theology's definition in this context see: Clooney, Francis, 1995, 'Comparative Theology: A Review of Recent Books', *Theological Studies*, 56, pp. 521–50; Clooney, Francis, 2010, *Comparative Theology: Meaning and Practice*, Chichester: Wiley-Blackwell; Nicholson, Hugh, 2007, 'Comparative Theology After Liberalism', *Modern Theology* 23:2, pp. 229–51; and, Knitter, *Introducing*, pp. 202–15

exploration of select areas. In this, it differs from the Comparative Theology of Keith Ward who seeks to show more general similarities between many religions.[97]

Another distinction within styles of Comparative Theology is that while Ward is more explicitly a Christian pluralist theologian who works in the theology of religions, Clooney, like Fredericks, has suggested that Comparative Theology differs from the theology of religions. This is related to a critique of the typological framework, already mentioned in passing, which is that it cannot precede actual dialogue. The encounter, it is argued, must happen first before we can decide how we relate to other traditions. I do not find this entirely convincing. To some extent a typology-inclined theology of religions judgement must come first, because unless we have decided that other religions are not completely Satanic or deluded human error (exclusivisms) then the very venture that Clooney has embarked on is untenable. Indeed, it is notable that as a Roman Catholic theologian, Clooney's work may be said to be heavily dependent on the inclusivist-style theology of religions propounded by Vatican II, and would have been deeply problematic, to say the least, within his tradition prior to that. In fact, Clooney has suggested his work is in accord with an inclusivist approach.[98] Of course, comparative studies may lead one to adopt an exclusivist or pluralist approach, and as such it is not to say that Comparative Theology in Clooney's style must be done within an inclusivist framework or any other; however, if, and in

97 Clooney's important and significant contributions includes 1993, *Theology After Vedanta: An Experiment in Comparative Theology*, Albany, NY: SUNY Press, 2002, *Hindu God, Christian God: How Reason Helps Break Down the Boundaries Between Religions*, Oxford: Oxford University Press, and 2005, *Divine Mother, Blessed Mother: Hindu Goddesses and the Virgin Mary*, Oxford University Press, and, *Comparative Theology*; Ward's include 1996, *Religion and Creation*, 1998, *Religion and Human Nature*, 2000, *Religion and Community*, all Oxford: Oxford University Press.

98 Clooney, Francis, 1990, 'Reading the World in Christ: From Comparison to Inclusivism', in D'Costa, Gavin (ed.), *Christian Uniqueness Reconsidered: The Myth of a Pluralistic Theology of Religions*, Maryknoll, NY: Orbis, pp. 63–80, p. 66, a position he has maintained in subsequent works.

as far as, it leads one to another position this would change the nature of the work done. Presumably if Clooney were to decide that no useful insights could be gained for Christian theology from Hinduism, that all truth lay within his own tradition, it would lead to an end to his practice of Comparative Theology, and lead perhaps to the writing of missionary apologetics on his part. To say that the typological framework of the theology of religions is a prerequisite for this kind of work is not therefore to limit or prescribe what it is or its goals; indeed, simply labelling it inclusivist will not tell us much – as we have seen between Farquhar and Rahner lies a vast gulf – but one must at least be playing within the parameters of the typology (even if one doesn't use the terms) to begin this kind of work. While to use the typology will help position it in relation to an ongoing conversation in the field.[99]

Rather than distinct, the kind of work Comparative Theology does is, I would suggest, vital and the very heart blood of the theology of religions. When Clooney and Fredericks suggest that Comparative Theology is distinct from the theology of religions it is to limit the latter to narrow confines. Rather, discussions of the typology are one narrow area within the broader framework of the theology of religions, which extends to suggest how and why Christianity is, and must be, in contact with other religious traditions and, as such, an integral part of systematic theology, while its remit extends to religious identity, how Christianity works in the public sphere, in ethics, etc. Comparative Theology is also a meeting place of the theology of religions and interreligious dialogue, being part of the dialogue of theological exchange (see Chapter 2). While Comparative Theology could be a purely textual encounter, and so not interreligious dialogue in the way I will define it, it generally involves a meeting and encounter with those of other religions. While this book is not explicitly a work of Comparative Theology, I hope it makes clear that such work is essential, even integral, to Christian theology (understood as Intercultural Theology). Indeed, in showing connections and

---

99 On this see Hedges, 'Reflection', pp. 25–6; see also Schmidt-Leukel, *Transformation*, pp. 90–104, and Knitter, *Introducing*, pp. 203–7.

relations between religions it is highly supportive of the proposals suggested here:

> These two dimensions of Clooney's theological challenge, namely, the destabilization and reformulation of Christian identity, together imply a relational conception of Christian identity. The recognition of other forms of religious identity forces a revision of one's own.[100]

Finally, we should note that the kind of work undertaken in Clooney's Comparative Theology is highly supportive of the nuanced readings of religions as not monolithic that we will address in Chapter 2. This is not, though, to undermine the more generalized work done by figures such as Keith Ward, because it is useful to have both particular and general encounters and perspectives.[101]

Conclusions

There may be those who may reject or find unconvincing the picture of Christianity portrayed here. For them, perhaps, Christianity may be a certain interpretation of that tradition alone, given inviolate by divine decree and not part of a negotiated and created set of identities.[102]

---

100 Nicholson, 'Comparative', pp. 244-5.

101 It is notable that those who deal with a particular religion tend to stress that their encounter has the most relevance/greatest challenge to Christianity, as such broader perspectives provide a necessary balance. Also we should not disparage unnecessarily many nineteenth-century works of Comparative Theology, such as that of Maurice who saw every religion as having one major idea or theme and hence is out of line with our suggestions, because these are works of their time and did sterling service in creating a more open approach to other faiths and increasing understanding and appreciation (on Maurice's 'theology of religions' see Hedges, *Preparation*, pp. 51-63, and for an appreciation of how we can approach the works of our forebears with an eye to their times, see Hedges, Paul, 2008, 'Post-Colonialism, Orientalism, and Understanding: Religious Studies and the Christian Missionary Imperative', *Journal of Religious History* 32:1, pp. 55-75).

102 In theology the strong appeal of neo-traditionalist positions is a sign of this, which would include Barth's Neo-orthodoxy, as well as what may be termed

Others may suggest I have offered a 'liberal' reading of Christian history, where the 'secularized' norms of historical criticism are prioritized over Christian readings. However, we cannot divorce Christianity from its historical construction, which involves the social and political world in which it developed. To attempt to do so is not true to the nature of the Christian tradition in its theological and religious integrity (a theme extended in the following chapters). As the American Roman Catholic theologian David Tracy has argued, we cannot simply bypass the modern to the post-modern and ignore the problems raised by the Enlightenment legacy of criticism with the fideistic retrenchment of a problematic appeal to 'tradition' or 'orthodoxy'.[103] This is not, though, to side with liberalism against post-liberalism for, as we will see in the following chapters, the modernist liberal tradition is deeply problematic for the theology of religions and interreligious dialogue. If we are to move beyond the impasse we cannot simply opt for one position or another, but must develop a contemporary theology. To this end, the historical creation of Christian identity will help show, as Schreiter says, that 'contemporary proposals that might seem daring become more modest in scope',[104] as we are just continuing the reworking of Christian identity in context. This means that instead of placing ourselves in camps with fixed answers, or extolling a 'true Christianity', we should extol a humble Christianity that says: 'I'm not sure I can tell the truth ... I can only tell what I know.'[105] This, I believe, is in line with what the tradition *authentically* demands of us (not to be confused with an 'authentic tradition'!). This may

---

the updated Neo-Orthodox positions of post-liberal theologies of all colours, especially Radical Orthodoxy. While I would not suggest such figures as Barth, George Lindbeck and John Milbank all essentially espouse the same theological position, there is in their defence of what they see as the undisputed truths of Christianity as the base-rock of theology a distinct theological lineage.

103 For a discussion around these issues see my forthcoming article, Hedges, 'John'. The reference is to Tracy, David, 1996, *Blessed Rage for Order: The New Pluralism in Theology*, London: University of Chicago Press, p. xv. On fideism in post-liberalism, see Tracy, David, 1985, 'Lindbeck's New Programme for Theology: A Reflection', *Thomist* 49:3, pp. 460–72, p. 465.

104 Schreiter, *New*, p. 68.

105 Cited from a Cree hunter in Clifford, 'Introduction', p. 8.

demand things which make us uncomfortable, yet we may feel led by the Holy Spirit to agree with the American Roman Catholic theologian Paul Knitter, who argues that we must allow ourselves to be disturbed by the religious Other, recognizing not strict identity, but an analogy of being, whereby we can be both fascinated and frightened by the other, that is truly Other yet united to us.[106]

To conclude I will give an extended quote from Oduyoye and the Dutch Protestant theologian Hendrik M. Vroom which raises the questions of this chapter precisely:

Can the tradition change like a chameleon? In asking such a question we should be conscious of the fact that our understanding of the Gospel is always one-sided, and falls short of its full depth, height, length and breadth. For this very reason we have opted to read Scripture time and again, carefully, learning from one another as we do so. If we abandon the idea that we can master the whole truth of the Gospel, we may also come to understand the need for the guidance of the Holy Spirit who will 'declare the things to come' (John 16:13). This belief is the theological equivalent of Gadamer's hermeneutical insight: '. . . we understand differently if we understand at all' (Gadamer 1965: 280). Thus our cultural context rightly plays a part in our understanding of the Gospel.[107]

106 Knitter, Paul F. 1995, *One Earth, Many Religions: Multifaith Dialogue and Global Responsibility*, Maryknoll, NY: Orbis, pp. 75–6, he credits David Tracy as an inspiration for this idea.

107 Oduyoye, Mercy Amba and Vroom, Hendrik M., 2003, 'Introduction', in Oduyoye, Mercy Amba and Vroom, Hendrik M. (eds), *One Gospel – Many Cultures: Case Studies and Reflections on Cross-Cultural Theology*, Amsterdam: Rodopi, pp. 1–12, p. 4, quotation from Gadamer, Hans-Georg, 1965, *Wahrheit und Methode*, 2nd edn, Tübingen: Mohr.

2

Conversing between 'Religions'
Exploring Interreligious Dialogue

Introduction

The practice of interreligious dialogue is a contested area. Questions of what it is, what it should be, and how it relates to mission, are all commonly invoked both by participants and critics. In this chapter I would like to begin by defining some important terms and issues, before turning to a fundamental, but rarely asked, question in relation to dialogue: what is 'religion'? In Chapter 1 we have already asked some questions about religious boundaries, and these will be taken further. We will then conclude the chapter with some reflections on ways religious encounter may occur, discussing the meaning of dialogue as well as examining Scriptural Reasoning and multiple religious belonging, as well as questions raised about power dynamics and dialogue's relation to mission.

Terms and definitions in dialogue

Interfaith or interreligious?

I have preferred to use the term interreligious dialogue rather than interfaith dialogue for various reasons. For one, it keeps the discussion centred upon the term 'religion' rather than involving us in discussions of how 'faith' and 'religion' relate. For another, the term 'religion' suggests a broad application not simply limited to having faith in particular ideas, but relates to practice, culture, custom, etc. Finally, this does not limit it to the subjective realm of individual meeting and faith, but implies the institutional level.[1] Other issues may also arise, for instance can a Christian and a Humanist or Marxist have 'interreligious dialogue'? I leave the question hanging, for it takes us beyond our present discussion.

What is interreligious dialogue?

Some have suggested that interreligious dialogue is an essentially modern affair, whereas in the past religions have generally come together in cultural clashes and in a spirit of hostility. This has not always been true, however, and we will see some examples of more peaceful and amicable meetings in this chapter. However, it is certainly the case that a large-scale and active movement for dialogue has a fairly recent pedigree in the organized Western Christian tradition. Some date the dialogue movement to 1893 when the World Parliament of Religions met in Chicago. This brought together representatives of many religious traditions to speak in an open and free way, which represents what many see dialogue as: an arena for openly expressing viewpoints.[2] It was only in the second half of the twentieth century, though, that dialogue as a primary way of engaging with other religious traditions was widely endorsed by the mainstream churches, in meetings of the World Council of Churches (WCC) on the Protestant and Orthodox side, and with Vatican II on the Catholic side. In all major traditions, mission remains important and has a somewhat problematic relationship with dialogue.[3] Nevertheless dialogue has led

---

1 A critique that has been used to prefer 'interfaith', but which relies on a problematic interpretation of 'religion' (Egnell, Helene, 2006, *Other Voices: A Study of Christian Feminist Approaches to Religious Plurality East and West*, Uppsala: Studia Missionalia Svecana, p. 25).

2 It should be noted, though, that an agenda of Christian supremacy and aspects of racial and cultural exclusion lay behind this event (see Nordstrom, Justin, 2009, 'Utopians at the Parliament: The World's Parliament of Religions and the Columbian Exposition of 1893', *Journal of Religious History* 33:3, pp. 348–65, pp. 351–3).

3 For an introduction to the issues, see Race, Alan, 2008, 'Interfaith Dialogue: Religious Accountability between Strangeness and Resonance', in Hedges, Paul and Race, Alan (eds), *SCM Core Text Christian Approaches to Other Faiths*, London: SCM, pp. 155–72. For mainly Protestant wrangling at the WCC see Ariarajah,

many Christians to re-evaluate their stance on mission, especially, as Wesley Ariarajah has observed, for Christians living in areas where religious plurality has always been normative (see below). Today, we live in a situation where no Christian anywhere in the globe can responsibly live without, at the very least, active consideration of dialogue with religious Others. On a practical level, the famous Swiss Catholic theologian Hans Küng has stated the truism: 'No world peace without peace between the religions.'[4] This means finding ways to live and work together.

Interreligious dialogue operates at various levels and comes in various kinds. For the sake of clarity this has been put into four main types:[5]

The dialogue of theological exchange: This is intellectual, and is generally concerned with discussing theological and philosophical concepts, comparing ideas and concepts, etc. It is also known as *discursive dialogue*.

The dialogue of life: Here, people are seen as central and it is the interaction between them on a personal level that is seen as important. It tends to dominate at grassroots levels being concerned with day-to-day

---

S. Wesley, 1998, 'The impact of interreligious dialogue on the ecumenical movement', in May, John D'Arcy (ed.), *Pluralism and the Religions: The Theological and Political Dimensions*, London: Cassell, pp. 7–21.

4 Küng, Hans, 1991, *Global Responsibility: In Search of a New World Ethic*, first published 1990 in German, London: SCM Press, p. xv. Others have suggested, less dramatically, that we need practical ways to live with religious others, for instance, Berling, Judith, 1997, *A Pilgrim in Chinese Culture: Negotiating Religious Diversity*, Eugene, OR: Wipf and Stock, p. 121.

5 See Race, 'Interfaith', pp. 161–3. The names used here relate to Roman Catholic usage, but have a wider application; on their appearance in Vatican documents and Papal encyclicals, see Barnes, Michael, 2002, *Theology and the Dialogue of Religions*, Cambridge: Cambridge University Press, p. 21, fn. 42. A different breakdown has been given by Knitter who sees six types: reading texts (relates to: dialogue of theological exchange); comparing doctrines or themes (theological exchange); comparing founders (theological exchange); story telling (theological exchange and/or life); sharing or appreciating experience (religious experience); he adds his own approach which he labels 'liberative or globally responsible dialogue' (action) (Knitter, Paul F., 1995, *One Earth, Many Religions: Multifaith Dialogue and Global Responsibility*, Maryknoll, NY: Orbis, p. 151).

meeting and encountering, and is therefore also appropriately termed *human dialogue*.

The dialogue of action: This is concerned with people coming together around areas not seen as primarily 'religious' (or 'sacred' – these terms are discussed later in this chapter), but with more 'mundane' affairs, such as human rights, ecological concerns, or other areas of social activism. This is not to say that there may not be common 'religious' values that inspire the work. It is also known as *secular dialogue*.

The dialogue of religious experience: This is where individuals or groups come together to share, either through explanation or practice, what are termed 'contemplative', 'spiritual', or 'mystical' experiences. It is also known as *interior dialogue*.

Obviously, these are not mutually exclusive. Neighbourhood groups engaged in the dialogue of life may find particular concerns that lead them into the dialogue of action, and this may draw them to pray together, thus leading to the dialogue of religious experience, and then perhaps to ask questions about how their beliefs relate, the dialogue of theological exchange. As such, we draw artificial barriers if we see the theology of religions and interreligious dialogue as separate areas. Indeed, to some extent, as discussed in Chapter 1, prior theological judgements (even if not formally made) will no doubt inform the dialogue of life: do we regard our neighbours as in desperate need of salvation; as religious equals; or as being led in good directions by their own religion (to give possible exclusivist, pluralist and inclusivist-style answers)? Whatever the case, patience and persistence are needed, any meaningful dialogue cannot rely on superficial understandings or be speedily digested.[6]

Various suggestions for how dialogue may proceed have been forwarded at different times, including the American Roman Catholic theologian Leonard Swidler's notable 'Dialogue Decalogue'.[7] Here, for a

---

6 A thought expressed by Judith Berling (see, *A Pilgrim*, p. 36).

7 Swidler, Leonard, 1983, 'The Dialogue Decalogue: Ground Rules for Interreligious Dialogue', *Journal of Ecumenical Studies* 20:1, pp. 1–4; see also his later 1990, 'A Dialogue on Dialogue', in Swidler, Leonard, et al., *Death or Dialogue? From the Age of Monologue to the Age of Dialogue*, London: SCM, and

useful brief summary, I will give a selection from the guidelines 'Building Good Relations with People of Different Faiths and Beliefs' from The Inter Faith Network for the UK:

Learning to understand what others actually believe and value, and letting them express this in their own terms.

Working to prevent disagreement from leading to conflict.

We have a great deal to learn from one another which can enrich us without undermining our own identities. Together, listening and responding with openness and respect, we can move forward to work in ways that acknowledge genuine differences but build on shared hopes and values.[8]

This suggests several important concerns about the authentic voice of the Other, action in dialogue, and seeking commonality without a suggestion of absolute similarity.[9] These, I would suggest, represent some of the key principles of dialogue.

2007, 'Seven Stages of Deep-Dialogue/Critical Thinking', in Swidler, Leonard, Reuven Firestone and Duran, Kalid, *Trialogue: Jews, Christians and Muslims in Dialogue*, Mystic, CT: Twenty-Third Publications, pp. 33–7; his 'Dialogue Decalogue' is also reprinted therein. See also: Mojzes, Paul, 1989, 'The What and the How of Dialogue', in Bryant, M. Darrol, and Flinn, Frank (eds), *Interreligious Dialogue: Voices from a New Frontier*, New York: Paragon House, pp. 199–206; Lande, Aasulv, 2005, 'Recent Developments in Interreligious Dialogue', in Jeanrond, Werner G. and Lande, Aasulv (eds), *The Concept of God in Global Dialogue*, Maryknoll, NY: Orbis, pp. 32–47; and, Heisig, James W., 2005, 'Six Sūtras on the Dialogue among Religions', in Jeanrond and Lande (eds), *Concept*, pp. 162–72.

8 The Inter Faith Network for the UK, 2005 [1993] 'Building Good Relations with People of Different Faiths and Beliefs', available at, http://www.interfaith.org.uk/pcode.htm, accessed 28 August 2009.

9 A further discussion of these in ways that relate to ethics can be found in Hedges, Paul, 2008, 'Are Interfaith Dialogue and a Global Ethic Compatible? A Call for an Ethic to the Globe', *Journal for Faith, Spirituality and Social Change* 1:2, pp. 109–32, pp. 117–18, available at, http://www.fsscconference.org.uk/journal/1-2/Hedges.pdf, accessed 12 August 2009 (see Chapter 7).

On the nature of dialogue and the theological impasse

Dialogue is in certain ways a separate activity from theology. I would suggest here that dialogue implies a meeting of minds and therefore people. That is to say, a person cannot (fully) engage in interreligious dialogue simply by reading books about another religion. To do this would probably lend itself to doing the theology of religions, though this also may be enhanced by face-to-face encounter.[10] I would suggest that Martin Forward's analysis of the roots of the term 'dia-logue' is useful here:

> What, however, of the first part of the word 'dialogue'? It is 'dia-', not 'di-' as many people wrongly infer. In Greek, 'di-' indicates 'two' rather than the 'one' that is signified by 'mono-'. But 'dia-' is a preposition that means 'through'. 'Di-logue' could mean *two* people conversing about a worldview; maybe amicably, maybe not; maybe with results, maybe not. But '*dia*-logue' signifies worldviews being argued *through* to significant and potentially transformative conclusions, for one or more participants. It involves a much more consequential encounter.[11]

Therefore, in terms of what we have said about the need to create and rethink identities, interreligious dialogue must be an act of radical thinking through our own tradition. We do not have a fixed identity to give others in dialogue, to make them become 'Christians' like us. Nor does it imply we must give up our own Christian identity; rather it means, if we authentically dialogue, to be shaped through the encounter – as well as to seek to shape others. Christianity is always culturally negotiated (Chapter 1), and in a globalized world it must be negotiated again. However, the theological impasse we have spoken of suggests what some see

---

10 However, even those geographically distant from religious Others can experience the dialogical challenge posed by them.

11 Forward, Martin, 2001, *Inter-religious Dialogue: A Short Introduction*, Oxford: Oneworld, p. 12.

as two extreme options. One is the giving up of any distinct Christian identity (as some see pluralisms suggesting, though that it does not entail this will be discussed further in Chapters 3 and 6), and the other that we cannot and should not be shaped by this encounter (the post-liberal approach, discussed further in Chapters 4 and 6). In some senses, the impasse we have discussed is bypassed through interreligious dialogue. To ask whether religions are characterized by difference or sameness as a theoretical starting point becomes taken over in the meeting of the religious Other. However, our theological presuppositions will affect the way we meet and engage in encounter with the religious Other. Again, this may affect the forms of encounter we engage in. Indeed the way we engage in and interact in interreligious dialogue, in any of the four types, will be affected by where we stand in relation to this impasse. However, the impasse and the way we dialogue is also bound up with how we construct the concept of 'religion'.

Religion

The issues

We come now to a key issue, which is how our understanding of 'religion' plays into the way we envisage and engage in dialogue. According to the Asian American Protestant theologian Kwok Pui-lan:

In most interreligious dialogues conducted in Western ecumenical or academic settings, a handful of Third World elites, usually all males, are invited to speak as representatives of their traditions to a largely white Christian audience . . . The different 'world religions' are reified as if they were distinct and insoluble entities, represented primarily by male elite traditions, while intrareligious differences are ignored and women's voices neglected. To the organizers, that one person or two have been invited to speak on behalf of 'Buddhism' or 'Hinduism' does not seem to be awkward or inadequate. Instead of promoting genuine understanding, such a kind of interreligious dialogue can be a device used by metropolitan centers to manage religious differences and to co-opt Third World elites in a postco-lonial world.[12]

Such approaches, she goes on to tell us, can 'preserve the status quo' and 'camouflage the real differences between Western dominant pow-ers and Third World societies'. Two imperative issues are raised in the critique that Kwok makes. First, there is the way our discourse creates a monolithic sense of 'religions' as fixed and identifiable entities. Sec-ond, such an approach can hide power differences and the construction of what is taken to be the normative discourse. These two issues are related. The way the discourse is created leads to the prioritizing of certain issues, while because of existing power relations the discourse has been constructed in a certain way. This, can, of course, become a self-perpetuating issue which can have wider implications. However, our focus is the construction and deconstruction of the term 'religion'. Here, Kwok rightly states that theologians need to be attuned to the way scholars of religion have problematized the term 'religion', warning that failure will lead to a distancing of theology from other disciplines in cultural studies.[13]

There are two basic issues to resolve in relation to the term 'religion' in our context. The first is whether there is such a category of things as 'religions'. That is to say, do the various traditions which we have come to label 'Hinduism', 'Buddhism', 'Islam', 'Judaism' and so on, belong to a common family of 'religions', or have we simply taken a vast amount of data and confusedly made it fit a single definition and falsely related them? This may, to some, seem a bizarre idea; how can the various 'reli-gions' of Sikhism, Buddhism and Islam which meet and talk together in encounters around the world not all be types of the same thing? Indeed, in its most radical forms, I believe the argument is simply misplaced. Nevertheless, behind this argument there are some important questions about how the whole cultural-social systems associated with the various

---

12 Kwok, Pui-lan, 2005, *Postcolonial Imagination and Feminist Theology*, London: SCM, pp. 202–3.

13 Kwok, *Postcolonial Imagination*, p. 204.

religions are understood. This second is what are we talking about when we use the blanket terms 'Hinduism', 'Islam', 'Judaism', etc.? Is there really such a thing as 'Buddhism' that can relate to 'Christianity', or are we creating huge monolithic unities out of what are, in fact, a diverse mass of beliefs, cultural forms, individuals, etc.? Does this then mean that we can never have a 'Christian' view of 'Islam', let alone other religions?

Critiques of 'religion'

Scholars have long recognized the problem of defining 'religion'. In 1912 James Leuba discovered over 50 definitions of 'religion', a finding long cited as proof that the term could not be defined, although it was taken for granted that we knew what 'religion' was. However, other scholars have suggested that the term itself is at fault, or, more radically, that there is no such phenomenon as 'religion'.

The tradition of criticizing the concept of religion finds its most well-known proponent in the person of Wilfred Cantwell Smith, one of the founding fathers of the modern discipline of the study of religion. In his groundbreaking book *The Meaning and End of Religion*, first published in 1962, Smith suggested that the term 'religion' had changed its meaning over time. From its Latin roots in the term '*religio*', which he suggested indicated 'a quality of men's lives or a colouring of the world that they perceive',[14] it came to mean, in the early church, either (*pace* Jerome) a rite, or (*pace* Augustine) piety or worship.[15] It kept similar meanings in the Renaissance and Reformation periods;[16] however, from the seventeenth century: 'They gave the name "religion" to the system, first in general but increasingly to the system of ideas, in which men of faith were involved or with which men of potential faith were confronted.'[17] This offers us a whole new meaning, rather than being particular acts or features of a religious world (such as a disposition, a rite or piety) we

14 Smith, W. C., 1978 [1962], *The Meaning and End of Religion*, London: SPCK.
15 Smith, *Meaning*, pp. 28 and 29.
16 Smith, *Meaning*, pp. 33ff.
17 Smith, *Meaning*, p. 38.

start to see the term becoming associated with a system. As we might expect, the rationalism of the Enlightenment period came to focus upon its cognitive aspects, whereby,

> the notion was driven home that a religion is something that one be-
> lieves or does not believe, something whose propositions are true or
> not true, something whose locus is in the realm of the intelligible, is up
> for inspection before the speculative mind.[18]

Alongside this, a 'parallel development' in seventeenth-century France detached the term from the realm of 'personal orientation' (piety and worship), to focus on a 'depersonalised intellectual systematisation'.[19] This allowed two new developments: the possibility of the plural form for various systems; and the term's usage to suggest a 'system of beliefs' as a generic entity.[20] Smith suggests some final notions, mainly originating in the nineteenth century, helped shape the modern concept of 'religion': 1) 'to expand the concept "religion" so that it has since, as an intellectual concept, included within its content the non-intellectual and the intellectual together'; 2) Hegel 'posited "religion" as a *Begriff*, a self-subsisting transcendent idea that unfolds itself in dynamic expression in the course of everchanging history'; and, 3) Feuerbach 'was suggesting that religion, and a religion, have an essence. Ever since the hunt has been on.'[21] Smith argued that 'religion' acquired a new meaning in the period from the seventeenth to the nineteenth centuries which is the application to particular systems of concepts, practices and ideas. Moreover, the idea arose that particular sets of data can be parcelled out and grouped as though they were something with their own inherent essence and identity. Identifying four main uses of the term religion – as: 1) personal piety; 2) system as an ideal; 3) system as empirical phenomenon; and, 4) religion in general[22] – he tells us that:

---

18 Smith, *Meaning*, p. 40.
19 Smith, *Meaning*, p. 40.
20 Smith, *Meaning*, p. 43.
21 Smith, *Meaning*, pp. 45–7.
22 Smith, *Meaning*, pp. 48–9.

I suggest that the term 'religion' is confusing, unnecessary, and distorting – confusing and unnecessary especially in the first and fourth senses, distorting in the second and third. I have become strongly convinced that the vitality of personal faith, on the one hand, and, on the other (quite separately), progress in understanding – even at the academic level – of the traditions of other people throughout history and throughout the world, are both seriously blocked by our attempt to conceptualise what is involved in each case in terms of (a) religion.[23]

Instead, he proposes we use the term 'faith', as a synonym for the original meaning of 'religion/religio' (piety and the inward aspects of worship), and 'cumulative tradition' for the accretion of historical events, practices and texts, etc. that we now term a particular 'religion'.

Contemporary critiques of 'religion'

Smith's arguments, though widely accepted among scholars of religion, have not led to the demise of the term 'religion'. However, assaults on the term have been renewed by a number of more recent critics, some of whom see their own critique as going into a theoretical space beyond Smith's.[24] This metatheory in religious studies is more radical, disputing any relation between what we call 'religions' and suggesting the term is simply a modern Western taxonomic invention with no basis at all; J. Z. Smith has put it strongly: 'there is no data for religion ... Religion has no independent existence apart from the academy.'[25]

Contemporary Religious Studies scholars such as Timothy Fitzgerald and Russell McCutcheon, two of the most significant scholars in the contemporary debate, argue that the term 'religion' as used to refer to a number of different and distinct sets of data which we might see as

23 Smith, *Meaning*, p. 50.

24 McCutcheon, 2003, *Manufacturing Religion: The Discourse on Sui Generis Religion and the Politics of Nostalgia*, Oxford: Oxford University Press, p. 14.

25 Smith, Jonathan Z., 1982, *Imagining Religion: From Babylon to Jonestown*, Chicago: University of Chicago Press, p. xi.

comparable is simply a construct of a particular set of agendas embedded within our modern Western worldview. This, it is suggested, is the view across other social science academic disciplines, and Religious Studies is therefore seen as part of the problem. Therefore, we had best abandon the term as distorting and problematic. However, others, such as Richard King and Kwok, believe we can still use the term in strategic ways.[26] While recognizing much truth in the criticisms raised by Fitzgerald, McCutcheon and others, I would side with King and Kwok, and will argue that the term has a legitimate usage as a distinct form of cultural phenomena. To some extent this involves arguing for things we may take for granted about 'religion', but to be able to use this term meaningfully, we must deconstruct and reconstruct the term. I have argued elsewhere for the application of the term 'religion' within the context of the study of religion, and so I will just outline the main arguments here. However, it is important that we do so to show the possibility of both the theology of *religions* and inter*religious* dialogue.[27]

A basic problem with 'religion' arises from the diversity of subject matter it is used to cover, from, for instance, the largely community-orientated Abrahamic monotheism of Islam, to the non-theistic system of life and more individualized spirituality of Theravada Buddhism, to the government and ethical-focused system of Confucianism. Indeed, most definitions of religion fail by either including too little, that is, if they

---

26   Kwok, *Postcolonial*, p. 204, reference to King, Richard, 2004, 'Cartographies of the Imagination, Legacies of Colonialism: The Discourse of Religion and the Mapping of Indic Traditions', in Evam, *Forum on Indian Representations* 3:1&2, pp. 272–89.

27   For my previous studies, and an extension of many of the arguments raised below, see Hedges, Paul, 2006, 'Defining Religion', Part I, *Interreligious Insight* 4:3, pp. 9–15; 'Defining Religion: A Religious Orientation Typology', Part II, *Interreligious Insight* 4:4, pp. 34–42; 2009, 'Understanding Religion as Culture in Academic Discourse', *Conference of the International Journal of Arts and Sciences*, 1:5, Gottenheim, Germany, 2008; and, 2010, 'Can We Still Teach "Religions"? Towards an Understanding of Religion as Culture and Orientation in Contemporary Pedagogy and Metatheory', in Durka, G, Gearon, L, de Souza, M, Engebretson, K (eds), *International Handbook for Inter-Religious Education*, New York: Springer Academic Publishers.

focus on a deity they discount Theravada Buddhism, or too much, like the most widely used definition, that of Ninian Smart, which includes such worldviews as Marxism, Humanism or being a skinhead. Obviously, then, there is a question as to whether we are discussing a meaningful set of data. I will argue below that we can have a meaningful definition. However, this argument against 'religion' is one of the least potent.

Stemming from the above problem, is the claim that the different things we call 'religions' are diverse sets of cultural spheres which have no common ground, and relate only to their own particular context. Implications of this feed into some contemporary versions of the theology of religions (particularities) which suggests that the differences show that each religion has different ends (we discuss this further in Chapter 4). This would clearly impact on what interreligious dialogue should and can be, or even whether it is a meaningful activity at all.

Another argument is that certain things termed as religions, notably Hinduism, can be seen as primarily Western constructions. Before outsiders came, India had many 'dharmas', a term with many meanings, but here equating to traditions, so one might follow the dharma of particular teachers, such as Shankara, Ramanuja, Gautama, or Nanak.[28] Thus, what existed were many paths, or traditions. When Westerners arrived they used an old geographical description, Hindu – those beyond the Indus River – to refer to the religion of these people, interpreting all dharmas as one 'religion', Hinduism. However, the dharmas of Gautama and Nanak came to be seen as different from Hinduism, and so two further 'religions' were 'created', Buddhism and Sikhism. Therefore, it is argued what we classify as 'Eastern religions' are constructs imposed upon data to fit Western presuppositions. Now, these claims are not just intellectual, they are also political, because, in response to Western colonialism, Hindu nationalist thought came to consider that being 'Hindu' was part of the ideology of being Indian; yet Hinduism is seen by many scholars as a recent creation in response to Western notions and interpretations, although many Hindus today would argue that everything we class as 'Hinduism' is

28 On usages of the term dharma see Flood, Gavin, 1996, *An Introduction to Hinduism*, Cambridge: Cambridge University Press, pp. 52–8.

part of one coherent system, often under the banner of the term Sanatana Dharma.[29] However, from an academic perspective, and also in response to the vast varieties of lived Hindu traditions, to engage in dialogue with Hinduism is to engage in dialogue with a family of related traditions rather than a single entity – although some contemporary Hindu apologetics may argue otherwise. Certainly, not all instances are like this; Islam had a more distinct notion of being something akin to a separate 'religion', and is more uniform, but this can lead to further problems.

One of these further problems is that in creating the notion of 'religions' as things of one type, J. Z. Smith argues that we have created 'religions' as we now know them. Hence, we think that Islam is somehow comparable to Hinduism which is somehow comparable to Confucianism which is somehow comparable to Judaism, etc.[30] This is how most textbooks discuss religions, as a set of comparable data patterns of a similar type; however, for many scholars, this is problematic. Why should we classify as being two types of the same phenomena such diverse things as, on the one hand, Confucianism, which incorporates an individualistic spirituality, but has been historically employed, perhaps primarily, for training civil servants in imperial exams in China, and has atheistic trends and, on the other, Islam, which is focused upon belief in a monotheistic God and requires communal worship. By classing them both as 'religions', it is argued that we have created a whole category of things which really don't exist. Put another way, we interpreted a set of multivalent data into homogenous patterns. In an important critique, McCutcheon has further argued that it helps create 'religions' as a *sui generis* category, that is to say, a set of data which is self-creating and self-referencing and essentially cut off and divorced from other phenomena.[31] This effectively

29 The best discussion of this is King, Richard, 1999, *Orientalism and Religion: Postcolonial Theory, India and 'the Mystic East'*, London: Routledge.

30 Smith, Jonathan Z., 1998, 'Religion, Religions, Religious', in Taylor, M. C. (ed.), *Critical Terms for Religious Studies*, Chicago, IL: University of Chicago Press, pp. 269–84, pp. 276–80.

31 McCutcheon, R., 2003, *Manufacturing Religion: The Discourse on Sui Generis Religion and the Politics of Nostalgia*, Oxford: Oxford University Press, pp. 3–26.

makes religion divorced from other aspects of culture and helps distance it from political and economic concerns (see below).[32]

We may extend this by noting that a number of critics have shown connections between aspects of modern ideology and the modern notion of religion; arguing that historical accident has given rise to our understanding of religion.[33] One consequence of this is what Jeannine Hill Fletcher calls the 'container-construction' conception of religion.[34] By this she means the ideology whereby each religion is seen as a fixed set of notions which are its own internal cultural island. For many critics, this idea of 'religions' as a fixed group of 'things', identified as a class of similar objects, 'tends to conceal rather than reveal aspects of the religions it interprets'.[35] The creation of a universal category of 'religion' is thereby seen to perpetuate a discourse based on certain Western modernist notions of universal norms and ideals which are claimed to be universal but just reflect a single cultural construct. This is the essence of Tomoko Masuzawa's critique, which is ably summed up by the American Comparative Theologian Hugh Nicholson: 'there is an intrinsic connection between . . . universalistic presuppositions . . . and . . . the perpetuation of imperialistic attitudes'.[36] These matters will be discussed further when we address power relations in dialogue.

Related to the Western modernist notion of religion is another important aspect of the critique, which argues that our notion of 'religion' is theological. The term 'religion' as well as much modern study of religion grew from a Christian worldview, in particular, a nineteenth-century liberal theology that believed every person and culture

---

32 On such issues see Masuzawa, Tomoko, 2005, *The Invention of World Religions, Or, How European universalism was preserved in the language of pluralism*, Chicago, IL: University of Chicago Press.

33 See, for instance, D'Costa, *Christianity*, Part II.

34 Fletcher, Jeannine Hill, 2008, 'Religious Pluralism in an Era of Globalization: The Making of Modern Religious Identity', *Theological Studies* 69, pp. 394–411, p. 401.

35 Nicholson, Hugh, 2007, 'Comparative Theology After Liberalism', *Modern Theology* 23:2, pp. 229–51, p. 237.

36 Nicholson, 'Comparative', p. 232.

had a similar religious experience at root.[37] Hence, an inbuilt quasi-theological agenda has shaped our understanding of 'religion'. Certainly, in the study of religion, some legitimacy attaches to this with noted scholars of religion such as Mircea Eliade believing that a common spirituality pervaded all religious phenomena.[38] Indeed, D'Costa takes up this particular argument and argues that the notion of the similarity of all religions is part of the problem of liberal theologies of religions, in particular pluralisms.[39] Therefore, for him, this argument from religious studies becomes an argument against pluralisms which have taken their own measure of 'religion' and applied it to others, a measure which is based, as he sees it, upon certain false Enlightenment/modernist premises. To some extent this is a valid critique; however, as we will see, D'Costa and other particularists too have failed to really tackle the issues raised by the critique against 'religion', and fall prey, perhaps even more so, to similar problems.

Assessing the critique

As can be seen, powerful arguments exist contending that the category 'religion' is an imposition of Western academic taxonomies. However, while accepting aspects of this critique, I suggest its most radical conclusions, that is to say that there is simply no common area or groups we may loosely term 'religious/religions', are wrong for at least three reasons.

First, the noted anthropologist Pascal Boyer has argued that 'although anthropology generally assumes that the systems of ideas grouped under the label "religion" are essentially diverse, a number of recurrent themes

---

37 This important argument is developed most especially in Fitzgerald, Timothy, 2000, *The Ideology of Religious Studies*, New York: Oxford University Press, and Asad, Talal, 1993, *Genealogies of Religion: Discipline and Reasons of Power in Christianity and Islam*, London: Johns Hopkins University Press. Such a notion is obviously tied to the 'father' of liberal theology, Friedrich Schleiermacher.

38 See McCutcheon, *Manufacturing*, pp. 158–9.

39 D'Costa, 2009, Part II. He provides a good overview of many of the arguments raised against 'religion' as a construction of a modern worldview.

and concepts can be found in very different cultural environments'.[40] This is important because part of the claim against 'religion' in both the study of religion and theology is that the social sciences generally have come to realize that there is no such thing as 'religion', therefore it is methodologically problematic for these areas to keep speaking of this area as something self-contained and unified. However, the arguments for the distinct nature of all religions are based upon outdated and deeply suspect models of closed cultural islands (this is explored further in Chapter 4).

Second, the notion of the similarity of what we term 'religions' is not a unique Western academic perspective; they have related to each other throughout history as similar areas. To take some examples: 1) Islam came to regard both Zoroastrianism and the Hindu family of faiths as 'religions of the book', indicating it found them comparable to Christianity and Judaism; 2) Sikhism was founded from the Sant tradition which drew from Islamic and Hindu roots showing unities of ideas and origins; 3) the fiercest debates Buddhism had in entering China were with the Daoist tradition, as its nearest rival; 4) there is a tradition of equating the gods of different religions stretching back in the ancient Middle East of the last three millennia BC, where 'religion appears to have been the promoter of intercultural translatability'; and, 5) religions and religious ideas have long interwoven histories of encounter and mutual learning.[41]

Third, we will address the arguments about the modern Western creation of the term 'religion'. Essentially, as Christian Europe developed it became a monoreligious area, the only religious Others being known were Jews and Muslims, who, respectively, were seen as precursors of

---

40 Boyer, Pascal, 1994, *The Naturalness of Religious Ideas: A Cognitive Theory of Religion*, Berkeley, CA: University of California Press, p. 4.

41 On point 4 see Assmann, Jan, 1996, 'Translating Gods: Religion as a Factor of Cultural (Un)Translatability', in Budick, Sanford and Iser, Wolfgang (eds), *The Translatability of Cultures: Figurations of the Space Between*, Stanford, CA: Stanford University Press, pp. 25–36, p. 27; on point 5 see Fletcher, 'Religious', p. 408 and Clarke, J. J., 1997, *Oriental Enlightenment: The Encounter between Asian and Western Thought*, London: Routledge; on the first three see Hedges, 'Can We Still Teach'.

Christianity who had failed to become Christians, and heretics within the Christian system. Hence, use of the term 'religion' at this stage was an intrareligious affair. Therefore, when other traditions were encountered terminology was needed to address this, and this is what 'religion' does. As Fitzgerald has shown, use of the term 'religion' referring to a plurality of different traditions can be traced back to the early seventeenth century, though widespread usage was later (becoming normative in the eighteenth and nineteenth centuries).[42] This usage seems to be related to a recognition, through an ecumenical tolerance, of a variety of Christian denominations as ways of being religious.[43] So, we move from a concept of a single Christian narrative (of course, Europe never had a monolithic Christianity, but this was the ideal) to a recognition that there are other ways of being religious, meaning, first, different ways of being Christian, which is extended by analogy outwards. Now, this clearly is not a 'neutral' thing, because assumptions from the internal intra-Christian debate get applied, while, in its construction, each religion is grouped into respective 'container-constructions', to use Fletcher's term. However, rather than simply seeing the story as the creation of something, we could cast it as the discovery of something. From a (supposed) mono-tradition context, the West had to find terminology to speak of a plural-tradition world. 'Religion' is simply a tool for this, one which may be both misused as well as suitably employed. Indeed, as I will argue shortly, we can see analogies between 'religion' understood as an equivalent to the Indian term 'dharma', mentioned above, and also the Chinese term 'jiao', both of which are used to denote various traditions. Certainly there is a lot of baggage tied to our term 'religion' which does not relate, and different border areas get drawn, but what is clear is that having a term to name traditions, associated either with particular teachers or sets of teachings, is not a modern Western innovation, but a millennia-old worldwide preoccupation. It is not my aim, however,

---

42 Fitzgerald, *Discourse*, Chapter 7.

43 Fitzgerald, *Discourse*, pp. 263 and 301ff. The story can be told in slightly different ways and with different emphases; see for instance, D'Costa, *Christianity*, Part II, and Fletcher, 'Religious', for two recent versions.

to defend all the particular and problematic baggage associated with 'religion'.

Considering these three arguments, that recent scholarship in the social sciences identifies similarities, that throughout history religions have recognized and related to each other, and that the naming of traditions is a cross-cultural phenomenon, I would contend that when we speak of the traditions we commonly label 'religions' we are speaking, in some meaningful sense, about a group of phenomena that can be related (I will argue this further in Chapter 4). However, we can go back to Kwok's earlier quotation, that bringing together groups of people as representatives of different 'religions' may not always be 'promoting genuine understanding'. Here, I think we need to attend to the insightful things to be learned from the criticisms of 'religion'. First, it is not clear, that, although related (an issue we will return to below), all the things we call 'religions' are directly comparable. Second, we have to understand that in seeing 'religions' as closed blocks we are creating problems of understanding. As we saw in Chapter 1 it is not easy to say when or where Christianity and Judaism split into two distinct 'religions', and that the two traditions were enmeshed for centuries (a more Jewish-focused Jesus movement co-existed alongside what was becoming a more Gentile-focused Jesus movement). Third, to see each religion as monolithic also creates problems that will gloss over the vast differences, as well as changes that occurred within each religious tradition over time. These issues obviously create problems for dialogue. What, however, can it mean to dialogue with somebody of another religious tradition when we realize that the terms and traditions we see as dividing us are not fixed and immutable barriers? Therefore, when we speak of 'Christianity' in dialogue with 'Hinduism' or 'Islam' we need to be very careful what we mean. I will therefore now suggest a working definition of religion.

Towards a working definition of 'religion'

If we are seeking to define the role and nature of interreligious dialogue we must recognize that we need to have an adequate categorization of religion which does not misrepresent the nature or relationship between the different traditions. It is in the light of this that I present the following definition. It may also be useful to add a few other notes. First, in giving a definition I do not wish to downplay the vast diversity between different traditions. Second, we must recognize that religions are intimately entwined with cultural and social networks, indeed, in ways that mean we cannot really distinguish between what is 'religious' or 'cultural'. Third, it is important to note that it is not my argument that there are a set of essentialist and monolithic entities such as 'Judaism', 'Hinduism', etc. that can clearly be labelled as essentially similar and relatable phenomena. Rather, there are areas of cultures that are 'religious', and that when these come together in institutional, or more dispersed, forms we can label these, for convenience, as 'religions'. In this sense, I would argue that 'religion' can be seen both as a discrete group of phenomena that occupy a particular place within human culture, but also as a particular emphasis given to culture – recognizing, though, that the term 'culture' itself is much disputed, and in relation to these disputes I use the term to refer, generally, to societies and their symbolic norms of acting and thinking.[44] Indeed, this may be seen to accord with David Chidester's definition of religions as 'intrareligious and interreligious networks of cultural relations'.[45]

In the light of my comments above, I now propose that what characterizes the religious realm is an emphasis of culture as the tendency, or orientation, towards transcendence. By this I mean aspects which claim that the meaning or fulfilment of human life goes beyond the limits of the ordinary bounds of physical and phenomenal existence. The nature of this will be made clear through the typology offered below, which,

---

44 See Ward, Graham, 2005, *Cultural Transformation and Religious Practice*, Cambridge: Cambridge University Press, pp. 4–6, and Cobb, K., 2005, *The Blackwell Guide to Theology and Popular Culture*, Oxford: Blackwell Publishing, pp. 41–5. Also, I think the term 'culture' offers a clarity that is lost if we use other terms; as such I will not adopt Joerg Rieger's otherwise insightful suggestion that we replace 'culture' with 'empire' (Rieger, Joerg, 2007, *Christ and Empire: From Paul to Postcolonial Times*, Minneapolis, MN: Fortress Press, p. vii).

45 Chidester, David, 1996, 'Anchoring Religion in the World: A Southern African History of Comparative Religion', *Religion* 26:2, pp. 141–59, p. 155.

I believe, avoids casting religion as a *sui generis* phenomenon, avoids monolithic traditions, and does not prioritize modernist Western (liberal Christian) norms, being based in factors from across religious spectrums. The typology has six factors, based on a notion of Wittgensteinean family resemblances, of which any system which has over half would seem to be what we normally term a 'religion'. I will briefly outline the typology.[46] The six factors are:

1   Belief in a spiritual power or being(s).
2   Interest in the afterlife.
3   Guiding societal and/or ethical norms.
4   It is transformative.
5   Methods or procedures for prayer or meditation.
6   It explains the human and natural situation.

I will briefly describe each, though emphasizing that not all are necessary to define something as a 'religion', and that many 'religions' or 'religious' areas will not relate to all of them.

Belief in a spiritual power or being(s): Belief in (perhaps) a supreme God, or some form of spiritual power pervading the universe, or in lesser deities or spiritual beings. The core of this factor is a belief in something that transcends the purely physical or phenomenal universe. It is not just a belief that something directs or guides the course of phenomenal events, but is itself phenomenal. It suggests that there is another 'transcendent' layer to the universe.

Interest in the afterlife: Teachings on what happens after this life, suggesting that individual human existence is not the end. Teachings may offer rewards or punishments for our behaviour in this life. Normally, the continuity involves a fixed 'soul' that links the 'I' in this life with the 'I' in the next, but not always.

Guiding societal and/or ethical norms: It provides a 'way of life'. This may be guidelines for the individual, or social and cultural systems into

---

46   Space does not permit a full extrapolation, so I refer readers to my fuller accounts: Hedges, 'Defining', Part I, and 'Can We Still Teach'.

which the individual is bound. In different settings, and at different times, the same religious tradition may function in both ways. This way of life will be determined by the other factors, such as belief in deity, the afterlife, the way to transformation, etc. This factor, perhaps, shows most fully where the 'religious' impinges on the 'secular', although, often, this impinging will mean the secular becomes 'religious' (we discuss this further below).

It is Transformative: The reorientation, or transformation, of the devotee is sought. Generally, it is recognized that the way we live, or our essential nature, is impure or not correctly aligned or adjusted. Therefore, a solution is offered to orientate the devotee in a manner determined by the other factors. Exactly how this happens can vary within traditions. Three aspects exist: 1) *forms*; 2) *timescales*; 3) *types*. Forms: 'weak' transformation is where the devotee decides to follow the religious path, but, she is not inherently changed except by commitment; 'strong' transformation fundamentally alters the devotee, perhaps, with direct 'mystical' contact with the divine, she is 'reshaped' or 'reformed'. In the former, the devotee follows the religious path because it is required, in the latter, once transformed, the devotee follows the religious path because that has become her nature. Timescales: before and after death. Types: 'sudden', where the devotee is catapulted by an 'instant experience' into a new state; 'gradual' where the devotee has an ongoing process of alteration. Each of these is not necessarily exclusive of any other, some traditions seeing various transformations happening at different times or in different ways.

Methods or procedures for prayer or meditation: Apart from ethical behaviour, the devotee shows her orientation through 'religiously orientated actions'. These behaviours may include giving adoration or thanks, making petitionary intercessions, seeking to 'attune' oneself with the divine, community festivals, pilgrimages, etc. In seeking to orientate the devotee towards that which the religion sees as most important within life, it must be placed in relation to factors 1, 2 and 4.

It explains the human and natural situation: Teachings describe where the devotee is and what she or he should do in this situation. Explained in terms of other aspects of the religion's orientation, it may discuss the causes or origin of such things as the world, human suffering, etc. Some cosmo-theologic questions may be described as beyond human knowing or simply not important.

Elsewhere I have suggested this typology distinguishes those phenomena we commonly define as religions, from those we don't, thus Marxism or forms of nationalism do not fit, although there clearly are close affinities.[47] It should also be stressed that I understand the typology as, primarily, about institutional traditions; it does not directly give some insight into what 'religion' as a 'thing' is in and of itself (or if it even exists).[48]

This typology, I hope, helps explain why we have groups of traditions in different cultural situations which have, historically speaking, related to each other in terms of kinship and relationship – though this may be marked out in terms of contestation rather than partnership. To use the term 'religion' therefore is to speak about these traditions, which, I postulate, are orientated to the transcendent along the lines described within the typology. However, such a typology gives us only certain, limited, data. As far as Kwok is concerned, theology should be concerned with asking broader questions about how religions relate to culture, an area which can be cut off if theology envisages its task as asking questions of truth in spiritual realms.[49] While I recognize that my typology might be used to favour what may be seen as 'spiritual' concerns, and could also be used to support the kind of elite traditions which Kwok has spoken of, we should recognize that 'religion' is not a monolithic structure and, indeed, as my typology suggests, has a vast diversity of forms and structures embedded within it which must be considered as part and parcel

47 Hedges, 'Defining', Part II.

48 I have discussed the nature of 'religion' and its problematic discussion in a conference paper, 'Religious Difference and the Difference of Religion: An Initial Reply to the Cultured Despisers of the Category "Religion"', Australian Association for the Study of Religion Conference, 2009, Melbourne, which I hope to develop into an article at some stage.

49 Kwok, *Postcolonial*, pp. 204–5, see also p. 208. This is a concern raised by Fitzgerald and McCutcheon, whose views we will discuss at various points in this work.

of any religious tradition.[50] We will therefore proceed to consider this alongside asking how and why interreligious dialogue is intimately related to the kinds of answers I have given to the question of what religion is. This will involve refining our definition.

Contesting the secular: refining our definition

At this stage it would be useful to introduce another important aspect of the critique against our contemporary usage of the term religion, which is that it plays into a very problematic portrayal of the terms 'secular' and 'religious'. This argument has been most fully developed by Fitzgerald.[51] He argues, most persuasively, that in much contemporary discourse and understanding we have divided the world into two realms that, to us, appear 'natural' and 'neutral'. That is, a 'secular' realm related to politics, economics, law and order, etc., and a 'religious' realm to do with faith and is essentially private and should not interfere with the former. He sees it enshrined most notably in the US Constitution where state and religion are divorced, and where it helps play an international role in establishing this division as normative. Through historical studies he shows us how such an assumption has not existed in previous times; indeed, at least into the nineteenth century in the United Kingdom he shows that religion and political power were intimately related. Therefore, he argues, to continue to use the term 'religion' helps perpetuate, as normative, a language that maintains this created divide. In practical terms we get a discourse in the media that speaks of, for instance, Islamic 'religious' authorities becoming 'illegitimately' involved in 'secular' spheres such as politics, schooling, dress codes and other such matters. Such a distinction, of course, disregards the way Shariah law is intimately tied up with what we may see as 'secular' affairs. We therefore

50 My working definition of religion, while I suggest helpful, stands no doubt in need of refinement and development in relation to these and other factors.

51 See Fitzgerald, Timothy, 2007, *Discourse on Civility and Barbarity: A Critical History of Religion and Related Categories*, Oxford: Oxford University Press; it is also a theme in Fitzgerald, *Ideology*. I am currently preparing a review article of *Discourse* for the *Journal of Religious History* (hopefully 2011).

see, in very concrete terms, the way our theoretical production of the term 'religion' has very real effects in areas of interreligious/intercultural encounter. Indeed, such issues become pressing for interreligious dialogue, and D'Costa argues it is perhaps through religions meeting in the Public Square that we can most readily deal with such problems, in ways that a secularized discourse cannot adequately do.[52]

Certainly, it is clear that the notion of 'religious' and 'secular' areas of culture, which is essentially a modern distinction, is not recognized in many traditional cultures, where each interpenetrates the other. This may seem to be a problem with the definition of religion which I have proposed; however, I would suggest that it is not, and clarifying why not will also bring to light several important factors for dialogue. To this end, we may note:

while, for many traditional societies, divine laws or energy may permeate, saturate, or be completely interwoven into the area we would in modern Western cultures call 'secular', there is still a demarcation in most, if not all, societies and cultures. For instance, while a Hindu vaishya householder may be following his dharma by being a merchant in the world, his way of life is still distinguished from the temple officiating Brahmin priest or the sunnyasi (renouncing holy man). Again, while Shariah law and the Sunnah of the Prophet is woven into the whole of a Muslim's life, time given over to prayer or recitation of the Qur'an is still distinct from this.[53]

Hence, despite the way that the 'religious' and 'secular' divide creates a false and quite untenable category, there are still areas we may speak of as more or less 'sacred' or 'profane' – a distinction Fitzgerald suggests we maintain.[54] This 'sacred' arena, the 'transcendent' of our definition, may relate to what Joerg Rieger refers to as a 'theological surplus', the

---

52 D'Costa, *Christianity*, Part III. I consider this to be, in many ways, the strongest and most important part of this book.

53 Hedges, 'Can We Still Teach', note 14.

54 Fitzgerald, *Discourse*, pp. 25, 55 and 76ff.

additional meaning that lays on top of what might be given within the 'mundane'.[55] This may be considered significant for dialogue in at least two ways:

1   Religions in dialogue need to understand where they stand in relation to the standards of the 'secular' world and present, from their own standpoint, an alternative vision.

2   It helps clarify some possible misunderstandings in areas of discussion, for instance, where specifically 'political' or 'social' questions arise, which may not seem explicitly 'religious' to someone from certain Christian or Buddhist standpoints, but are considered as such by a Muslim or Jew. Moreover, if no clear line stands between 'religion' and other areas of 'culture' or 'society' then we will not see interreligious dialogue as simply a discussion about 'spiritual' concerns constructed along certain frameworks.[56] This suggests that the varieties of dialogue, whether it be the dialogue of life or religious experience are not distinct and separate spheres or areas of encounter, but places that meet and crossover.

The 'religions' and identity: refining our definition

We have addressed above the concern raised by McCutcheon and others that the modern notion of religions creates 'essentialist' identities of each religion, such that we can talk in uniform ways about 'Hinduism', 'Islam', etc. I believe that my typological suggestion avoids this, speaking instead of a religious orientation. Therefore, I have even suggested we can still continue to speak of 'religion' and the 'religions'. I see this as historically grounded; for instance, in Indian parlance the teachings of the Buddha would have been called Buddha Dharma (the 'tradition of

---

55   Rieger, *Christ*, p. 31; see his discussion of 'surplus', pp. 9ff.

56   The way 'religion' and 'culture' are bound is discussed in Schreiter, Robert J., 2004, *The New Catholicity: Theology between the Global and the Local*, Maryknoll, NY: Orbis, p. 53.

the Buddha'), and someone could choose to follow this dharma, as opposed to, for instance, Shankara Dharma (the 'tradition of Shankara, a foundational figure for Advaita Vedanta) or another tradition. In China, a similar motif was used: what we call Buddhism, or the Indians call Buddha Dharma, would have been termed *'fojiao'* ('Buddha tradition'), which roughly translates as tradition of the Buddha as well, while we also have *rujiao* (the scholar's tradition) for Confucianism.[57] In terming this Buddhist tradition as Buddhism we are simply following this tradition, and something similar may apply elsewhere.[58]

To move to a key issue, Christian identity, as we saw in Chapter 1, is not a solid fixed boundary, but it is always constructed in relation to other religious boundaries and identities. Indeed, this understanding avoids constructing such identities as *sui generis*, that is to say they are not created in a vacuum that is a purely spiritual place; rather our religion 'becomes' at the intersection of various 'sacred' and 'mundane' concerns and affairs (see Chapter 5). Religious identities are always created and negotiated in context. Indeed, when we come to speak of religions in context we should consider this in relation to the impasse and what this may mean for dialogue. Fletcher has suggested that much of the problem comes from the following problematic attitude:

Christian identity . . . is shared among all Christians in distinction to other religions. From among the many ways of being human in

---

57 Certainly our term 'Confucianism' is a misnomer for it suggests the figure of Confucius is a founding figure in a way he would certainly not accept. In China he was seen as a consolidator of a tradition, and we may suggest it would be like calling Judaism 'Mosesism'. However, regardless of the inadequacy of our term it can still be used as a functional equivalent to *'rujiao'*.

58 This approach is not, though, without its problems. As we have noted, 'Hinduism' is more of a family of traditions, but one which has become accepted by modern-day Hindus. Also, boundaries are not clearly defined; under the Indian constitution, for instance, Buddhists and Sikhs are regarded as Hindus – their religions being seen as belonging to the same Indic source. The construction of the terms is therefore political; however, if we do not wish to constitute the religions as fixed and unchanging entities this problem does not necessarily discredit our usage of the terms.

the world, the categories 'Hindu', 'Christian', 'Jewish', 'Buddhist', 'Muslim' or 'indigenous/tribal' emerge as identifiable collectivities each of which is defined by a unique set of features shared among the members of the group. The collectivity of persons who share these features make up a given 'religion'.[59]

Referencing McCutcheon, she goes on to discuss how these manageable categories are used to suggest 'religions' with fixed essences which can either be brought into relation with one another or clearly distinguished.[60] We must recognize that each religion is far from monolithic, but is rather a collected set of communal and individual identities. Therefore when, as a Christian, I engage in dialogue with a Hindu, for instance, we do not stand as polar opposites: a 'Christian' and a 'Hindu' with no clear meeting place. First, as I have suggested, we share at least some commonality through religious identities and, indeed, we need to recognize that throughout history our religions have interacted and conversed.[61] Second, as Fletcher points out, our identities are complex matters; we are never simply 'Christians', but Christians from a particular country, with a particular job, social class, gender, family background and so on. Applied to religions in dialogue, we do not have fixed essences existing in relation to each other. Rather 'religions' are aspects of identity markers within cultures and part of a nexus of related concepts. Indeed, because we all exist as groups of multiple identities, Fletcher further suggests that creating a 'Christian' view of, for instance, 'Islam' may not be helpful, we have created two boxes that divide. However, when we meet a particular Muslim we may find points of contact, yet because of the convoluted natures of our identities we should not expect to find the same points of contact when we meet another particular Muslim.[62] This relates directly to interreligious dialogue as we dialogue not just as people with

---

59 Fletcher, Jeannine Hill, 2005, *Monopoly on Salvation? A Feminist Approach to Religious Pluralism*, New York, London: Continuum, pp. 77–8.

60 Fletcher, *Monopoly*, pp. 79–80.

61 Possibly the best study of this is Clarke, J. J., 1997, *Oriental Enlightenment: The Encounter Between Asian and Western Thought*, London: Routledge.

62 Fletcher, *Monopoly*, p. 94.

a religious identity, but as people with a range of identities. As Fletcher expresses it, recognition of this gives us an 'Openness to the unanticipatable multiplicity inherent in each person [which] allows the encounter to take place in freedom.'[63] Dialogue, indeed, must be open to a challenging of religious identities, and Ian Markham has suggested that one problem with the way interreligious dialogue is commonly constructed is that 'Even though the dialogue will change the faith of the individual, no one is allowed to challenge the appropriateness of the label', by which he means the defined religious boundary named as 'Christian', 'Hindu', 'Sikh', 'Muslim', etc.[64] The boundedness of such labels becomes less clear in the light of the critique of 'religion'.

To relate the discussion above to the previous point, religious identity seen as being simply bound up with a 'spiritual' or 'theological' realm is misconceived, because there is no natural space between this and other aspects of life. Indeed, the typology in seeing the religious sphere as part of the cultural sphere emphasizes that no real distinction between the 'secular' and 'religious' realms exists. While religion operates as a useful term to determine a range of activities, beliefs and influences of a particular type, we must not close it off, because our identities, including our religious identities, are multivalent phenomena (the experience of Christianity of a black, female, working-class, Pentecostal American will of necessity be different to that of a white, male, middle-class, Catholic Austrian). Religion's sphere includes political, cultural, social, artistic and other realms, yet is not readily dividable into its own distinct realm, so we cannot speak of what is solely 'religious' as opposed to any other of these.

I should stress here that I do not mean that our Christian identity is just one minor factor among others. Christians will, or should, see their Christian identity as a positioning factor that shapes, to some degree, other identities. I have purposefully underemphasized this aspect

---

63   Fletcher, *Monopoly*, p. 94.

64   Markham, Ian, 2004, 'The Dialogue Industry', Lecture One of the Teape Lectureship in India, available from, www.hartsem.edu/centers/markham_article1.htm, accessed 9 June 2009.

because, with our modern construct of religion, it tends to be overemphasized as though it existed alone or out of relation to all other identities. Although, ideally, Christians may see themselves as under Christ above and beyond all else, especially rather than as party members (see 1 Cor. 1.12), it is inevitable that we always bear that identity in a particular place, at a particular time, and in relation to a particular embodiment. Moreover, this boundedness as being 'in Christ' does not erase all other contexts (see Chapters 1 and 6), but exists incarnationally and historically. These two factors in Christian theology mean that we cannot, in accordance with tradition, take a Christian identity divorced from its context, but must see it in direct relationship to the full extent of God's revelation and creative activity in the world. This restates, in more theological terms, my above argument.

The activity of dialogue

Dialogical encounter

To speak of interreligious dialogue in relation to religious identities we may therefore make a number of points, some of which we have already discussed in some detail, others are ones which will be discussed further on or developed more as we proceed:

1   The Christian tradition is a multivalent and pluriform set of traditions which have an open-ended relationship, in their origins, with other religious traditions such as Judaism, the mystery religions of the first centuries, and Neoplatonic thought.
2   Christian orthodoxy, in a historically nuanced and ecumenical context, does not consist in adherence to a single dogmatic formula, whether this be Chalcedon orthodoxy or anything else, and various factors such as political debates have shaped notions of 'orthodoxy' and 'heresy'.
3   To adopt a Christian identity today is to be in dynamic relationship with other traditions in a global and intercultural context.

4   Dialogue demands a radical openness and thinking through of our own tradition in recognition of its permeable barriers in relation to the religious Other.

5   We cannot usefully speak of ourselves as 'Christians' in relation to 'Hinduism' or even 'Hindus', etc. but rather as individuals and communities, each in relation to variously formed sets of religious communities and identities.

6   All religious identities, including our own, are not 'pure' religious/theological/spiritual things with some inviolate way of being 'Christian' but rather multivalent, created and dynamic interrelationships.

This is, evidently, not a set of clear or obvious standpoints upon which to base the activity of interreligious dialogue. It is easier to think of convenient blocks of Christians viewing Muslims or Hindus through an inclusivist, exclusivist or pluralist lens. However, to do so is to do an injustice both to our own religious traditions and identities and also to the religious traditions and identities of those Others we encounter. We may, however, see this encounter in terms of a radical openness to religious Others in which we realize the porous edges of our identities. However, this does not entail any particular end result. It does not entail that we allow our tradition to drift amorphously into a homogenous unitary religion. Each tradition has got its own integral structures.

Scriptural Reasoning

Some may think that Scriptural Reasoning does not belong within the areas of the theology of religions or interreligious dialogue as it does not come from an angle that specifically sees itself as dealing with Christianity's encounter with other religions. Born at meetings of the American Academy of Religion it began with a group of Jewish scholars seeking to read their own scriptures from within the integrity of their own religion in traditional ways (although inspired by post-liberal Christian hermeneutics). Later, both Muslim and Christian scholars joined these groups, and so the venture become a multireligious (composed of many religions) one.[65] Inevitably, this has interreligious overtones, and although it can be seen as a means for each tradition to find resources to learn more about their own scriptures and traditions, rather than relating to other traditions, the multireligious nature of it means that it is from other traditions that resources may come to assist in reading one's own scriptures. While, in bringing traditions together, it is, and can be stressed as, a more explicitly interreligious encounter; indeed, for many who practise it if has become primarily an interreligious venture.[66] Whether it is a multireligious or interreligious venture, will depend upon the nature of particular groups, individuals, and how one interprets these two terms.

The nature of Scriptural Reasoning gives it some distinctive features, which may be seen as deeply beneficial. For one thing, it tends to involve what may broadly be termed more 'conservative' figures within the traditions it represents, who may well have no interest in being engaged in other kinds of 'interreligious' encounter. It therefore provides a valuable service in bringing different communities into relationship particularly in terms of the more conservative ends of the spectrum.[67] It also represents itself as a 'civic practice', by which it seems to mean that it is not simply an academic venture, but one that works in the community and, indeed, it seems aimed to position itself as a major framework for creating

---

65 Ford, David, 2006, 'An Interfaith Wisdom: Scriptural Reasoning Between Jews, Christians and Muslims', *Modern Theology* 22:3, pp. 346–66, pp. 347–8. This edition of *Modern Theology* was devoted to Scriptural Reasoning, with all the articles subsequently published as Ford, David and Pecknold, C. C. (eds), *The Promise of Scriptural Reasoning*, Oxford: Blackwell.

66 See the *Journal of Scriptural Reasoning* website, http://etext.lib.virginia.edu/journals/jsrforum/gateways.html and Adams, Nicholas, 2006, 'Making Deep Reasonings Public', *Modern Theology* 22:3, pp. 385–401, especially pp. 396–401. As adopted and practised beyond the academy it is often explicitly seen as primarily a form of interreligious dialogue.

67 In this it is useful, as much dialogue may be seen to prohibit conservatives (see Markham, 'Dialogue'). Notably a fatwa, a Muslim legal opinion, has been issued in the UK to make Muslims comfortable with this type of dialogue and which has permitted meetings in mosques (see Williams, Jenny, 2009, 'Sense and Spirituality', *The Baptist Times*, 12 March, available at, http://www.scripturalreasoning.org.uk/the_baptist_times_12_march_2009.pdf (last accessed 27 April 2010)).

meetings between the Abrahamic faiths.[68] It is here, perhaps, that it most clearly becomes a form of interreligious dialogue. Within this, some of the major figures seem to have an almost evangelical desire to see Scriptural Reasoning spread through as many communities as possible; although much interreligious work is at a grassroots level and so it is not unique in this, but it does offer a unified platform for local meetings.

Yet, Scriptural Reasoning is not without its downsides as well. For one thing, by being composed of many figures who proclaim little interest in interreligious dialogue, it can leave those who engage in it with little awareness either of the other traditions they encounter, or the sensibilities needed to encounter the religious Other.[69] For another, by so heavily foregrounding scripture and certain forms of reading it leaves little place for those outside the Abrahamic family of religions to engage with it, which is not to decry the importance of trialogue between these three groups, but limits the wider interreligious applicability of Scriptural Reasoning.[70] Finally, by emphasizing the need for participants to read and understand the scriptures deeply from within their own tradition it favours certain readings, groups and traditions. These will normally be male (some traditions will not allow women the training needed to engage with scriptures at this level) representatives of the 'great' tradition, with the 'little' tradition being ignored (on this distinction see Chapter 5). It therefore tends to reinforce certain elitist hierarchical readings and

---

68   Scriptural Reasoning website, http://www.scripturalreasoning.org/index. php.

69   For instance, one notable Christian proponent of Scriptural Reasoning, speaking of reading the Hebrew Bible, remarked that it was very strange because although these are *our* books they also in some sense belonged to Jews as well. The audacious claim that these Jewish books belonged primarily to Christians is shocking to interreligious sensibilities, let alone the offence it could cause. Perhaps this was just an unconsidered phrase, but it may indicate some issues about the competency of Scriptural Reasoning as an approach when it comes to the practicalities of community cohesion and relating sensitively to communities outside its own sealed hermeneutical practice.

70   That it is a particularly Abrahamic enterprise is emphasized by several figures; see, for instance, Kepnes, Stephen, 2006, 'A Handbook for Scriptural Reasoning', *Modern Theology* 22:3, pp. 367–83, p. 367, and Ford, 'Interfaith', p. 346.

traditions in ways that may seek to override the multivalent nature of religious traditions, and the disparate groups that compose them. Therefore, it makes it a problematic basis for any genuine interreligious encounter and dialogue to take place as it can favour conformity (this is not to deny that Scriptural Reasoning is very much aware of, and attuned to, the variety of ways scriptures have been read, but in so far as these are raised within such groups it will reflect a multivalent set of readings only inside the elite traditions that it foregrounds).[71]

Multiple religious belonging

The act of belonging to two religious identities at the same time is not, of itself, an act of interreligious dialogue, in the sense of a meeting of two individuals or two communities. However, an internal dialogue must take place within the existential context of the multiple religious belonger herself, and presumably takes place in a context of exposure to the lived reality of these different traditions. Moreover, it has important implications for interreligious dialogue and the theology of religions in general.

In recent years there has been an increasing interest in multiple religious belonging.[72] It is increasingly recognized that multiple, or dual,

---

71 For some related critiques of Scriptural Reasoning as an interreligious practice see Lambkin, Magdalen, 2010, 'Can Scriptures Unite? A Hiedogical exploration of the irreligious practice of Spritual Reasoning', *eSharp*, 15, pp. 42–64.

72 The major work is Cornille, Catherine (cd.), 2002, *Many Mansions? Christian Identity and Multiple Religious Belonging*, Maryknoll, NY: Orbis; see also, Drew, Rose, 2009, *An Exploration of Buddhist Christian Dual Belonging*, unpublished PhD thesis, University of Glasgow, UK (publication with Routledge due in 2011); Schmidt-Leukel, Perry, 2009, *Transformation by Integration: How Inter-faith Encounter Changes Christianity*, London: SCM, pp. 46–66, 110–11, 187–93; Gooses, Gideon, 2007, 'An Empirical Study of Dual Religious Belonging', *Journal of Empirical Theology* 20:2, pp. 159–78. Academics who claim dual or multiple identity include Julius Lipner an Indian and Czech professor of Hinduism at Cambridge who calls himself a Hindu-Catholic (see Lipner, Julius, 1994, 'ISKCON at the Crossroads', *ISKCON Communications Journal* 2:1, available at, http://www.iskcon.com/icj/2_1/lipner.html, accessed 14 September 2009), and Bettina Bäumer, an Austrian Indologist (see Schmidt-Leukel, *Transformation*, pp. 63–4).

religious belonging is not the preserve of a few exceptional and gifted individuals at what may be seen as the levels of 'mystical' attainment or exceptional theological refinement, exemplified by such figures as Abhistikananda, Bede Griffiths or Aloysius Pieris.[73] Rather, as our discussion of the nature of religion and religious identity suggests, it is a viable option for a greater number and, indeed, appears to be part of an increasing trend, perhaps made possible by our increasingly multicultural and multireligious societies. In exploring this area, we must disagree with John Cobb that people 'deeply rooted in one tradition' will not be attracted to this path, as many prominent figures who speak of dual belonging are 'deeply rooted' in their own tradition, especially in non-Western, but increasingly also Western, contexts.[74] Moreover, if we take seriously what I suggested was intended by dialogue, that it 'signifies worldviews being argued *through* to significant and potentially transformative conclusions', then in the light of a more nuanced understanding of religions we would not see it as, of itself, giving up a Christian identity in a sense that may be seen as infidelity to the tradition; indeed, as Clooney argues, God will meet us where we are even across boundaries.[75]

We can note affinities to Comparative Theology, where in seeking actively to create a conversation between religions, the possibility of boundary crossing is opened. In some ways, we may contrast Comparative Theology and multiple religious belonging with the conceptions behind Scriptural Reasoning: reading across traditions versus within traditions; religious boundaries being seen as open versus fixed. An increasing number of figures are involved in Comparative Theology. Figures who

---

73 See Dupuis, Jacques, 2002, 'Christianity and Religions: Complementarity and Convergence', in Cornille (ed.), *Many*, pp. 61–75, pp. 69–71 for a discussion of Abhistikananda, or Harris, Elisabeth, 2002, 'Double Belonging in Sri Lanka: Illusion or Liberating Path?', in Cornille (ed.), *Many*, pp. 76–92, pp. 85–9 for a discussion of Pieris.

74 Cobb, John B. Jr, 2002, 'Multiple Religious Belonging and Reconciliation', in Cornille (ed.), *Many*, pp. 20–43, p. 24.

75 Clooney, Francis, 2002, 'God for Us: Multiple Religious Belonging as Spiritual Practice and Divine Response', in Cornille (ed.), *Many*, pp. 44–60, pp. 45 and 59.

would be seen as being in complete fidelity to their own tradition and within the bounds of orthodoxy as traditionally envisaged, yet are engaging in the sympathetic and humble study of different religious traditions to find not just points of comparison, but also areas where insight and inspiration may be found. Indeed, Clooney relates his practice of reading texts across traditions to a form of multiple religious belonging.[76] If we take it that we are not dealing with fixed and impermeable religious boundaries where 'Christian' attitudes are one thing, and 'Hindu', 'Buddhist', 'Muslim', 'Daoist', etc. attitudes are something else, then we can see where religious distinctions may cross, grow, evolve and develop. To suggest that we can remain wholly within one tradition, yet truly open and sympathetic to another is, according to Perry Schmidt-Leukel, a 'hardly convincing compromise', who argues we can radically enter into different identities.[77] As we have seen (Chapter 1) this is the pattern of development that marked out Christianity's origins. Why should we assume that such development stopped with the early church; indeed, we know for a fact that it did not: Thomas Aquinas, for instance, was inspired by Aristotle through Jewish and Islamic lenses – in some senses he was a boundary crosser. However, even when we consider the more radical move of a dual or multiple belonger it does not necessarily entail losing one's primary identity within one tradition, with many of the main Christian dual belongers seeing their primary, Christian, identity enriched by contact with another (which in turn may provide resources for that other religion).[78]

Another very pertinent issue is that if we accept, as I have argued, that Christian identity is bound up with cultural identity, then the notion

---

76 Clooney, 'God', p. 57; he speaks here of being 'intertexted'.

77 Schmidt-Leukel, *Transformation*, pp. 50–1, the particular instance that causes him to use this phrase is Catherine Cornille's suggestion that we should have 'complete openness' to another tradition combined with 'total commitment' to one's own (Cornille, Catherine, 2005, 'Conditions for the Possibility of Inter-religious Dialogue on God', in Lande, A. and Jeanrond, Werner (eds), *The Concept of God in Global Dialogue*, Maryknoll, NY: Orbis, pp. 3–18, p. 8.

78 See Jacques, 'Christianity' (on Abhistikananda), Harris, 'Double' (on Pieris and Michael Rodrigo), and Jeanrond, Werner, G., 'Belonging or Identity? Christian Faith in a Multi-Religious World', in Cornille (ed.), *Many*, pp. 106–20 (on Hugo M. Enomiya-Lassalle).

of multiple religious belonging would appear natural for many Asian Christians, especially within the Chinese and Japanese world. To be Chinese or Japanese culturally is to inhabit a world steeped in values that owe much to Confucianism (and to Daoism and Buddhism).[79] The same applies to India, where, again, religious and cultural aspects of identity cannot be disentangled. Moreover, for centuries, multiple belonging has been the norm in parts of East Asia.[80] Today, we may ask if this is true in just this context; could multiple belonging be a norm in a globalized world?[81] While some would see this as a possible syncretic watering down of 'pure' Christian identity, and the exclusionist principle these have been supposed to entail, I have argued against such a view from grounds internal to Christianity as well as on an academic basis concerning the nature of religion (related themes will also be argued in subsequent chapters).

Power and dialogue

We must issue a caveat here. So far our discussion has been related to mainly theoretical concerns, but behind this lies a realm of politics and a

---

79   The Rites controversy dealt with just this issue. In eighteenth-century China, Jesuit missionaries argued that Chinese converts could make sacrifices to Confucius as he was regarded as just a great teacher not a deity, and the ancestors as this was simply an act of filial piety not religious observance to the spirits (a stance supported by the emperor Kangxi (1654–1722) who wrote to the Pope outlining this position). Enemies of the Jesuits ensured, however, that their petitions were rejected, and the Roman Catholic Church rejected these ideas, effectively destroying decades of missionary work, and ensured that a Christian presence would not be significant in China for many years (see on the debates and issues, Cummins, J. S., 1993, *A Question of Rites: Friar Domingo Navarrete and the Jesuits in China*, Aldershot: Scolar Press, and Whyte, Bob, 1988, *Unfinished Encounter: China and Christianity*, Glasgow: Collins, Ch. II. An excellent recent volume on the Jesuits in China is Brockey, Liam M., 2007, *Journey to the East: The Jesuit Mission to China, 1579–1724*, Cambridge, MA: Harvard University Press, see pp. 184–94 on this issue).

80   See Berling, *Pilgrim*, pp. 8–9, and, Bragt, Jan Van, 2002, 'Multiple Religious Belonging and the Japanese People', in Cornille (ed.), *Mansions*, pp. 7–19.

81   Schreiter, *New*, p. 26; see also Clooney, 'God'.

history of colonialism, while a continuing cultural imbalance in terms of power relations persists. While interreligious dialogue may seem to be a matter of 'spirituality', the way it is described and mediated is bound up, as we have already hinted, in a whole network of other factors.

One aspect is our understanding of 'religion', which, as we have seen, has been written by a dominant Western discourse that shapes our understanding of other traditions. The effects of this are not neutral. For instance, as we have discussed, in China multiple religious belonging has been the norm; however, the author has been informed that today Buddhist and Daoist teachers in temples will tell their devotees not to frequent other places of worship or to consult with the increasing number of popular religious teachers found on the mainland.[82] This might suggest that indigenous religions are trying to remodel themselves as closed realms imitating a Western understanding of religious identify, at least from a top-down level. This I believe is becoming seen as normative in China, and certainly I have met Chinese who believe that people should belong to just one 'religion'.[83] Therefore, writing from a Western Christian perspective, it must be acknowledged that the lingering effects of Western imperialism need to be considered as a factor in the power construction of religious identity. Within our current world situation, Western culture has a powerful dominant hegemony which is tied to the economic and military power of the West.

Western culture has been a dominant cultural export since the time of the Portuguese and Spanish colonial ventures of the fifteenth century, becoming more pronounced in the global economic and military

---

82 I have also heard Chinese Christian priests give similar directions in sermons, something that is, perhaps, less surprising. Elisabeth Harris observes something comparable in Sri Lanka. When missionaries first arrived, Buddhists there assumed that one could be both Christian and Buddhist; however, pressures have led to the assumption that one cannot be both (see Harris, 'Double', p. 80).

83 This seems to be the view of the government, perhaps to make 'religion' more manageable; however, it is clear that such distinctions do not exist at many popular levels (see Hedges, Paul, 2010 'China', in Biondo, V. and Hecht, R. (eds), *Religion and Everyday Daily Life and Culture*, Vol. 1: 'Religion in the Practice of Daily Life in World History', Santa Barbara, CA: Praeger, pp. 45–82).

dominance of the British Empire in the nineteenth, shifting to the dominance of the American dollar in the twentieth. Various media and commercial exports have enhanced this process, such that certain global brands, be it Coca Cola, MTV, Kentucky Fried Chicken or others, have become almost universally known and associated with 'modernization', 'development', and other such motifs. It may be asked what has this got to do with religion? Surely the spiritual and transcendent values of religion exist within another sphere, or may even be seen to offer a counter narrative against such commercialism. While this may be so to some degree, we exist in a world not of cultural diversity, but of what Homi Bhabha has termed cultural difference, a term he suggests 'focuses on the problem of the ambivalence of cultural authority'.[84] Rather than simply proclaiming 'diversity', he believes we must stress the power asymmetry that exists between cultures. Within this we must recognize that a Western (Christian/academic) discourse has a power as a norm associated with progress, modernity, development, even power and technology that may be aspired to. This is not to suggest, though, that counter currents do not exist, which we will address shortly. However, we must recognize that the Western 'container construction' image of religion is a powerful and dominant cultural export.

Although interreligious dialogue seeks to bring religions together on a level of equality, it cannot escape these power dynamics. Indeed, Wesley Ariarajah has suggested that it tends to neglect the 'power dimension'.[85] One aspect of this is revealed in the quote that began our discussion on 'religion' from Kwok, where Third World elites are co-opted to represent an entire tradition. In this way, it may be suggested that dialogue tends to efface intrareligious difference, where powerful patriarchal figures from elite traditions give a definitive version of how their religion should be

84   Bhabha, Homi, 1994, *The Location of Culture*, London: Routledge, p. 34. See on this Kwok, *Postcolonial*, pp. 42–3.

85   Ariarajah, Wesley S., 2002, 'Power, Politics, and Plurality: The Struggles of the World Council of Churches to Deal with Religious Plurality', in Knitter, Paul F. (ed.), *The Myth of Religious Supremacy*, Maryknoll, NY: Orbis, pp. 176–93, p. 176; he references the work of Felix Wilfred in this regard (Wilfred, Felix, 2002, 'Interreligious Dialogue as a Political Quest', *Journal of Dharma* 28:1).

(see Chapter 5). Indeed, in as far as the discussions tend to take place within an atmosphere that is often seeking to promote unity and show similarity, we should heed Schreiter's warning: 'Denial of difference can lead to the colonization of a culture and its imagination.'[86] Indeed, we should be aware that in wanting to be included Third World cultural representatives may well, even if only implicitly, shape their tradition to fit the expectations of the dominant Western cultural discourse.[87] We therefore have to be aware of our discourse, critiques of it, and the fact that 'Postcolonial criticism bears witness to the unequal and uneven forces of cultural representation involved in the contest for political and social authority within the modern world order.'[88]

In respect of this, I would like to highlight several dangers that can easily intrude. First, Markham warns that individualism marks many dialogic principles.[89] It is about free-floating 'modern' individuals without societal or communal ties who can pick and choose among a range of religious options, altering their religious identity as they go. Such a luxury exists through the creation and maintenance of certain discourses and forms of social control, found primarily in Western nations, and in many traditional societies such an option is not possible. Indeed, for many, from more communal societies, such a notion may be considered 'anti-religious': how can someone operate without regard to their community, society, etc. It presupposes, it may be suggested, in Geert Hofstede's scales of cultures, an individualist and low-context society, such as the United States of America, as opposed to a collectivist, high-context society found, for example, in East Asia.[90]

Second, if Western norms do dominate, we must be aware that a danger of liberalism is to recognize tolerance but in a patronizing way that assumes others (non-white societies) are less advanced, or stuck in the

---

86 Schreiter, *New*, p. 43.

87 See Hedges, Paul, 2008, 'Concerns about the Global Ethic: A Sympathetic Critique and Suggestions for a New Direction', *Studies in Interreligious Dialogue* 18:2, pp. 153–68, pp. 160–1.

88 Bhabha, *Location*, p. 171.

89 Markham, 'Dialogue'.

90 On Geert Hofstede's series of scales, see Schreiter, *New*, pp. 36–8.

past.[91] Whether this pressure is to become more individualistic, to demarcate religious boundaries in non-traditional ways, or to adopt a pluralist model to enter dialogue, the West has, in part at least, created the modern religious scenery. As Bhabha has argued, power does not just reside in direct coercion but also in the myths, fantasies, dreams and obsessions of the dominant discourse which can affect the way the other understands and presents itself.[92]

Third, the inherent danger is that a Western Christian model of 'religion' becomes predominant and shapes our understanding of what religion is and does. Moreover, the mainly English-language medium for discussing dialogue can result in a certain shape being given to the discussion which will result in the creation of the outcome in a fixed 'design'.[93]

Fourth, it must be emphasized that we need to be aware of subtle imbalances and the way context creates our discourses. In particular, our social, economic and political background will create a context out of which our religious discourse will grow. In this regard Kenneth Surin's warning (although one that is highly contestable!) that Hinduism is generally expressed from the standpoint of a Third World person, while Christianity is expressed from the West is important.[94] Associating dialogue with the pluralistic hypothesis (a move Markham makes and Surin

---

91 See: Kwok, *Postcolonial*, p. 199, who references the work of Rey Chow in this regard (Chow, Rey, 2002, *The Protestant Ethnic and the Spirit of Capitalism*, New York: Columbia University Press, pp. 13–14, 28–9); and Surin, Kenneth, 1990, 'The Politics of Speech: Religious Pluralism in the Age of the McDonald's Hamburger', in D'Costa, Gavin (ed.), *Christian Uniqueness Reconsidered: The Myth of a Pluralistic Theology of Religions*, Maryknoll, NY: Orbis, pp. 192–212, p. 201.

92 See on this, Kwok, *Postcolonial*, p. 118 who references Bhabha, *Location*, p. 71. We can no doubt see the influence of Michel Foucault in this, whose work, while historically flawed, is important in emphasizing the way the dominant discourse creates power in understanding.

93 See Kwok, *Postcolonial*, pp. 43–4; here she discusses the notion of a 'global design' of Christianity becoming a norm. This term she takes from Mignolo, Walter, 2000, *Local Histories/Global Designs: Coloniality, Subaltern Knowledges, and Border Thinking*, Princeton, NJ: Princeton University Press.

94 Surin, 'Politics', p. 201. Of course, many globally known representatives of Hinduism work within the Western world, while Christianity is today mainly

appears to share), they are seen as linked in an indifference to the political, economic and social dimensions behind dialogue.[95] The danger being that many of those who most desire to embrace the religious Other with radical openness may be blind to the way the discourse is shaped through an imbalance of power.

Having outlined some dangers we must, though, issue a caveat to our caveat. As has been convincingly argued the portrayal of power as a one-way stream is extremely misleading, especially when seen as a transmission of West to East.[96] Indeed, the religious and cultural Other serves as a critique of Western and Christian norms. This is particularly the case within dialogue, which seeks to negotiate difference. While we must not ignore the warnings of post-colonial and feminist critics (see Chapter 5) about the way dialogue cannot erase power asymmetry, it provides a place where a counter discourse can be heard. If we assume that dialogue can result in taking on new identities we do not just need to read this as either an act of colonial imposition or consumerist religion, but as a sign of a wider and changing discourse.[97] We can link this to the act of taking on an ethnic identity in a diasporic situation:

> such a process of assuming an ethnic identity is an insistence on a pluralist, multidimensional, or multifaceted concept of self: one can be many different things, and this personal sense can be a crucible for a wider social ethos of pluralism.[98]

---

a Third World religion (though Kwok's notion of the Western normativity that shapes much of this should be borne in mind).

95 Surin, 'Politics', p. 204.

96 For a discussion of the relations between 'Orient' and 'Occident' over history, especially in modern times, J. J. Clark's *Oriental Enlightenment* (1997, *Oriental Enlightenment: The Encounter Between Asian and Western Thought*, London: Routledge) is a classic work debunking many myths and false assumptions.

97 On the consumerization of religion see Carrette, Jeremy and King, Richard, 2004, *Selling Spirituality: The Silent Takeover of Religion*, London: Routledge; see also Bruce, Steve, 1995, *Religion in Modern Britain*, Oxford: Oxford University Press.

98 Fischer, Michael M. J., 1986, 'Ethnicity and the Post-Modern Arts of Memory', in Clifford, James and Marcus, George E. (eds), *Writing Culture: The Poetics*

PAUL HEDGES

To engage in dialogue with the definition of religion I have suggested is to recognize the challenge to one's own cultural norms, which can, in turn, lead one on to challenge other factors within society, especially with a renewed openness to other religious and cultural forms. I would also like to raise a few other issues that would correct what is sometimes the one-sided critique of dialogue from hostile standpoints:

1 The criticism that it promotes an individualistic religion may be somewhat misplaced. An aspect that many people see as important in dialogue is the actual face-to-face meeting; as such, it is as much about individual people meeting as religious institutions meeting. Indeed, as we have suggested, the notion that huge monolithic traditions are in dialogue is simply misplaced. Moreover, the idea that religion is in some places a social-communal activity with no individual element is too extreme a view. Schmidt-Leukel has shown that religious individualism has a strong place in the Buddhist tradition; we may say that while people traditionally take refuge in the *sangha* (the community [of monks]), it is always stressed that the search for enlightenment is something you must do for yourself (to extend Schmidt-Leukel's argument, I would suggest, this is also the case in the Pure Land School, where 'other power' rather than 'self power' is a theme, as it is the individual's devotion that is stressed).[99] It is wrong to contrast a modern Western ideology (individualist) with all other traditions (communal) in simplistic dichotomies.

2 Just as some have suggested that the Western discourse is about theory, while the Third World seeks activism, we can note Bhabha's observation that they cannot be so clearly divided.[100] Such portrayals run the risk of reinforcing a problematic sense of distance and distinction, dividing the world into discrete blocks.

and Politics of Ethnography, Berkeley: University of California Press, pp. 194–233, p. 196.

99 Schmidt-Leukel, *Transformation*, pp. 55–8.
100 Bhabha, *Location*, p. 19.

3   O'Leary usefully observes that it is not a desire for philosophical unity, to erase difference, but the excitement of meeting the
religious Other that can lead to pluralism.[101] Indeed, this insight
can lead us to see that it is not modern liberals inspired by the
Enlightenment being against traditional Christians, rather the
desire to know the religious Other is a challenge, in truth, to all
universalizing standpoints.

Having noted these points we may even note that despite some problems
inherent in a traditional liberal modernism (as a universalizing model that
may, in certain senses, seek to write out difference, and has, in the past,
imposed its own ways of seeing the world) it also opens up new lines of
thought. It is a 'liberal' dialogic approach within Christianity that has
opened itself to other cultures. As Oduyoye has observed, a culturally exclusive stance on African issues has been unhelpful.[102] Meanwhile, while
Schreiter suggests a 'liberal' 'denial of difference' could lead to cultural colonization, he also criticizes 'post-liberal' alterity: 'Denial of difference promotes an anomic situation where no dialogue appears possible and only
power will prevail.'[103] I would argue that without dialogue, without listening to the other as an equal, then we have no way to critique ourselves.

We may even go further and suggest that to deny meaningful dialogue,
which we must understand as radical openness, will create other problems. John Milbank claims that dialogue is only possible if we treat the
other as a mirror of ourselves. Clearly, discussing on this basis is antithetical to dialogue for, as we have seen, dialogue is not about, as Milbank
seems to suppose, finding that we all say the same things (he seems to operate with a caricature of a pluralist-dialogue model). Instead, he takes it
upon himself to pontificate on truth and falsity in another tradition, and

---

101   O'Leary, Joseph Stephen, 1996, *Religious Pluralism and Christian Truth*,
Edinburgh: University of Edinburgh Press, see Chapter 1 'Interreligious Space'.

102   Oduyoye, Mercy Amba, 'African Culture and the Gospel: Inculturation
from an African Woman's Perspective', in Oduyoye, Mercy Amba and Vroom,
Hendrik M. (eds), *One Gospel – Many Cultures: Case Studies and Reflections on
Cross-Cultural Theology*, Amsterdam: Rodopi, pp. 39–62.

103   Schreiter, *New*, p. 43 (see Chapter 6).

even suggests that different answers in various areas shows the 'futility of "dialogue"'.[104] However, he seems to view both cultures and religions as monoliths that cannot legitimately be in dialogue.[105] Rather than beginning with the monolithic view of cultures and religions that has marred some approaches to dialogue and post-liberal views, a better starting place, Kwok observes, would be asking questions about why Western Christianity has constructed a hierarchy of religions, which Fletcher relates to historical reasons.[106] As such, by deconstructing the impasse between similarity and difference in terms of 'religion' we may open the way to a genuine dialogue, but one that still needs to attend to 'cultural difference' (see Chapters 6 and 7).

Dialogue and mission

What I have said about dialogue may seem at odds with what some see as the essence of the Christian faith and proclamation: mission. According to Andrew Kirk, 'Mission is so much at the heart of the Church's life that, rather than think of it as one aspect of its existence, it is better to think of it as defining its essence',[107] while a recent Vatican document says: 'dialogue . . . remains oriented towards proclamation in so far as the dynamic process of the Church's evangelizing mission reaches in it its climax and its fullness'.[108] This, of course, can be seen to reflect the concluding words of Matthew's Gospel, traditionally expressed in the words: 'Go ye therefore, and teach all nations, baptizing them in the name of the Father,

104 Milbank, 'End', p. 185.

105 See Chapter 4.

106 Kwok, *Postcolonial*, p. 205; Fletcher, 'Religious', p. 399, referencing the work of Ulrich Beck (2006, *Cosmopolitan Vision*, trans. Ciaran Cronin, Cambridge: Polity).

107 Kirk, J. Andrew, 1999, *What is Mission: Theological Explorations*, London: Darton, Longman and Todd, p. 30.

108 Pontifical Council for Inter-Religious Dialogue, 1991, *Dialogue and Proclamation: Reflection And Orientations On Interreligious Dialogue And The Proclamation Of The Gospel Of Jesus Christ* (1), 34, 82, available at, http://www.vatican.va/roman_curia/pontifical_councils/interelg/documents/rc_pc_interelg_doc_19051991_dialogue-and-proclamatio_en.html, accessed 24 July 2009.

and of the Son, and of the Holy Ghost' (Matt. 28.19 KJV). Is this compatible with the radical thinking through of tradition in the face of radical openness to other religions which I have suggested dialogue entails?

For biblical literalists the question may not seem open; however, as I will suggest in the next chapter a serious and devout reading of scripture would lead us to a radical openness to the religious Other. Moreover, if the Gospels, and other early Christian writings, are records of the community transcribed and reworded as they passed on, then the question is open. Are these the words of Jesus, or the words of the Gospel's author reflecting upon what his community and their experience has come to tell them, but not the final and definitive version of Jesus? Biblical scholars may argue either way, but we should remember that the early church collected the New Testament canon not as a selection of 'inspired' or 'revealed' works, but as the works that came from those closest to the first generation disciples of Jesus. They are collected, then, not as flawless divine works but as the words of men passed on to one another. Indeed, we should note that the strong Protestant emphasis on biblical texts as inspired revelation comes close to 'heresy' in creating an idol.[109] Moreover, in seeking to understand Jesus, it is notable that the Church came to recognize four Gospels, each a portrait from a different angle, rather than accepting a *diatessaron*, a single summation of all the truths in one text or version. This suggests that there are different stories we can tell of Jesus and the Christian tradition, and so we should not limit ourselves to one vision.[110]

---

109 On the collection of the New Testament canon and the nature of biblical texts see the very accessible account in Barton, John, 1998, *How the Bible Came to Be*, Louisville, KY: Westminster John Knox Press, pp. 13–24, 36–52 and 53–72. Regarding emphasis on the Bible as a Protestant heresy, depending on how it is interpreted (Christian theology is as we've seen multivalent), the emphasis on the Bible as sole authority: a) transfers knowledge of revelation from God's work in Jesus and the Holy Spirit to a text; b) changes the focus from Jesus as God to the Bible as guiding focus in Christian life; c) makes a man-made text the arbiter of things divine. In all these cases 'Biblicalism' (the belief that the Bible alone is the source and knowledge of God) induces what could be seen as idolatry.

110 I would like to thank the Austrian Catholic intercultural theologian Judith Gruber for highlighting to me the applicability of this to an interreligious context (personal email correspondence).

Yet even an approach of radical openness does not preclude some form of evangelization. John Cobb has argued that deeper dialogue, once one has moved with one's dialogue partners to an attitude of trust and co-operation, involves a more 'confrontative' stance, where representatives challenge us on their values (see Chapter 6).[111] Moreover, it is worth noting that evangelism in itself should not be seen as a bad thing, and may even, at times, be a positive. As an instance of what may be seen as 'positive' evangelism I offer the following quote from Oduyoye, a well-known Christian proponent of indigenous African ways of life and religiosity:

> The Wesleyan Methodist Missionary Society's encounter with Fantse culture . . . took a dramatic turn when the missionaries were able to demonstrate that the fearsome noises and humming that emanated from the ancestral grove did not come from spirits but from human beings. The grove was a burial ground deep in the forest, and also the site of a powerful cult. The spirits were literally unmasked and the grove destroyed (cf. Mackenzie 1970). This blatant disrespect for, and desecration of, a holy place should make one angry. Yet I am using it to illustrate, not only the confrontation of the Gospel and Religious culture, but specifically the liberating element of the Gospel ... The point is that, when that which is sacred is used to domesticate and to exploit it, it ceases to deserve the label religion and becomes an ideology. Here we encounter the Gospel as it challenges the misuse of belief in a spirit world ...[112]

This instance is not offered as an example that 'primitive' (indigenous) religions should give way to a 'major world religion', simply as an example of a case where what seems to be 'foul play' is at work to keep people in thrall to a particular cultus. In one sense, I would suggest that mission

---

111 Cobb, John B. Jr, 1990, 'Dialogue', in Swidler, Leonard, Cobb, John B. Jr, Knitter, Paul F., Hellwig, Monica K., *Death or Dialogue? From the Age of Monologue to the Age of Dialogue*, London: SCM, pp. 1–18, p. 8.

112 Oduyoye, 'African', p. 43, reference to Mackenzie, R. P., 1970, 'Thomas Freeman's Attitude to Other Faiths', *Ghana Bulletin of Theology* 3:8.

is imperative, in that each religion needs to confront the world with its values and principles. Conversion is a possibility, yet, at the same time, there is a need to recognize the values of religious Others with respect, meaning the arrogance of personal correctness disappears – moreover, we must be open to the possibility of our own conversion in this encounter. It must never be a one-way evangelization, for 'Good News' is found in many places.

We should also consider what mission and dialogue may mean. Mission is far more than simply trying to convert others, as has been observed, 'most of the people who are today called "missionaries" are not Christians working to convert "non-Christians" but foreign pastoral workers'.[113] This, of course, is linked to the recognition that evangelizing mission itself is not very effective (see below), and that medical and educational missions are more effective. Yet, through this style of mission a close encounter with other cultures and religions is also possible, which in turn opens up the possibility of depth encounters. Indeed, as Werner Ustorf has argued, an intelligent missiology today must, in response to dialogue and pluralism, 'end up with a revision of the missionary mandate by assuming God's wider mission'.[114] We must therefore be careful not to draw a sharp dichotomy between mission as one thing and dialogue as something else.

I would like to end with a few closing thoughts on mission and dialogue, partly inspired by Ariarajah's deep consideration of the matter:

1   Mission is not unrelated to power, and that when power is not present many aspects of mission are not so apparent.[115] On this several points are in order. For one, history shows that a strong missionary imperative is generally associated with some colonial

---

113   Burrows, William R., 1997, 'Christian Mission and Interreligious Dialogue: Mutually Exclusive or Complementary?', *Buddhist-Christian Studies* 17, pp. 119–30, pp. 124–5.

114   Ustorf, Werner, 2008, 'The Cultural Origins of "Intercultural Theology"', *Mission Studies* 25, pp. 229–51, p. 245.

115   Ariarajah, 'Power', pp. 180–1.

or cultural superiority, and that when not present some form of integration tends to take place. The case of the Thomas Christians in India or the indigenization of the Nestorian Church in China are two instances of the Christian tradition taking on local colouring when unsupported by imperial power.[116] For another, history tells us of the failure of mission to make headway against other substantial religious cultural systems; where mission has worked it has been when faced with the collapse of another worldview.

2   That the mission imperative could not be questioned seemed obvious when European power was still strong, especially in terms of cultural hegemony, but in our days of growing post-colonial attitudes, the loss of Western cultural hegemony, and the rise of plurality we find something different.[117] Importantly, dialogue was stressed by what Ariarajah terms 'Southern' churches in contrast to 'Northern' ones (by which we may, roughly, read 'Third World' and 'Western' respectively), especially at the WCC Nairobi debate.[118] As such, we may suggest it is not so much a lack of fidelity to Christ but the real encounter with the religious Other that leads us to stress dialogue over mission.

3   Related to our above two concerns is the question of religion, mission and culture. When mission is strongly linked to power we find a demand that converts take on the culture and social norms of the evangelizing nation. Fitzgerald, with strong evidential support, has argued that traditionally to become 'converted'

---

116   On Thomas Christians see: Collins, Paul M., 2007, *Christian Inculturation in India: Liturgy, Worship and Society*, Aldershot: Ashgate; Aleaz, K. P., 'Pluralism Calls for Pluralistic Inclusivism: An Indian Christian Experience', in Knitter (ed.), *Myth*, pp. 162–75, pp. 62–4. A good account, though somewhat uncritical in places, of Nestorian Christianity in China is Palmer, Martin, 2001, *The Jesus Sutras: Rediscovering the Lost Religion of Taoist Christianity*, London: Piatkus.

117   See Ariarajah, 'Power', pp. 183, as well as Ariarajah, Wesley S., 1998, 'The impact of interreligious dialogue on the ecumenical movement', in May, *Pluralism*, p. 7 on Visser't Hooft.

118   Ariarajah, 'Power', p. 185, Ariarajah, 'impact', p. 11.

has meant not just to take on a religious identity but also a cultural one – to become 'civilized' is to take on appropriate forms of behaviour.[119] It has been observed that, in the past, when missionaries lost control they accused the indigenous peoples of 'syncretism'; today, however, loss of Western control (inculturation) is positively encouraged.[120] However, if religion and culture are related what can this mean? Aleaz argues that in India religion and culture are so closely related that you cannot simply remove one religion and replace it with another, to become an Indian Christian is to some degree to become a Hindu Christian.[121] For an Indian, to become a 'Western-style' Christian is to some extent to lose an Indian identity – I was shocked when I first visited the Anglican Cathedral in Calcutta at the way walking through the doors removed one from India to an English location, with notice boards displaying flower-arranging rotas, sidemen's lists, all within the context of Gothic architecture, stained glass and rows of pews approaching the high altar; it was as though I had stepped into a grand old Cotswold church in rural England having been transported halfway round the world by stepping through those doors. I am glad to say that when I attended an early morning service there (I cannot speak for their main Sunday morning services) I had to remove my shoes and sit on the floor with the other congregants in an area behind the pews as I (attempted to) join in a service said mainly in Hindi. If religion and culture are tied, then, without imperial power we find that mission and conversion are always about Christianity taking on new inculturated forms.

4   The current worldwide spread of Christianity is clearly the flipside of Westernization, and with it a perceived modernization. In

---

119   Fitzgerald, *Discourse*, Chapter 4.

120   On the first point see Obuyoye, 'African', p. 47, on the second see Collins, *Christian*, pp. 76ff.

121   Aleaz, 'Pluralism', p. 172. John Thatamanil's experience relates to this (see, http://sitemason.vanderbilt.edu/vanderbiltview/articles/2009/05/01/deep-and-wide.79026, accessed 16 September 2009).

turn, Spanish and Portuguese, then Dutch, British and German, and now American money and power have transformed (Western/Chalcedon) Christianity from a regional religion (with some outposts elsewhere) to the world's largest religious tradition. Indeed, more than this: 'what prevents the Christian worldview from being turned inside-out in its encounter with other worldviews is Christianity's association with the global hegemony of Western civilization'.[122]

Conclusions

Ariarajah suggests that Western Christian theology has set the cart before the horse in its attitude to the religious Other, which is to say from a position of historical dominance it has arranged a religious hierarchy with itself at the top, but fails, in the light of experience, to re-evaluate this.[123] I would argue that the challenge that interreligious dialogue should present to us (in the context of what we have seen of Christian identity and religion) suggests that we need to rethink the whole set of concepts whereby we have traditionally considered these questions. What does it mean to be a Christian or to have a Christian identity: it is not, whatever else it may be, to think we can sit tightly in a closed-off box that separates us distinctly from the religious Other. This will, in turn, lead us to ask new questions, or address old questions in new ways. We will address these issues in the following chapters.

---

122 Nicholson, 'Comparative', p. 238.
123 Ariarajah, 'Power', reference to Nirmal, p. 190.

3

Radical Openness to Religious Others
Assessing the Pluralist Hypothesis

Some issues in the debate

Religious plurality and Christian integrity

Christianity grew up in a religiously plural world, and many Christians throughout history have experienced religious plurality. However, we need to readdress this question today for several reasons, which include, at least, the following five:

1   Our knowledge, and appreciation, of other religions is at a much greater level than at any other point in history.
2   There is a recognition that without peace between religious worldviews we will not have peace within the global community.
3   Our thinking on other religions has, mainly, not been conditioned by those who have experienced plurality, but those whose experience is mono-cultural/religious.
4   We have a greater historical awareness of the inter-relationship of religions and religious identity.
5   Christian theology and integrity should lead us to reassess the religious Other.

We will briefly unpack each of these. First, the last couple of centuries (admittedly often through imperialism) has led us to a greater awareness of the teachings, spiritualities and lifeways of other religious communities and cultures. This has led to modern academic religious studies, which, unlike previous approaches, attempts to undertake neutral and phenomenological studies without the baggage of ideological or theological interpretation – I purposefully say 'attempted' as a whole literature exists arguing that such an approach is not neutral.[1] Space does not permit us to rehearse the arguments here; however, little controversy surrounds the notion that, in many ways, our qualitative and quantitative knowledge of the various global religious traditions is tremendous, and allows the resources to help enter into an empathetic yet critical understanding.

The second brings to mind Hans Küng's famous quotation: 'no world peace without peace between the religions'.[2] Quite simply, we know that we must relate to our religious neighbours, often in areas of mutual interest, in ways that go beyond polemic, criticism and rejection.[3]

Third, due to political factors, what has become the mainstream Christian discourse of recent centuries has emanated from the European and American spheres, where Christianity has been experienced, largely, as the major, or only, religious grouping (at least of any significance to the Christians) until very recent times. Encounter with religious Others has largely happened in the sphere of 'empire', and in generally negative terms. Even for those who have written on the theology of religions and interreligious dialogue, the experience has also largely been from an experience of Christian predominance. As such, the encounter of religious plurality has not been taken seriously in Christian theology (see Chapter 1). We should acknowledge the experience of Christians

---

1 Much of this is discussed in Chapter 2. Also, within this modern 'secular' study Christian scholars and missionaries have played a vital part in building up this storehouse of knowledge and making it possible. Indeed, in large part, it was nineteenth-century missiological agendas to know the religious Other to help overcome them that helped lay much of the basis for the growth of modern religious studies.

2 Küng, Hans, 1991, *Global Responsibility: In Search of a New World Ethic*, first published 1990 in German, London: SCM Press, p. xv.

3 Such sentiments are common among many, see for example Todd, Douglas, 2001, 'Arinze: hard-liners make interfaith relations hard', *The Christian Century* (12 December).

who now, and for centuries, have lived in religiously plural societies, whose experience can develop our understanding of how Christianity can respond to different religio-cultural systems.

Fourth, Christian tradition has effaced Jesus' Jewish identity, while socio-political factors distanced us from the Jewish 'Other', resulting in a legacy of anti-Semitism culminating in the atrocities of the last century. Christians must be aware and alert to the way their discourse, almost 2,000 years of tradition, has been complicit in this. The problem lies in part within an exclusional creation of Christian identity, tied into battles for control of Church and complicity with empire, which runs contrary, I would argue, to a correct understanding of Christian and religious identity (see Chapter 1).

Fifth, recognizing that Christianity is a syncretic creation with elements from many traditions already bound within it, we must accept an Intercultural Theology (Chapter 1). This will demand that we do not insist on a European colonialism in theology, exporting our 'global design' (see Chapter 2). Here, I will argue that the pluralist option of radical openness to religious Others is not a watering down or betrayal of Christian witness but, rather, a demand necessitated by Jesus' example and Christian tradition.

Open and closed Christianities

I have spoken already of pluralisms as a radical openness to religious Others. It is my contention that an authentic Christian witness in contemporary society will exemplify such a radical openness. Our first two chapters have set out some arguments which move in this direction. However, questions arise as to what this might mean, whether this is possible and, assuming it is, what form it may take? This chapter will start to explore these issues. A radical openness to other faiths is, I would suggest, found not just in the pluralisms of such figures as John Hick, Paul F. Knitter, Leonard Swidler, Rosemary Radford Ruether, Alan Race, Kwok Pui-lan, Perry Schmidt-Leukel, John Cobb Jr, Stanley Samartha, Ursula King, K. P. Aleaz, Diana Eck, and a host of others too numerous to mention – although including many other leading international lights

in the theological world.[4] It is also found in many others who would disavow the label of 'pluralisms', especially those who adopt a Comparative
Theology approach, because they allow a permeable and open border to
exist between the Christian faith and other religious traditions; so such
figures as Francis Clooney, James Fredericks, John Keenan, Judith Berling, John Thatamanil and Joseph Stephen O'Leary also take what could
be seen as a pluralistic style in their writing and theologizing. This is
not to say, though, they could be classed within the usual pluralisms
definition (Chapter 1). Meanwhile others within the churches, including
those in senior positions, are led by their experience of dialogue towards
a radical openness in relation to religious Others, even if their expressed
theology is inclusivist or particularist. This openness was suggested in
the words of Rowan Williams when addressing the World Council of
Churches in 2006:

when others appear to have arrived at a place where forgiveness and
adoption are sensed and valued, even when these things are not directly spoken of in the language of another faith's mainstream reflection, are we to say that God has not found a path for himself?[5]

Landmark events under Pope John Paul II, such as the Assisi interreligious prayer meeting in 1986 and his entering a mosque in Damascus in

---

4 For a good overview of roots that have led people to a pluralist stance,
as well as some within these lines, see Schmidt-Leukel, Perry, 2008, 'Pluralisms: How to Approach Religious Diversity Theologically', in Hedges, Paul
and Race, Alan (eds), *SCM Core Text Christian Approaches to Other Faiths*,
London: SCM, pp. 85–110, pp. 88–92. For a powerful and personal account
of finding 'God' in other traditions, see Eck, Diana, 2003 [1993], *Encountering
God: A Spiritual Journey from Bozeman to Benaras*, Boston, MA: Beacon Press,
esp. Chapters 4 and 5.

5 Williams, Rowan, 2006, 'Christian Identity and Religious Plurality', Plenary
Session Paper from the World Council of Churches Assembly, Porto Alegre,
available at http://www.oikoumene.org/en/resources/documents/assembly/porto-
alegre-2006/2-plenary-presentations/christian-identity-religious-plurality/rowan-
williams-presentation.html, accessed 4 August 2009.

2001, also suggest this openness.[6] Despite such openness being increasingly found in mainstream and orthodox Christian witness, with many seeing it as imperative, the pluralist approach has been subject to a vast number of criticisms which must be addressed to justify a pluralist radical openness to religious Others.[7]

Problems with pluralisms

Having suggested that Christianity calls for a radical openness to other religions, we must address criticisms raised against the pluralist option. To do this we need to frame a concept of pluralisms, so we will begin by outlining Hick's version of the pluralistic hypothesis – without suggesting it has a normative status as the correct or best version of a pluralist theology, simply the best known. We then address different interpretations of pluralisms as possible critiques of Hick. Next, we consider philosophical issues concerning the coherence of a pluralist worldview. After that, we address the question of whether pluralisms are a Western imposition. Finally, we discuss an important critique, whether it is, or can be seen to be, a Christian standpoint.

John Hick's pluralistic hypothesis

When referring to pluralisms, commentators tend, at least implicitly, to mean the theological pattern laid down by John Hick, whose views are most fully expressed in his magnum opus on the theology of religions, *An*

---

6 See Fitzgerald, Michael and Borelli, John, 2006, *Interfaith Dialogue: A Catholic View*, London: SPCK, pp. 1, 85, 150; see also Kasimow, Harold and Sherwin, Byron L. (eds), 1999, *John Paul II and Interreligious Dialogue*, Maryknoll, NY: Orbis.

7 Indeed, so numerous are pluralism's critics that, with a touch of irony, Paul Knitter says that if to be taken seriously is to be criticized, pluralism is blessed to be taken so seriously (Knitter, Paul F., 2005, 'Is the Pluralist Model a Western Imposition? A Response in Five Voices', in Knitter, Paul F., *The Myth of Religious Superiority: A Multifaith Exploration*, Maryknoll, NY: Orbis, pp. 28–42, p. 28).

Interpretation of Religion.[8] Hick began life as an exclusivist-style thinker from a Presbyterian background. However, his experience of religious Others led him, as a Christian, to believe that the God he believed in was not compatible with such a view.[9] Through a series of stages, Hick expanded his vision from seeing truth centred in Christianity alone, to being located in a common experience of God and then, recognizing the nontheistic nature of some religious traditions, to what he terms the Real.[10]

Hick suggests that it seems most plausible that all religions are responses to the same ultimate reality, and explains the varied natures of descriptions of the Real being due to diverse human expressions of this in different cultures. He therefore makes a distinction between the real *ein sich* (as it is in itself), and the Real as experienced, supporting the distinction with reference to the theologies and philosophies of various religions which suggest that the absolute can never be fully comprehended or expressed in human terms. As to other doctrinal matters, such as whether there is reincarnation or only one life, he argues these are of secondary importance.[11] Of primary importance, for him, is what he sees as the empirical evidence that we have of the religions. This includes common ethical values, their capacity for producing 'saints' (people who live holy and virtuous lives in response to the Real), as well as the deep conviction, devotion and piety that each produces in its followers.[12] He describes the salvific movement in each religion as being a move from self-centredness to reality-centredness.[13] Hick argues we must remain rooted within one tradition, because that gives us a coherent and integrated transformative path towards the Real.

---

8 Hick, John, 1989, *An Interpretation of Religion: Human Responses to the Transcendent*, Basingstoke: Macmillan, Part Four. An important addition to this is his reply to his critics, Hick, John, 1995, *The Rainbow of Faiths: Critical Dialogues on Religious Pluralism*, London: SCM.

9 See: Hick, John, 2005, *An Autobiography*, Oxford: Oneworld, see, for instance, pp. 33-5 and 160; and Cheetham, David, 2003, *John Hick: A Critical Introduction and Reflection*, Aldershot: Ashgate.

10 Hick, *Interpretation*, Part Four.

11 Hick, *Interpretation*, Chapters 19 and 20.

12 Hick, *Interpretation*, pp. 303-5 and 307-9, see also Chapters 17 and 18.

13 Hick, *Interpretation*, Chapter 3.

As the best-known proponent of pluralisms, Hick has found his hypothesis open to numerous assaults from many angles. We shall deal with these below; although the critiques arising through the particularist challenge are addressed later (Chapter 4). Also, Hick's work is a pioneer effort to express radical openness towards religious Others, so cannot be expected to be the final word – as Judith Berling has noted, the pluralistic hypothesis is still in the early stages of development.[14]

Other pluralisms

While Hick is the most widely known pluralist he is far from being the only one, while some other pluralists find his version of pluralism insufficiently pluralistic or otherwise inadequate.

According to Heim, pluralistic theologies are not truly pluralist because they see all religions as responding in a fairly similar way to one goal. The result he says is not 'religiously pluralistic at all'.[15] That is to say, they don't offer enough options. Heim does not offer a pluralist theology, but rather a quasi-particularist inclusivist approach.[16] He does, though, raise a question as to how pluralist should a pluralist theology be. David Ray Griffin distinguishes what he sees as two types of pluralisms: *identist* pluralism, which sees all religions orientated on the same goal; and, *differential* pluralism, which sees their different language and approaches referring to a variety of absolutes or salvations.[17] Favouring

---

14 Berling, Judith, 1997, *A Pilgrim in Chinese Culture: Negotiating Religious Diversity*, Eugene, OR: Wipf and Stock, p. 31.

15 Heim, Mark S., 1995, *Salvations: Truth and Difference in Religion*, Maryknoll, NY: Orbis, p. 129, see also p. 123.

16 See: Cheetham, David, 2008, 'Inclusivisms: Honouring Faithfulness and Openness', in Hedges and Race (eds), *SCM Core Text Christian Approaches*, pp. 63–84, pp. 76–7; and Hedges, Paul, 2008, 'Particularities: Tradition-Specific Post-modern Perspectives', in Hedges and Race (eds), *SCM Core Text Christian Approaches*, pp. 112–35, p. 112.

17 Griffin, David Ray, 2005, 'Religious Pluralism: Generic, Identist, Deep', in Griffin, David Ray (ed.), *Deep Religious Pluralism*, Louisville, KY: Westminster John Knox Press, pp. 3–38, p. 24.

the latter, he endorses a form of pluralism advanced by John Cobb Jr, based in Whiteheadian Process Theology.

Cobb's pluralist theology of religions speaks of at least two, if not three, forms of the absolute. This follows Process Theology's distinction of God and creativity as two absolutes, the universe being a third. Cobb's emphasis upon Buddhist–Christian dialogue leads him to emphasize the first two, wherein, he claims, the Christian language of a personal God refers to an experience of God, whereas Buddhist language of *Shunyata*, or emptiness, refers to creativity.[18] The possibility of two distinct and contrasting absolutes has been disputed by Schmidt-Leukel. He takes issue with what he terms 'polycentric pluralism' on the grounds that, logically, the absolute must be one, else none is truly *absolute*.[19]

Another worry raised by Cobb is that pluralistic approaches can lead to a meaningless relativism (we address this further below as a philosophical problem). If everything is true, then why strive or commit to any path?[20] This is a common worry that accepting all religions as valid leads to no truth or claim being seen as truly binding or worthwhile. Cobb's resolution of pluralisms' incipient relativism is an appeal to Christianity's norms as absolutely binding, in particular the justice embodied in the biblical deity. Griffin expresses this in somewhat paradoxical language:

---

18 The best synopsis of Cobb's thought is found in Griffin, 2005b, 'John Cobb's Whiteheadian Complementary Pluralism', in Griffin, *Deep*, pp. 39–66, and I use this as my main source here for Cobb's thought. That it represents a fair and accurate summation of his thought is acknowledged by Cobb in the same work; see Cobb, John, 2005, 'Some Whiteheadian Assumptions about Religion and Pluralism', in Griffin, *Deep*, pp. 243–62, p. 243.

19 See Schmidt-Leukel, 'Pluralisms', pp. 96–9. I suspect that, humanly speaking, we cannot truly solve this dilemma in relation to the dispute. However, from a Process-based starting point Cobb's makes sense, otherwise Schmidt-Leukel's objection is logical. We will address issues related to this below concerning philosophical objections.

20 For a recent critique of pluralism from this point of view see Keenan, John, 2009, *Grounding Our Faith in a Pluralist world – with a little help from Nāgārjuna*, Eugene, OR: Wipf and Stock, pp. 21–30.

As Cobb puts it elsewhere, to enter into dialogue 'we do not need to relativize our beliefs.' Rather, '[w]e can affirm our insights as universally valid! What we cannot do, without lapsing back into unjustified arrogance, is to deny that the insights of other traditions are also equally valid.'[21]

The seeming paradox is resolved by Griffin and Cobb through the belief that each religion has a set of unique and specific insights which its adherents should advance. Each should also be ready to listen to other insights, for they may have truths which can be learned from. Difference is not minimized but brought together as strong demands. This accords with my own views, as well as some feminist and other approaches.[22] Within the context of Process Theology there is a strong emphasis upon creative and dynamic development and, speaking of Christ, Cobb and Griffin say the following:

Creative transformation is the essence of growth, and growth is of the essence of life. Growth is not achieved by merely adding together elements in the given world in different combinations. It requires the transformation of those elements through the introduction of novelty. It alters their nature and meaning without suppressing or destroying them.[23]

A similar critique of Hick's static model of pluralism, which although acknowledging the equality of religions sees each remaining as an integral block, is found in K. P. Aleaz's work which suggests a 'pluralistic

---

21 Griffin, 'John', p. 63, citing Cobb, John, 1999, *Transforming Christianity and the World*, Paul F. Knitter (ed.), Maryknoll, NY: Orbis, p. 137.

22 I have suggested that the motif of mutual fulfilment may be useful in relation to different faiths; see Hedges, Paul, 2001, *Preparation and Fulfilment: A History and Study of Fulfilment Theology in Modern British Thought in the Indian Context*, Bern: Peter Lang, p. 397. For feminist theology, see Chapter 5 herein. I develop this idea further in Chapter 6.

23 Cobb, John and Griffin, David Ray, 1976, *Process Theology: An Introductory Exposition*, Philadelphia, PA, p. 100.

inclusivism', where, in the Indian context, Christian thought would be re-expressed in Indian religio-philosophical terms.[24] This could be seen as an intercultural approach, where we see the religions not as many divergent and incompatible standpoints, but as related patterns of thought within and between diverse cultural forms.

This shows some other ways the pluralist stance has been advanced; however, if we believe there is an essential place for a radical openness to religious Others within contemporary Christian theology, we must answer some serious questions about the very viability of any pluralistic approach.

Are pluralisms philosophically viable?

Pluralisms have been subjected to a variety of philosophical critiques, mostly attacking Hick's version of pluralism, or what is taken as his version of pluralism. It is important to address these attacks as they claim to undermine the pluralist endeavour, although some do not apply to non-Hickean versions of the pluralistic hypothesis.

Many books, chapters and articles have been written giving philosophical critiques and defences of religious pluralisms, and we cannot deal with them all here. For this reason we will concentrate on several prominent arguments, placing them in three broad categories:

1   It falsely supposes that all religions have a common set of teachings.
2   It has an untenable notion of the unity of deity and/or experience that underlies all religions.
3   It does not represent our best option in the face of religious diversity.

---

24 See Aleaz, K. P., 2008, 'Hinduism: We Are No Longer "Frogs in the Well"', in Hedges and Race (eds), *SCM Core Text Christian Approaches*, pp. 212–33, pp. 226–7, which references many of his more substantial outworkings of this idea. See also Aleaz, K. P., 2005, 'Pluralism Calls for Pluralistic Inclusivism', in Knitter (ed.), *Myth*, pp. 162–75.

First, it is commonly asserted that pluralists consider all religions to have certain common values. To assess this I will look at Keith Yandell's analysis of pluralisms.[25] He begins with a discussion of morality in relation to truth claims. According to him we must consider the core values on which faiths act, where, he asserts, we see a vast disparity. For instance, in Advaita Vedanta and Theravada Buddhism personal individuality is lost in liberation. He therefore suggests that for these traditions the individual has no intrinsic value, while liberation is about a return to the absolute, and therefore individual extinction. Contrariwise, he suggests both Jainism and Christianity keep individuality in liberation. Therefore, the individual has intrinsic value. Consequently, liberation is seen as the individual in relation to the divine. Any attempt to match these two contrasting ideas must, he feels, be incoherent. Therefore, he concludes, the core values between these religions are utterly distinct. He does, however, recognize a possible objection that he might face, that perhaps a religion may embrace one set of values but that its adherents follow another, and so he argues:

> The values a religion embraces are those its authoritative texts sanction [he notes the possibility that there may be contradictions in texts in which case this doesn't apply] . . . Attempts to evaluate religious traditions by looking at the behavior of its adherents is worthless as evidence regarding the tradition; what is evidentially relevant is what values the tradition's authoritative texts sanction.[26]

Before replying to Yandell's arguments in relation to pluralisms, it is worth making four key points about his basis of analysis:

1   It makes an assumption that all religions value texts as the supreme authority (which they do not).

---

25 In what follows I am making use of his arguments found in Yandell, Keith, 1999, *Philosophy of Religion: A Contemporary Introduction*, London: Routledge, pp. 57ff.

26 Yandell, *Philosophy*, p. 61.

2   It assumes there is a self-evident meaning to texts apart from those embodied in the interpretative acts of the reading community (however, any text's meaning is embedded within the context in which they are read and written – there is no free-floating and self-evident meaning that can be accessed 'objectively' (this is not to endorse an absolute post-modern relativism that texts have no meaning, but simply to insist upon the importance of contextual reading)).

3   It ignores the fact that religions, their beliefs and ethics change and evolve over time (there is no 'essence' of religion that defines what it is and does).

4   It assumes there can only be one way to read and interpret the beliefs and core values of texts (it ignores the little traditions, as well as the multitude of variations between sects and groups).

As such, when we are faced with a claim that different religions embody different values we must ask ourselves what this says about the claim, which makes an essentialist judgement divorced from the actual practice of communities. Even given this, I would suggest that the critique does not necessarily apply to pluralisms. We will now address the three lines of critique outlined above.

As we have seen, Hick believes that certain doctrines, which he sees as secondary, can be left as unknowable. However, Yandell's point is that this applies to fundamentals, and, certainly, the question of liberation and the individual in relation to this is central to Hick's notion of our change from self-centredness to reality-centredness. Various replies could be made. A Hickean could reply that despite various expressions of form, the move from individualistic ego-centredness to focus upon the transcendent is highlighted in each tradition, with each tradition also saying the exact nature of this final state is utterly unknowable and so disagreements are just culturally specific expressions of an unknown.[27] For Cobb,

---

27 Such a claim is made by Perry Schmidt-Leukel; see, for instance, 'Pluralisms', and 2009, *Transformation by Integration: How Inter-faith Encounter Changes Christianity*, London: SCM.

the two approaches Yandell highlights are seen as centred upon different absolutes, and so the problem is answered by saying they refer to distinct experiences. Either way, it is certainly the case that a major problem is raised but one that is not unanswerable. This critique is related to particularist objection and so will be addressed more fully in Chapter 4.

We should also address another objection concerning the vast variety of claims made by religions about ethical and moral terms; what we may call their core values. Here, it has been argued that the pluralist belief means that we must accept 'all claims to revelation, however contradictory or morally repugnant'.[28] This is essentially the claim to relativism, that is, if we accept an open approach then we have no boundaries. However, for Hick, pluralisms do not propose relativism, but, by seeing the ethical commands of each religion as vital, it foregrounds what he sees as common imperatives so they are not relative but mutually reinforced. The core values he proposes belong to the major traditions, that is those religions which have lasted through time and have a widespread basis. Therefore, Hickean pluralism states that not just anyone who claims a revelation, or propounds any religion, must be responding to the 'Real'. Rather, by reference to what are seen as mutually supporting ethical claims in major traditions (empirical and evidential), grounds to distinguish between true and false claims can be made. In general, we may say that the variation of values is not in itself a philosophically compelling argument against a pluralist approach, though it does raise some serious problems about practical resolution of these differences (see Chapters 6 and, especially, 7).

Second, Hick's Real, the supposed transcendent centre, or goal, of all religions is disputed. This is, perhaps, the central issue: can there be one absolute reality to which all religions respond? We return to Yandell to start fleshing out these issues. According to Yandell, one problem with pluralisms is that of applying concepts to the Real. However, some of his arguments seem to take a straw-man approach. He suggests that the Real cannot have humanly applied properties (as these are subjective and culturally specific), only logical ones (as these are universal),

---

28 Trigg, Roger, 1998, *Rationality and Religion*, Oxford: Blackwell, p. 58.

but then complains that the qualities of such a Real cannot be gained by logic but come from specific traditions, or else he proposes that we can only either apply the concepts of one religion, because to apply them all would result in contradictions.[29] These approaches set up his own self-generated interpretation of the pluralist hypothesis, and ignore what Hick and others actually say, that the Real itself is beyond our comprehension – although at least one of his points could be developed as a critique, and to which we will return. Nevertheless, despite the weakness of Yandell's argument here, behind these issues is a very telling point, which he elaborates elsewhere, which is that the kind of Real we may end up with is a 'thin' concept.[30]

If no religion refers with absolute certainty to the 'Real' then we are left with the problem of not having reference to anything substantial. While pluralists rightly note that every religion speaks of their absolute as ultimately unknowable, we are left within a pluralist framework, it can be claimed, with very little idea of what it is we claim to be speaking of as the absolute of all religions. Are we, then, instead of being brought closer to the truth through pluralisms actually even further removed from the object supposedly referred to? Against this, Peter Byrne suggests that the unknowable nature of the divine already has a central place within many religions.[31] As such, pluralisms do not further denude the idea of the absolute; indeed, it could even be claimed that they support, through their radical questioning of all bases, the approach of the *via negativa* (way of negation), which is discussed further below. Also, contra Yandell, pluralisms are not intended to supply a new religion as he suggests. Rather it is a meta-system to make sense of all religions, while, in the praxis of faith, Hick and others endorse following one particular religion which supplies a 'thick' context of religious meaning for personal transformation.

---

29 These arguments can be found in Yandell, *Philosophy*, pp. 70ff.

30 Yandell, Keith, 2004, 'Can Only One Religion Be True?', in Peterson, Michael and Warragon, Raymond (eds), *Contemporary Debates in Philosophy of Religion*, Oxford: Blackwell, pp. 191–201, p. 197.

31 Byrne, Peter, 2004, 'Reply to Yandell, in Peterson and Warragon, *Contemporary*, pp. 215–17, pp. 216–17.

The philosopher Roger Trigg, however, allows us to take this critique further by attacking the Kantian basis he sees as underlying Hick's thought, which distinguishes between a noumenal (transcendent) realm of the Real as it truly is, which is unknowable, and a phenomenal (physical) realm of the manifestation of the Real in concrete religious traditions. According to Trigg, 'the great problem with Kantian views of reality is that they can easily appear to make noumenal reality seem redundant', such that 'his [Hick's] pluralism leads to a downgrading of the role of Reality in our thinking'. [32] Trigg suggests that all religions become weakened by Kantianism as it makes the focus merely what we can know, not any reference to what truly is. For instance, in Hick we see his stress upon ethics as common ground, which is divorced from questions about what 'Truth' is, in its absolute sense. Hence, the human phenomenon of religion rather than the Real becomes the focus. Therefore, returning to Yandell's arguments, if we have a Real about which we cannot validly postulate anything, and therefore no absolute basis for judgement, it could be argued that: 'Wishing one were torturing one's enemies, enjoying mugging a helpless victim, or happily kicking a dog is *as* reasonably viewed as an experience that is a response to . . . the Real.'[33]

We have addressed relativism above, but here it is approached from another angle. In reply, it is not clear that Hick endorses what is often claimed to be a distinct Kantian standpoint, that without access to the noumenal realm we must work on the basis of the phenomenal alone (although his ideas are clearly based upon this Kantian distinction, it does not follow that he endorses all positions that could be associated with this basic distinction; we must distinguish between basic propositions and higher-level interpretations based upon these). For Hick, religious experiences mediated from the Real can be a basis for us to have some knowledge, hence his claims about saintliness and common ethical viewpoints. Hick does not say we have no knowledge of the divine, but

---

32 Trigg, *Rationality*, pp. 61 and 62.
33 Yandell, *Philosophy*, p. 78.

says we must take seriously the imperatives within each religious tradition. I would like, also, to offer an analogy about direct knowledge of the Real and what we may say of it. I have never personally met Hick, although I have attended talks by him and read numerous books and articles penned by him, and so can meaningfully be said to know something of his views (that is, by analogy, I do not know the Real *ein sich*, but know something of the traditions that mediate it). If I were to suggest that Hick endorses kicking dogs and mugging hapless victims then this may be said not to reflect a true representation of his position. Obviously, there is a distinction between this and knowledge of the noumenal, but we can draw an analogy. Given the fact of well-established traditions which, while not identical, give some broadly comparable ways of living in community (that is, they do not endorse kicking dogs and mugging defenceless victims), it would seem odd, to say the least, if we met someone who claimed this and said it was a revelation from the 'Real'.[34] Internally, religions have criteria to judge authentic and inauthentic witnesses to their message. Recognizing that often these may manifest as forms of social control or hierarchical dominance, we can still, probably, say that grounds exist, whether in a pluralist or non-pluralist setting, to determine between religious claims. Indeed, to some degree it should be noted that this philosophical argument is based upon a suspect notion of monolithic religions, because the arguments against religious pluralisms

---

34 It may be noted in passing, related to this, that a well-known recent critique of religion as a whole has been based upon the individual nature of experience. However, Hick's argument that we do find common traditions would count against this (especially spurious assessments of religious experience's reliability based on probability – we may note that a mathematical understanding of the basis of statistics is vastly different from a philosophically/rationally sound employment of it). My reference is, of course, to Dawkins, Richard, 2006, *The God Delusion*, London: Bantam Books. It would take us beyond the scope of this work to address it further; moreover its largely philosophically facile and undeveloped approach has resulted in an array of works pinpointing errors; for a general overview, the atheist Terry Eagleton's review in the *London Review of Books* picks up many points ('Lunging, Flailing, Mispunching', 19 October 2006, available at, http://www.lrb.co.uk/v28/n20/eagl01_.html, accessed 1 September 2009).

could, at least with almost equal force and validity, be applied intra-religiously to various sects, denominations and interpretations (see Chapters 1 and 2).

I would suggest that it may well be the case that Hick's expression does not give us the strongest basis as a foundation for an argument that we have a provisional, yet adequate, mediated knowledge of the Real. The doctrine of the analogy of being, or *analogia entis* (favoured in a number of recent, broadly post-liberal, theologies), speaks of the way we partake, though in a limited way, in knowledge of God, and forms a way forward from within the Christian tradition. Meanwhile, from elsewhere, it has been argued that Christians could adopt aspects of a Mahayana Buddhist philosophy to understand the mediated and partial nature of all religious revelations without thereby needing to give up claims to truth and validity for their own tradition.[35]

We return, though, to the claim that to apply all the possible notions of the divine/absolute/God would result in contradiction. Yandell's expression of this, it seems to me, is inadequate, because he says the Real must be everything that Muslims claim about Allah, Jews claim about Yahweh, Christians claim about God, Vaishnavites claim about Vishnu, Advaita Vedantins claim about nirguna (without qualities) Brahmin, Mahayana Buddhists claim about the Dharmakaya, Theravada Buddhists claim about nirvana, etc. Two responses may be made. First, it ignores the fact that each religion says its absolute is ultimately unknowable

---

35 On some uses of analogy and knowledge in the Christian tradition, see Williams, Rowan, 2000, *On Christian Theology*, Oxford: Blackwell, pp. 22–7, and Oliver, Simon, 2009, 'Introducing Radical Orthodoxy: From Participation to Late Modernity', in Milbank, John and Oliver, Simon (eds), *The Radical Orthodoxy Reader*, Abingdon and New York: Routledge, pp. 3–27, pp. 15ff. (for those who find Radical Orthodoxy an unlikely partner to bring into a defence of pluralistic approaches, see Hedges, Paul, 2010, 'Is Radical Orthodoxy a Form of Liberal Theology? A Rhetorical Counter', *Heythrop Journal*, 15:5, pp. 795–818. For Christian uses of Mahayana philosophy, see Keenan, *Grounding*, and O'Leary, Joseph Stephen, 1996, *Religious Pluralism and Christian Truth*, Edinburgh: University of Edinburgh Press, esp. Chapters 5 and 6.

and inexpressible in human terms, as such all this language is merely approximations or analogical. Second, Yandell does not face the issue that even if we just stuck to everything the vast variety of Christians say and believe about God we would be faced with a vast diversity of conflicting and contradictory images.[36]

It is worth addressing here a related critique, for Harold Netland has cogently asked whether Hick's claim that the Real can be both personal and non-personal is coherent, suggesting that there must be 'significant continuity' among the various images held of the absolute.[37] Indeed, he asks:

Now it is not just a question of whether the Eternal One can be experienced as personal and non-personal, it is a question of whether its ontological status is such that it can correctly be described as both personal and non-personal.[38]

His question then leads us on to ask simply whether we are faced with an unintelligible set of propositions about the Real? In short, although he does not raise it this way, we have reached a statement that would appear to run against one of the most basic notions of all logic, Aristotle's principle of non-contradiction: we cannot affirm two opposite assertions at the same time.[39] Although seemingly strong, such a charge is not insuperable. As Twiss has argued, one of Hick's own analogies could answer this. The analogy in question is the way light, when seen in different ways, can behave as

---

36 As Paul Badham has pointed out the divergence in worldview between a Christian who believes God wishes to send those who don't believe in him to hell, and another who understands God as a benevolent deity who wishes all to be saved is, in many ways, as vast a divergence of understanding as can be found between different religious traditions; however, in many churches such people will sit side by side as co-religionists (Badham, Paul, 1980, *Christian Beliefs about Life after Death*, London: SPCK, pp. 10–11).

37 Netland, Harold A., 1986, 'Professor Hick on Religious Pluralism', *Religious Studies* 22:2, pp. 249–61, p. 258.

38 Netland, 'Professor', p. 259.

39 Aristotle, *Metaphysics* IV 6 1011b13–20.

both a wave and a particle: two contradictory modes of being.[40] Indeed, it may even be asked if what appears to be contradictory on the pheneomenal level is really contradictory on the noumenal level. Building from the Christian tradition, John Cottingham argues that the apophatic root, the mysticism of the *via negativa*, which experiences God as beyond all dualities, may provide an answer.[41] However, he feels while this may answer the problem, it might sacrifice too much, and so argues 'there must, if theism is to retain any distinctive character whatsoever, be some road back, some road for religious faith to return from the darkness of unknowing and locate itself within the domain of workable human language'.[42] He finds this within liturgy and cultural expressions – an attention to the need for contextualization within an intercultural context. We may even say it is a need to attend both to the plurality and particularity of religions (see Chapter 6). Whatever the case, it appears that we can find ways to philosophically deal with the plurality that Hick wishes to attribute to the Real. Moreover, Cobb's polycentric pluralism would avoid some of the problems altogether.

Third, there is the question of whether pluralisms represent the best option when faced with religious plurality. In some ways this problem is a theological one, but often expressed with a distinctly philosophical voice. This question does not attend to the internal coherence of pluralisms, as the previous two questions have, but is more concerned with whether it negates other stances and, as such, whether we should move to it. Expressed in this form, the query finds its best-known proponent in the analytic philosopher of religion Alvin Plantinga of the Reformed theological tradition. In a well-known essay, Plantinga defends an exclusivist position, interpreted as *the* authentic Christian position, as the most

---

40 Twiss, Sumner, 2000, 'The Philosophy of Religious Pluralism: A Critical Appraisal of Hick and His Critics', in Quinn, Phillip and Meeker, Kevin (eds), *The Philosophical Challenge of Religious Diversity*, Oxford: Oxford University Press, pp. 67–98, p. 85 (this paper first appeared in *The Journal of Religion* 70, 1990, pp. 533–68).

41 Cottingham, John, 2005, *The Spiritual Dimension: Religion, Philosophy and Human Value*, Cambridge: Cambridge University Press, pp. 159–61.

42 Cottingham, *Spiritual*, p. 162.

evidentially likely, asking whether the fact of religious plurality really leads us to reject exclusivisms.[43] His claim, simply put, is that pluralisms are not a rational response to religious plurality. Hick, in some earlier works, suggested that he finds the pluralist option more convincing,[44] and so the question is whether there is 'evidence that makes the pluralistic hypothesis . . . "considerably more probable" than exclsuivism?'[45]

The best and most thorough account of the dispute between Plantinga and Hick is offered by David Basinger. Here, we may usefully note his conclusions and some general points. First, and perhaps self-evidentially, there is no universally agreed way to distinguish the validity of various religious truth claims, and so we cannot prove, in philosophical terms, that either exclusivist, pluralist, or any other standpoint is correct. Second, while not saying that a strong Hickean position (pluralism is more likely) is correct, he does conclude, as Plantinga in places concedes, that there are certainly factors which should lead an exclusivist to revisit their position, and in this he says:

> In short, it seems to me that Hick has tried to prove too much. I agree . . . that the experiential factors he has identified do give the exclusivist good reason to engage in the type of belief assessment Hick desires. However, even if such assessment did require the rejection of exclusivism (which I have argued is not the case), Hick has not given us sufficient reason to embrace pluralism. He has at best given us only a sufficent reason to affirm some form of non-exclusivism.[46]

---

43 First published as Plantinga, Alvin, 1995, 'Pluralism: A Defense of Religious Exclusivism', in Senor, Thomas D. (ed.), *The Rationality of Belief and the Plurality of Faith*, London: Cornell University Press, pp. 191–215; the first section has been reproduced recently in Hedges, Paul and Race, Alan (eds), 2009, *SCM Reader: Christian Approaches to Other Faiths*, London: SCM, pp. 12–21.

44 See Hick, John, 1980, 'Whatever Path Men Choose is Mine', in Hick, John and Hebblethwaite, Brian, *Christianity and Other Religions: Selected Readings*, Philadelphia, PA: Fortress Press, pp. 171–90.

45 Basinger, David, 2002, *Religious Diversity: A Philosophical Assessment*, Aldershot: Ashgate, p. 57.

46 Basinger, *Religious*, p. 75. For his assessment of the dispute between Plantinga and Hick see pp. 53–75.

As such, if we accept Basinger's argument, this is not a strong argument against pluralisms. Indeed, it could even be an argument in their favour.

Assessing the three types of argument considered, philosophically, we may conclude that there are no compelling arguments against pluralisms. Accepting many religions as equal paths to one Real, in a Hickean manner, is not incoherent; moreover, other forms of pluralisms bypass various arguments raised against Hick. However, at the same time, we are not driven, philosophically, towards a pluralist answer either – although the questions raised may lead us to reject an exclusivist answer. If we are, from a Christian standpoint, going to argue for radical openness to religious Others, we must turn to theological arguments. Therefore, we will shortly address the criticism that the pluralist option is not compatible with Christian belief. Before we do so, however, we should address the imperialist and colonialist charges ranged against pluralisms.

Imperialism and pluralisms

In Chapter 2 we addressed dialogue and power, notably the way a dominant Western discourse shapes and creates the field; indeed, many of the criticisms raised there were, implicitly or explicitly, directed against a pluralist-style approach. However, we must deal with criticisms raised directly against pluralist theologies.

Critics argue that 'pluralist theologies often fail, despite their pretensions to the contrary, to transcend the particular perspectives of their proponents'.[47] That is, although they try to make a 'universal' system they fail, creating one bound up within a Western Enlightenment standpoint. Indeed, Kwok says of Hick's glossing over of differences that it 'smacks of the patronizing tendency of white liberals'.[48] Yet few, if any, would see the main proponents of pluralisms as actually being covert

47 Nicholson, Hugh, 2007, 'Comparative Theology After Liberalism', *Modern Theology* 23:2, pp. 229–51, p. 234.

48 Kwok, Pui-lan, 2005, *Postcolonial Imagination and Feminist Theology*, London: SCM, p. 199.

imperialists; the charge is more that they are well-intentioned liberals who have failed to see that their attempts to include others actually involve subsuming them into their own worldview. Meanwhile, pluralists in different religions are sometimes accused of becoming embedded into a Western Enlightenment worldview, and so no longer represent the integrity of their own system (on issues around this, see Chapter 2). We must therefore address such criticisms. It would be wrong, though, to suggest that pluralists are not aware of the issues involved, and some have addressed such issues.[49]

It is argued that pluralisms, especially Hick's version, are inherently an act of intellectual colonialization by explaining how religion should be understood. Put another way, it posits its own religious meta-system as an explanation and meta-narrative over and against all others. However, the title of Hick's magnum opus in the area, *An Interpretation of Religion*, should tell us that he is not imposing the only interpretation, but suggesting *an* interpretation which makes sense from his position but is not asserted as the absolute truth (this is made abundantly clear in the Introduction). Another related argument is that pluralisms are forms of exclusivisms (or inclusivisms). Schmidt-Leukel has given short shrift to this by pointing out that any meaningful statement excludes certain others.[50] It is therefore meaningless to say all statements or claims are of the same type. For instance, to say 'Spain is in Europe' is to exclude it from being in Asia, but it is not to take an exclusivist or closed stance on Asians in the way that the statement 'the people of Spain are superior to the people of Asia' would. The two statements are clearly saying different things. Again, a lesser charge, to say pluralisms (and exclusivisms) are types of inclusivisms would be to reinterpret the typological framework for rhetorical effect; in one sense they are 'inclusive' in that they include other explanations, or systems, within their preview, but clearly each stance says something different. As has been observed, the terms exclusivisms, inclusivisms and pluralisms clearly intend different

---

49 See Knitter, Paul F., 1995, *One Earth, Many Religions: Multifaith Dialogue and Global Responsibility*, Maryknoll, NY: Orbis, pp. 87–8 and 93–6.

50 Schmidt-Leukel, *Transformation*, p. 95.

things.[51] This is not to deny that, as sometimes expressed, pluralisms do not have the exclusive claim that it has the absolute correct solution, but this is not the claim made by Hick or other sophisticated advocates of the pluralist hypothesis.

We turn to a significant set of critiques, although they challenge the way pluralisms are expressed rather than the radical openness underlying it. As we have seen, the term 'religion' has been created in a particular context, and Kwok believes that it is only an uncritical usage of the terms 'religion' and especially 'world religions' that makes pluralisms possible.[52] 'World religions' is particularly interesting as Hick, like many other pluralists, bases his ideas upon the 'major world religions'.[53] Only by accepting, it is claimed, that we have a similar genus with a similar set of concepts can we easily speak of the pluralist option as a way to view these together.[54] Yet, it is not naive to group 'religions' together, but actually historically reflective of their interactions (see Chapter 2). Nevertheless, particular problems with the Western construction of religion infects the way the pluralist option is constructed. Jeannine Hill Fletcher uses the term 'sameness solidarity' to discuss this, while she also notes that, for Hick at least, religions appear 'bounded'.[55] By

---

51 Berling, *Pilgrim*, p. 29.

52 Kwok, *Postcolonial*, p. 202.

53 These are variously recorded, but in its widest usage represents all the religions that have survived for a significant period through time with a major following, hence it is not just the 'big five', Christianity, Islam, Judaism, Hinduism, Buddhism (in the UK Sikhism is often added to make six), but includes smaller and lesser-known traditions such as the Bahais, Jains, etc.

54 There is a growing literature in the study of religion, criticizing the way 'World Religion' textbooks do this, for instance grouping all religions into chapters that shows how they all talk about 'salvation', 'deity', etc. See, for instance, McCutcheon, Russell, 2005, 'The Perils of Having One's Cake and Eating It Too: Some Thoughts in Response', *Religious Studies Review* 33:1 & 2, pp. 33–6, available at, http://www.as.ua.edu/rel/pdf/mccutchrsrreply.pdf, accessed 11 September 2009.

55 Fletcher, Jeannine Hill, 2008, 'Religious Pluralism in an Era of Globalization: The Making of Modern Religious Identity', *Theological Studies* 69, pp. 394–411, pp. 401 and 402.

the former she intends that the way in which difference is glossed over is problematic. That is to say, pluralisms do not sufficiently attend to the problems of interreligious hermeneutics, the way we discuss the differences. To be sure, Hick does note there are very real differences and never suggests we can blend all religions into one master religious narrative or theology. Nevertheless, by, for instance, suggesting that there is a common motif of 'salvation' from self-centredness to reality-centredness much nuance and individual difference is lost. By the latter, Fletcher argues that pluralisms have tended to see each religion as a fixed and monolithic entity, which fails to be responsive to the way that religion is a much broader and more flexible entity. Indeed, it represents a very static and problematic notion of religious identity, one formed within a single all-encompassing tradition, rather than one founded in relation to the boundaries beyond it and also, of course, in relation to other identities. I would suggest, though, that these problems attend to some early expressions of the pluralist standpoint (and, indeed, given that the concept of religion being criticized represented the prevailing discourse about the nature of 'religion' when Hick created his theories, it is not so much a critique of him as the problematic category 'religion' as it played out in his theory) and is not inherent in expressions of the pluralist standpoint (see Chapter 6).

To turn to broader questions, though, is a pluralist stance inherently colonial or imperialist or domineering in some way? It is interesting that D'Costa has recently argued that exclusivisms need not be so, because although they can make claims for their own positions they can do so with a sensitivity and respect for others. Despite this, he still hurls the claim that pluralists are 'colonial' as though this standpoint must inherently be done in a disrespectful way.[56] It is hard to see how this can be maintained, especially if the pluralist model used seeks to be respectful to and learn from other religious traditions. We must not, though, neglect the power dynamics, and recognize that being a standpoint largely developed and propagated by a

56 D'Costa, Gavin, 2009, *Christianity and World Religions: Disputed Questions in the Theology of Religions*, Chichester: Wiley-Blackwell, pp. 10–12.

white, male, intellectual, Christian elite[57] it will, at the very least, be open to suspicion and the danger of exerting an influence tied to the cultural superiority that is its home ground. Indeed, as McCutcheon has argued, a liberal pluralism can be seen to give voice only to those who share within its viewpoint.[58] A pluralist standpoint must therefore make its case in a humble, sympathetic manner of learning rather than preaching or dogmatizing (on the whole it has strived to do so even if not successfully).[59] However, this must always be done from somewhere, rather than nowhere and, as such, this work, as already noted, will make an ecumenical Western Christian case for pluralisms, within the context of an Intercultural Theology, and respecting the particularity of religions.

Is the pluralist option Christian?

If radical openness to religious Others is to be understood as a Christian option within the debate, then it has to be made clear that it is not contrary to what most Christians would recognize as a Christian standpoint. There are certainly many who would maintain it is not, and cannot be, a Christian theology from quite polemical stances.[60] However, even among theologians who recognize the contextual nature of Christian identity and the ecumenical imperative, a pluralist stance is not necessarily endorsed. According to the Asian American Roman Catholic theologian Peter Phan:

---

57 I do not wish to downplay the contribution of non-Western and female pluralists; however, my claim is simply that its best-known spokespeople primarily belong to this class. I could list John Hick, Leonard Swidler, Paul Knitter, Perry Schmidt-Leukel and Alan Race as, perhaps, the key spokespeople for this stance. I hope the evidence of this book will show that I do not thereby limit my discussion to this Western male tradition.

58 McCutcheon, Russell T., 2002, 'The Category of "Religion" and the Politics of Tolerance', in Greil, Arthur L. and Bromley, David (eds), *Defining Religion: Investigating the Boundaries Between the Sacred and the Secular*, Amsterdam: JAI, pp. 139–62, pp. 152–9.

59 See the discussion on power in Chapter 2, and also Chapters 6 and 7.

60 See, for instance, Carson, D. A., 1996, *The Gagging of God: Christianity Confronts Pluralism*, Grand Rapids, MI: Zondervan.

The imperceptible slippage from Christianity to Jesus, whether intentional or not, is, in my opinion, the Achilles' heel of the pluralist stance, for, and this is my contention, while it is not possible to claim that Christianity is unique in the sense of definitive, absolute, normative and superior to other religions, it is legitimate to claim that Jesus is the only Christ and savior.[61]

Phan's wording suggests that in moving from a focus on Christian teachings (around Jesus) to the person of Jesus himself (presumably with something like a Hickean metaphorical Christology – see below) is the flaw. His claim is that Jesus, understood as the Christ of tradition, is central to being Christian, yet that Christianity, as a historical phenomenon, is not definitive. There is, though, a tension here: how do we accept the Christ mediated in tradition as non-negotiable but not the tradition which mediates him? In Chapter 1 we explored the issue that Christian identity is a contextual matter, and I would suggest we need to take this further in relation to our views of Christ (Christology). However, this is a very delicate issue, and for many Christians it goes too far to suggest that we can negotiate on the position of Christ. Pluralisms do not, however, necessitate that we must do so. However, if we accept the contextual nature of Christianity then I think we need to take a move towards allowing us to rethink how Jesus has been mediated to us in the tradition. To this end, I will argue two points below:

1   That there is a legitimate Christian way to take another look at how we understand Jesus.
2   To show that a pluralist stance is possible within the accepted boundaries of traditional Christology.

61 Phan, Peter, 1990, 'Are There Other "Saviors" for Other Peoples? A Discussion of the Problem of the Universal Significance and Uniqueness of Jesus Christ', in Phan, Peter (ed.), *Christianity and the Wider Ecumenism*, New York: Paragon, p. 168. Phan has further developed his position in his impressive exposition, Phan, Peter, 2004, *Being Religious Interreligiously: Asian Perspectives on Interfaith Dialogue*, Maryknoll, NY: Orbis, a work which has faced censure from his church for the subtle and sympathetic way he has tried to balance a Christian stance on Jesus with a radical openness to other religions.

One problem is that the kind of thinking around Christ that many associate as necessary for being a pluralist is not seen by them as compatible with the Christian heritage. This is despite the fact that there are very good and faithful Christian ways of reading who Jesus was, which have long been recognized in theological circles. This problem was long ago recognized by Knitter who suggests that 'if these new christologies . . . have any future within Christian theology, they need a better *ecclesial mediation* in order that they might be "received" by the faithful'.[62] This seems to be an idea shared by others, such as Judith Berling.[63] It is useful here to address one particularly controversial area of Hick's theology, in terms of it being seen as Christian, which is his belief that Christology must be rethought such that Jesus is seen simply as a human being. For him, Jesus' divinity, especially if he is understood as the definitive revelation of God as deity incarnate, is a major obstacle to pluralisms, for we cannot recognize that each equally mediates the Real if one holds its founder is truly God in a way no others are. His position is, of course, supported by many investigations into the historical Jesus which stress reading him in Jewish context (see Chapter 1).[64] I would stress that there

---

62 Knitter, Paul F., 1988, 'Toward a Liberation Theology', in Knitter, Paul F. and Hick, John (eds), *The Myth of Christian Uniqueness*, Maryknoll, NY: Orbis, pp. 178–200, accessed from, http://servicioskoinonia.org/relat/255e.htm, 11 September 2009.

63 See Berling, *Pilgrim*, pp. 26ff.

64 This is not to deny, though, that some major biblical critics do not argue for contrary views. Therefore against the arguments that Jesus clearly never claimed messiahship or divinity, cogently argued by the likes of Marcus Borg (1992, *Jesus: A New Vision – Spirit, Culture and the Life of Discipleship*, San Francisco: HarperSanFrancisco), Dominic Crossan (1991, *The Historical Jesus: The Life of a Mediterranean Jewish Peasant*, Edinburgh: T. & T. Clark), and Geza Vermes (2003, *Jesus in his Jewish Context*, London: SCM), we find serious scholars like Tom Wright (1997, *The Original Jesus: The Life and Vision of a Revolutionary*, Grand Rapids, MI: Wm. B. Eerdmans), James Dunn (2005, *A New Perspective on Jesus: What the Quest for the Historical Jesus Missed*, Grand Rapids, MI: Baker Academic), and John P. Maier (1996, *A Marginal Jew: Vol. 1: Rethinking the Historical Jesus*, New York: Bantam Doubleday Dell) arguing for a more traditional case. However, serious biblical scholarship, like Wright's, must concede that many traditional claims that Jesus claimed full divinity are suspect, and that

is certainly an arguable biblical warrant for Hick's position and, if, as we have seen, we must accept many different versions of Christianity, then we cannot simply classify this as unchristian, especially, as we have seen, it was strong Christian belief that led Hick to this position.

Recognizing that many Christians would have problems accepting this stance, we move to our second point, that other pluralists will defend a Chalcedon orthodoxy in Christology. In particular, Roger Haight and Schmidt-Leukel have written at length on this.[65] Clearly, then, it is possible to be a Christian and a pluralist. Indeed, among the major proponents of pluralism we see that many are not nominal Christians but committed believers, even priests or theologians within their own tradition.[66] However, the case for a pluralist approach does not just need to be made at the level of this or that doctrine, rather a more radical readjustment within Christianity is needed, a new Reformation even. Whereas most previous landmark events in Christianity have marked moves to greater exclusion or schism, whether it be the Councils of Nicaea and

---

we can only surmise, rather than prove, that Jesus claimed, or believed himself to be, the Messiah. This still, of course, leaves us a long way from the possibility that Jesus endorsed anything like a fully developed Chalcedon Christology!

65 See Haight, Roger, 1999, *Jesus: Symbol of God*, Maryknoll, NY: Orbis; Haight, Roger, 2005, 'Pluralist Christology as Orthodox', in Knitter (ed.), *Myth*, pp. 151–61; Schmidt-Leukel, *Transformation*, pp. 159–70; Schmidt-Leukel, 'Pluralisms', pp. 95–6; see also the reading from Haight in Schmidt-Leukel, Perry (ed.), 2009, 'Pluralisms' in Hedges and Race (eds), *SCM Reader: Christian Approaches*, pp. 50–8.

66 As I have mentioned, it was Hick's strong Christian commitment that led him to pluralism (see Cheetham, David, 2003, *John Hick: A Critical Introduction and Reflection*, Aldershot: Ashgate). A strong Christian commitment can also be found in other pluralists, such as Alan Race who is a parish priest and interreligious activist seeking to bring religions together in a spirit of co-operation, while Paul Knitter wished to become a missionary to 'save' the religious Other before his calling led him to pluralisms (see Knitter, Paul, 2004, 'The Vocation of an Interreligious Theologian. My Retrospective on 40 Years in Dialogue', available at, http://www.crcs.ugm.ac.id/news.php?news_id=173, accessed 20August 2009, first published in *Horizons* 31:1, pp. 135–49).

Chalcedon,[67] the events that divided Catholic and Orthodox worlds, or the Reformation that split the Catholic world, we need now to move to a greater ecumenism. Therefore we will argue that a pluralist, or radically open, attitude is in the very nature of the Christian tradition and, moreover, is what I believe Christians must move towards.

Christian foundations for pluralisms

It is commonly felt that the pluralist option is somehow a watering down of Christian commitment. It has been argued that it stems from an acceptance of modern notions of indifferentism into the 'pure norms' of Christian theology where it does not belong.[68] However, many pluralists found that it was their radical commitment to the Christian gospel that led them to acknowledge a wider range to God's work in the world. Therefore, almost in reverse, for this is perhaps where we should begin (?), we end with a reflection on the Christian foundations for radical openness to the religious Other. I will do this with relation first to Jesus, then some other biblical texts, and will end with some brief comments on the later Christian tradition.

Was Jesus a pluralist?[69]

In one sense my heading here is clearly rhetorical. Jesus was not a pluralist in the same sense as such figures as Hick or Knitter; this worldview is contextual to our times (and is envisaged in concepts that would, perhaps, not even be translatable in ways readily understandable to a first-century

---

67 These councils sought to define correct belief as the hallmark of Christian belonging (as though God depended on us to work out how exactly s/he worked in the world and was incapable of saving whomsever s/he wished as and how s/he wished) and divided Christianity into Chalcedonian and non-Chalcedonian camps (see Chapter 1).

68 See D'Costa, *Christianity*, Chapter 6.

69 I develop the themes more fully here in a paper I am working on, provisionally entitled: 'Was Jesus a Pluralist? A Christian Meditation on Openness to Other Religions and Fidelity to the Gospel'.

Aramaic speaking Jew). However, what I wish to argue is that Jesus' worldview, contextual to his times, was marked by an incredible and radical openness to the religious Other. Indeed, I would suggest that Jesus' openness allows us to regard the exclusivist option as not only untenable but also radically unchristian.

The 'proof text' most readily cited by exclusivists for Jesus' exclusivist stance is found in John's Gospel: 'I am the Way, the Truth, and the Life. No one comes to the Father except through me' (John 14.6). However, various problems arise with this, such as the very Protestant (but a tendency found throughout Christianity) habit of prooftexting, taking passages of scripture out of context and using them to 'win' arguments in a put-down fashion. Not only must we use texts in context, but we also need to examine the theological presuppositions of the book from which the text is taken. If so, we find John's Gospel is widely cited by inclusivists because of the quite startling theology that shapes the whole book expressed in the prologue: 'That was the Light which Lights every man that comes into the world' (John 1.4). Christian theology has understood by this that the Logos, the pre-incarnate Jesus, exists in all people as their inner source or guide. In case it be supposed that I too am prooftexting, having just cited one verse from John's Gospel, there are other verses which would also support an openness to the religious Other. Perhaps, most notably his conversation with the Samaritan woman at the well (John 4.1–42; I shall say more on Samaritans in due course). However, there is much else to suggest Jesus has a radical openness.[70]

To take the argument forward, let us examine Jesus' interactions with religious Others. We begin with the centurion found in chapter 7 of Luke's Gospel, a non-Christian and possibly a polytheist, though he may, like other educated Romans, be a monotheist, or even a God-fearer (a term for Gentiles converting to Judaism), but we must speculate for we simply are not given this information. What we are told is that he comes to Jesus because he has heard of his miracles of healing and, seeing

---

70 For another reading of John 14.6, I would direct the reader to Chapter 8: 'Uniqueness: A Pluralistic Reading of John 14.6,' in Schmidt-Leukel, *Transformation*, pp. 146–58.

himself as unworthy, asks Jesus to cure his servant at a distance. Jesus does this because of the man's faith, and remarks, 'I tell you, not even in Israel have I found such faith' (Luke 7.9). That we do not have the details on this person's religious affiliation is itself significant, for it implies (for the author) information about this was irrelevant. Jesus was moved to compassion by the man himself. Also, what is his 'faith'? Certainly not Christian faith, in Jesus as *the* Son of God (in a Christian rather than Jewish sense of the term), but faith in his ability as a miracle worker, a healer, a holy man. We therefore find an acceptance of the religious Other on their own terms as persons of faith.

Another example of Jesus' attitude is his view on Samaritans. In Jesus' day, the Samaritans were, for Jews, not just the religious Other (other), but a particular example of those who had rejected God and the path to salvation.[71] It is therefore illuminating that they appear quite often. That Jesus could find virtue in such despised religious Others is shown in his parable of the Good Samaritan (Luke 10.25-37).[72] Moreover, a positive assessment is also found where we see the only leper, in one healing story, returning to thank Jesus is the Samaritan (Luke 17.11-19). What this tells us is that Jesus found virtue, as seen in the Good Samaritan parable, in people following the ethical codes of innate goodness and natural human decency. Certainly, we cannot deny that there is a polemical side to this story against the Levite and priest who walk by. However, considering the priest and Levite, both concerned with the purity of their tradition, who do not reach out, can lead us to read Jesus' message as telling us to move beyond what we see as the edges of our understandings. Expressed another way, holiness of life does not lie with those who would traditionally be seen as defining the truths (ritual purity, doctrinal correctness, etc.) of our religious world but may lie beyond it, and this should allow us to see spiritual truth in the religious Other. We may consider it our

---

71 Coggins, Richard, 1993, 'Samaritans', in Metzger, Bruce and Coogan, Michael, *The Oxford Companion to the Bible*, Oxford: Oxford University Press, pp. 671-3.

72 A reflection on the interreligious implications of this is found in Berling, *A Pilgrim*, p. 122.

religious duty to ignore the religious Other, but Jesus suggests otherwise, to embrace them as our neighbour (this forms the context of this passage: see Luke 10.25–29).

Our examples so far have all come from Luke's Gospel, but we find the same Jesus, marked by radical openness, across both Mark and Matthew. In Matthew, we find Jesus encountering the Canaanite woman (Matt. 15.22–28), another religious Other and, after a dispute on whether Jesus' message is simply for the people of Israel, he extends this outwards. Indeed, we see here what Durwood Foster has referred to as an instance where 'actual interreligious dialogue takes place' between Jesus and a religious Other (see Chapter 6 on biblical hospitality).[73]

Indeed, I would suggest that the whole tenor of Jesus' teaching leads us to see this openness. The Sermon on the Mount collection of sayings (Matt. 5—7) leads us to see that anyone who does virtuous actions, of whatever faith, creed or denomination, is doing what Jesus asked. Taken in the light of Logos theology this leads us to, at least, a Christian theology of inclusivisms.[74] Again, Jesus saves the woman being stoned for adultery (John 7.53—8.11) an example of his openness not to correctness of belief, form, or even ethical practice, but of his compassion to all, and a recognition of our failings – an openness which we have suggested extends to his dealings with religious Others.

We should, also, briefly, attend to some possible instances of Jesus' more negative views, in particular against Jewish figures. The critique of the scribes and Pharisees is not, I would suggest, in Jesus' context an

---

73 Foster, Durwood, 1990, 'Christian Motives for Interfaith Dialogue', in Phan, Peter (ed.), *Christianity and the Wider Ecumenism*, New York: Paragon House, pp. 21–33, p. 26. In his interpretation he even suggests that, at some point, the Canaanite woman's understanding exceeds Jesus' own, for she realizes the possible extent of his Christ role through challenging him to extend beyond the Jewish borders.

74 See Cheetham, David, 2008, 'Inclusivisms', in Hedges and Race, *SCM Core Text Christian Approaches*, pp. 66–9. For a more detailed exposition of some of these themes, see Hedges, Paul, 2001, *Preparation and Fulfilment: A History and Study of Fulfilment Theology in Modern British Thought in the Indian Context*, Bern: Verlag Peter Lang, pp. 17–21 and 36–7.

assault upon Judaism (this tradition is the basis of Jesus' own thought! (see Chapter 1)), but rather an assault upon a certain interpretation of Judaism, or, more broadly, a type of theology and religious thinking – one marked by a closed attitude and lack of generosity, in contrast to the openness and generosity that I have suggested characterizes Jesus' teaching. Jesus also seems opposed to those with exclusivist tendencies. It is in this light that we need to understand Jesus' words: 'But woe to you, scribes and Pharisees, hypocrites! Because you shut the kingdom of heaven against men; for you neither enter yourselves, nor allow those who would enter to go in' (Matt. 23.13). Here, we may say literally, we see Jesus complaining about the way that a closed system is created. As he continues in this collection of anti-Pharisaic sayings collected by Matthew (no doubt collected and brought together as a whole as part of the dispute with the emerging Rabbinic school within Judaism, as is the collection in Luke 11) we see Jesus complaining of their lists of laws and regulations, and saying: 'You blind guides, straining out a gnat and swallowing a camel!' (Matt. 23.24).[75] We may take this as opposition to a legalistic religious worldview that believes that divisions should be drawn up to divide and separate. Indeed, Jesus' condemnation of a closed system of religiosity can lead us to support an open view to religious Others. We may prooftext either way ('He who is not with me is against me' (Matt. 12.30), or 'For he that is not against us is for us' (Mark 9.40)). However, taken as an integrated whole, Jesus' message, I would argue, is one of radical openness (see also Chapter 6 on biblical hospitality).

Openness and the earliest Jesus Movement

To turn from Jesus' views to those found within the early church, we may presume that Jesus' earliest disciples learned from him about religious Others. Therefore, we may expect to find, if our thesis is correct, Jesus'

---

75 See Chapter 1. Certainly, we should note both that in Jesus' day the Pharisees were seen as pillars of virtue, and that it was their interpretation of Judaism that was shaping Rabbinic Judaism (see Maccoby, Hyam, 2003, *Jesus the Pharisee*, London: SCM, pp. 1–14).

radical openness confirmed and continued. I believe we find this clearly in the case of Peter: 'And Peter opened his mouth and said: "Truly I perceive that God shows no partiality, but in every nation any one who fears him and does what is right is acceptable to him"' (Acts 10.34–35). Here, Peter is speaking about Gentiles, and hence his mention of different nations is not simply about Jews or Christians (indeed, at this stage, there is no distinct Christian identity), but people of all religions (nations). Tying this together theologically, it is the Light, the Logos, inside all people which directs them in ways acceptable to God. However, I do not suggest that the New Testament represents us with a unified theology of religions, nor that a Logos theology in any developed sense pervaded all these thinkers; my suggestion here is to tie these together theologically for our benefit, as a way Christians today may come to connect with religious Others.

It cannot be denied that in places negative attitudes appear, especially in Paul's condemnations of idolatry (1 Cor. 5.10, etc.), yet here we run the risk of prooftexting without appreciating Paul's underlying sympathy to the religious Other. Paul's famous discourse on the Areopagus seems to make an exclusivist interpretation of him impossible. In this instance, although we find Paul 'provoked' at Athens being full of idols (Acts 17.16), we find his view changing for, in speaking of the altar to an unknown God, he tells the Athenians that they are already worshipping Jesus (as the pre-incarnate Logos) unknowingly (Acts 17.22–23). They could only do so of course if the Light is already within them, and their yearning was for God. His approach is not simply, or primarily, to see what is wrong in other religious practices and to condemn it, but to show how and where this leads us: it requires an open mind to the value and worth of the religious Other.

A collection of other possible sources of openness in the New Testament texts has been assembled by Foster, who cites such texts as 2 Timothy 4.6, Romans 1.20, Acts 14.17 and others as examples of such openness. However, in suggesting that we should accept the good in other religions where we find it, we may cite one particularly significant text that Foster notes, Philippians 4.8: 'Whatever is true, whatever is just, whatever is pure, whatever is lovely, whatever is gracious, if there is any excellence, if there is anything worthy of praise, think about all these things.'[76] Foster also suggests that many Old Testament passages may also support a radical openness to religious Others, something he supports with further exegesis of a range of New Testament passages.[77]

Openness in church history

While space does not permit me to extrapolate, we find, in biblically based reflection, an insistence upon this openness is many subsequent Christian thinkers: Justin Martyr, for instance, developed a Logos theology; Augustine of Hippo thought we should mine for what was good in any system of thought; Thomas Aquinas spoke of natural theology available to all; Martin Luther accepted a general revelation; and, John Wesley believed in an accessible grace, to name but a few figures.[78] In recent times Christians have answered with different responses: do we reject any good outside the Church, or do we take radical openness as our stance?[79]

Jesus' openness, religious pluralism and the contemporary context

There is no doubt that many of the biblical passages we have cited and theological reflection upon them, alongside the example of the figures in church history, have led many to adopt an inclusivist stance. However, we must ask whether this is adequate. The question we must ask ourselves therefore is: what is the Spirit saying to us today? We live in a

76 We may apply this to Hick's notion that all religions produce 'saints' and lead people to live what can, cross-culturally, be seen as ethical lives (though, on some problems with this, see Chapter 7).

77 Foster, 'Christian', pp. 22ff. See also Schmidt-Leukel, 'Pluralisms', p. 88.

78 A brief overview of some of these can be found in Cheetham, 'Inclusivisms', pp. 63–84, pp. 66–8.

79 The two options are well represented in two contrasting documents given by: a) the 1970 Frankfurt Declaration of the Evangelical Church of Germany, which is utterly exclusive; against, b) the statement from the United Church of Canada in 1985 which asserts that a salvation that excludes is not one they find in Christ's spirit (both are found in Eck, *Encountering*, pp. 169–70).

globalized world, often in multicultural and religiously plural contexts. We find ourselves alongside religious Others, who we cannot distinguish from us in terms of the depth of their spirituality, commitment to their faith, nor in the ethical and moral lives they lead.[80] In such a circumstance what would Jesus' openness to the religious Other lead us to say, do and think? Should we, like the closed-minded representatives of the scribes and Pharisees of Jesus' day, insist that only those who follow to the letter the prescriptions we have laid down, and the doctrines we have created (the creeds, the doctrines, or other such things, we must never forget, are never Jesus' own words, but the response of the Church, of fallible humans, to how we feel God is leading us)? Or should we seek to follow the loving example of the one who never shut out the Other? I recognize that what is being asked is, in some ways, a great cultural leap, but we must ask ourselves the question, based upon what Jesus said and did. Could we imagine him saying, when faced with our neighbours, our colleagues, those about whose religious beliefs and practices we know so much more than did the early Christians, answering to them, 'He who is not with me is against me'; would he not rather say, 'For he that is not against us is for us'? It may be objected that here I am falling into the trap Phan noted for us, the move from Christianity to Jesus, which may be said to be painting an image of Jesus as he appeals to contemporary sensibilities of openness rather than what is said in the historic witness of the Church and Christianity. However, in as far as Christianity must always return to its roots and the identity and teachings of Jesus as its guiding light, I believe that it is not illegitimate to ask the question this way, especially, as we have seen, there is not simply, in our ecumenical context, one single Christianity given to us (see Chapter 1). As Rowan Williams puts it: 'If we are truly learning how to be in that relation with God and the world in which Jesus of Nazareth stood, we shall not turn away from those who see from another place.'[81]

---

80 This is an essential insight of John Hick, so often condemned by opponents of pluralisms as disregarding Christianity, but who, it must be seen, was dragged from a deeply committed Christian exclusivism to a deeply committed Christian pluralism, just because of such issues.

81 Williams, 'Christian'.

Conclusions

We have seen that no compelling reasons exist, either philosophically or theologically, for the pluralist position to be seen as either incoherent or unfaithful to Christian tradition. Moreover, we can see in Jesus' example a radical openness to religious Others that allows itself to be challenged, touched and extended by encounter with them; an approach that calls Christians today to adopt a radical openness in our dealing with the religious Others we encounter. However, much theology today seems to consider that a stance of radical difference is the one it must pursue. In the next chapter we will therefore address this contemporary trend and give an assessment of it. We will see that, as expressed, both the pluralist and particularist stances offer things we can learn from, and combined with what we learn from feminist positions, we shall seek to integrate this in Chapter 6.

4

Radical Difference and Religious Others
The Particularist Agenda[1]

Introducing particularities

An impasse exists between the pluralist and particularist worldviews, which I characterize as a clash between the motifs of 'radical openness' and 'radical difference' (Chapter 1). Having considered pluralisms, we will now outline and critically assess the characteristics of particularities.

The theological worldviews that endorse particularist positions are not a unified system of thought, with individuals having their own standpoints, some of which are contradictory. However, certain core assumptions allow us to describe it as possessing some common features. These have been classified into six key points:

1   each faith is unique, alterity[2] is stressed over similarity, as seemingly common elements in religious experience or doctrine are regarded as superficial;
2   it is only possible to speak from a specific tradition, there can be no pluralistic interpretation;
3   the Holy Spirit may be at work in other faiths, requiring them to be regarded with respect and dignity;

---

1 I have written two previous works (referenced below) outlining and critiquing particularities, and this chapter makes use of this while producing a new presentation of the argument, and adding a number of original critiques or comments.

2 A word frequently used in post-modern discourse, which may simply be read as difference – though various post-modern writers might give various sublayers of meaning to it.

4   no salvific potency resides in other faiths, though they are some-
     how involved in God's plans for humanity but in ways we cannot
     know;

5   we need to work from a position based in a post-modern and
     post-liberal worldview;

6   the orthodox doctrines of Trinity and Christ are grounding
     points from which to approach other faiths.[3]

We will explore particularities in relation to these six points, under the
headings of: Religion; Tradition-Specific; Holy Spirit; Salvation; Post-
modernism; and Orthodoxy. We will first outline the views of various particularists on these areas, before offering a critical assessment of each.

Religion

The particularist understanding of religion

Particularity builds, partly, on the critique of religion encountered earlier (Chapter 2). However, it is useful to spell out its specific arguments.
For particularists the term 'religion', when applied to a set of traditions
that can be enumerated under the names of Hinduism, Islam, Buddhism,
Christianity, etc., is simply meaningless. It is regarded, as the product of
the modern Western academic world with its obsession with categorization and taxonomy. Worse than this, it is seen as symptomatic of the
will to power, a concept taken from Nietzsche and given post-modern
expression most particularly by Michael Foucault, for whom all attempts
at knowledge are attempts to suppress and control the 'Other'. It finds its
most potent manifestation in the critique it offers of pluralisms. From the
particularist's own standpoint, its vision could be contrasted with that of
pluralisms in the following ways:

---

3 Hedges, P., 2008, 'Particularities: tradition-specific post-modern perspectives', in Hedges, P and Race, A. (eds), *SCM Core Text Christian Approaches
Other Faiths*, London: SCM, pp. 112–13 (this quote is set out here, in the original
it was presented in paragraph format).

1 Religion: for pluralism, all religions stem from one basic form, and are essentially compatible; for particularity, they are independent 'language games' and mutually incompatible.

2 Religious/mystical experiences: pluralism is seen as believing one core experience exists across religions, which is interpreted differently according to culture;[4] for particularity, each religion has its own core experience, and only superficial similarities exist.

3 Religious teachings/doctrines: for pluralism, these are cultural expressions of faith, an interpretation of the core mystical experience; for particularity, they are given, even fixed, as part of internally coherent systems which cannot be compared.[5]

Two strands of thought can be seen as leading to this position; one is theological, with antecedents in Karl Barth, the other comes from the social sciences and contemporary metatheory in the study of religion. We will briefly trace some outlines of the argument in each case to explain how this thought arises and, in so doing, recap some of the arguments found in Chapter 2.

Theology and the problematic category of 'religion'

The motto of this line of thought can trace a theological and intellectual antecedent to Tertullian's famous cry: 'What has Athens to do with Jerusalem?' This simple statement gives voice to a belief that the message of the Christian tradition is of a separate order from that found elsewhere. In the modern world, Barth has most famously advocated such a stance. For him, Christian revelation and religion are antithetical concepts,

---

4 'This is not the view of all pluralists, but is certainly how most critics of pluralism see *all* pluralists – see Schmidt-Leukel's chapter on pluralism herein on this' (Hedges, 'Particularities', p. 132, fn. 9). The chapter referenced in this note is: Schmidt-Leukel, Perry, 2008, 'Pluralisms: How to Appreciate Religious Diversity Theologically', in Hedges and Race, *SCM Core Text Christian Approaches*, pp. 85–110.

5 Hedges, 'Particularities', p. 115.

'religion is unbelief . . . [I]t is the one great concern, of godless man . . .'[6] What is meant by this is that while man may delight in making his own systems of belief and creating ideas of deity, these are a result of his own sinful nature and not the fruit of revelation, which, for Barth, is found only in its historical instantiation in the person of Jesus of Nazareth. As such, religion and revelation stand as opposites, not as part of one natural progression of thought.[7] Even Christianity, in as far as it is a system based around the figure of Christ, becomes part of 'religion' and so subject to decay and corruption.[8] The concept extends into contemporary thinking exemplified by a number of particularist writers. (Not that we can draw a straight line of influence from Barth to any or all particularist theologians; however, the theological thought patterns are shared.) For instance, D'Costa asserts:

> I suspect Hick's use of 'superiority' is a category mistake. One can say, 'This English apple is *superior* to other apples', when one is judging things in the same category. However, when we come to 'revelation' we are dealing with a *sui generis* reality which therefore admits no comparison.[9]

Here, D'Costa is seeking to reposition the particularist agenda away from the ground inhabited by exclusivist or inclusivist positions, which may assert, especially the latter, that Christianity is a higher form of religion compared to, for example, Judaism or Hinduism. D'Costa claims this is

6 Barth, Karl, 'The Question of Natural Theology' (*Church Dogmatics* I, 2), in Bromiley, G. W. (trans. and ed.), 1961, *Church Dogmatics: A Selection*, New York: Harper Torchbooks.

7 See Torrance, Thomas F., 2000, *Karl Barth: An Introduction to His Early Theology 1919–1931*, Edinburgh: T. & T. Clark, pp. 57ff.

8 Barth, 'Question', p. 53.

9 D'Costa, Gavin, '"Roundtable Review" of *The Meeting of Religions and the Trinity*', *Reviews in Theology and Religious Studies* (2001), p. 246. This review is particularly interesting as it presents three responses to this work, with D'Costa's reply to his critics.

the category mistake,[10] for Hick supposes that Christianity/revelation, as a religion, is being compared to another similar object, namely another religion. For D'Costa, revelation is *sui generis*, that is to say unique in type and kind. For him, we cannot compare religions, religious experience, or mystical experience, because we are not comparing like with like. Hence, the projects of pluralisms and inclusivisms are seen as fundamentally flawed and, in as far as exclusivisms see Christianity as the 'true religion' and others as 'false religion' it too is subject to the same objections. For D'Costa and others a number of consequences flow from this, which we will deal with in due course.

The study of religion and the problematic category of 'religion'

Particularity finds itself aligned with what may be termed aspects of a post-modern worldview (see below). This means that it seeks to align itself with critical thought in the contemporary discourses of sociology, anthropology and other social sciences – though it should be noted that a tension also exists between some exponents of particularity and these disciplines, but, nevertheless, they would (mostly) not find themselves in disagreement on the subject of 'religion'.[11] Points of agreement would include Talal Asad's claim that the term 'religion' operates within the realms of 'Orientalism', as defined by Edward Said, wherein it becomes

---

10 A category mistake is a philosophical term used to indicate a particular type of error in argumentation. It suggests that the argument in question has not understood the distinction between two or more separate things. A classic example is to imagine that a visitor has just been shown around Oxford University, where he has seen the various colleges, the Bodleian Library, the Examination Hall, but then turns in exasperation to his guide saying he has seen the colleges and other buildings, but not the university, which is what he came to see! Obviously, he has missed the point, for there is no single physical manifestation of the university, it is the collection of its constituent parts (see Ryle, Gilbert, 1949, *The Concept of Mind*, London: Hutchinson, p. 16).

11 In particular, Milbank and other thinkers associated with the Radical Orthodoxy project would see the social sciences as disciplines which can launch no legitimate critique against the Christian tradition; see Milbank, John, 1989, *Theology and Social Theory*, Oxford: Blackwell.

another manifestation of the Western world seeking to box in and confine the 'Other', in particular the Oriental.[12] For Timothy Fitzgerald, the term is quasi-theological, imbued with the sense of a unified transcendent essence that pervades all manifestations of 'religion'. This for him is a pervasive, and negative, leftover of the influence of nineteenth-century liberal theology.[13] Jonathan Z. Smith has argued that the terminology of religion is entirely the manufacture of the Western academic disciplines, axiomized in his now famous words, 'there is no data for religion . . . Religion has no independent existence apart from the academy.'[14] Perhaps most influential of all is Russell McCutcheon, who has argued that religion can only legitimately be seen, in the academic study of religion, as a manifestation of human culture and, as such, the data we pare off and bracket as 'religion' is merely an arbitrary distinction within the whole continuum of 'secular' human culture, society and behaviour.[15]

The particularist account of religion

Therefore, according to particularists, the latest critical thinking within the social sciences and the study of religion shows that inclusivisms, exclusivisms and pluralisms are on weak theoretical ground in claiming that all religions are of some similar type. However, it also develops its own specific critiques. The American Roman Catholic theologian Paul J. Griffiths has argued that the diversity between traditions demonstrates that the aims and orientations of any one are incompatible with the parameters of another:

---

12 Asad, T., 1993, *Genealogies of Religion: Discipline and Reasons of Power in Christianity and Islam*, London: Johns Hopkins University Press.

13 Fitzgerald, T., 2000, *The Ideology of Religious Studies*, New York: Oxford University Press.

14 Smith, J. Z., 1982, *Imagining Religion: From Babylon to Jonestown*, Chicago: University of Chicago Press, p. xi.

15 McCutcheon, Russell, 2003, *Manufacturing Religion: The Discourse on Sui Generis Religion and the Politics of Nostalgia*, Oxford: Oxford University Press, pp. 18–19, 107, 127ff.

> The features common to a form of life inhabited by a member of Gush Emmunim in Israel and . . . [the] form of life belonged to by a Theravada Buddhist in a forest hermitage in Sri Lanka . . . [are such that] the features that differentiate them are . . . more numerous (and . . . more significant) . . . than those they share.[16]

However, the foundational statement of the particularist position comes from the American Lutheran George Lindbeck, found in his seminal work *The Nature of Doctrine: The Church in a Postmodern Age*.[17] He argues that three main approaches have dominated Christian understandings of 'religion': the 'cognitive-propositionalist'; the 'experiential-expressive'; and, a third combining these two found in ecumenical Roman Catholics.[18] The first sees religion as primarily a set of doctrines to be believed and accepted, the second sees it as based in internal feelings with doctrine being secondary, while the third attempts to combine these two. He focuses on the 'experiential-expressive' model (liberal, modernist), which he contrasts with his own 'cultural-linguistic' model (post-liberal).[19] The latter he sees as theologically sound and based on a 'non-theological' set of factors, that is historical, anthropological and sociological, which show, he says, against the 'experientialist-expressive' model that we cannot speak of essences of religion across cultures.[20]

---

16 Griffiths, Paul J., 2001, *Problems of Religious Diversity*, Oxford: Blackwell, pp. 15–16. Griffiths was also a Buddhist scholar, a role he has largely given up to focus on theology after a conversion from Anglicanism. Notable religious studies works by him include: 1986, *On Being Mindless: Buddhist Meditation and the Mind-Body Problem*, La Salle, Ill: Open Court Publishing; 1994; *On Being Buddha: The Classical Doctrine of Buddhahood*, New York: SUNY Press; and, 1999, *Religious Reading: The Place of Reading in the Practice of Religion*, Oxford: Oxford University Press.

17 Lindbeck, George, 1984, *The Nature of Doctrine: The Church in a Postmodern Age*, Philadelphia: Westminster Press.

18 Lindbeck, *Nature*, p. 16.

19 Lindbeck, *Nature*, pp. 31–3.

20 Lindbeck, *Nature*, pp. 30ff.

The core of Lindbeck's argument is that we should understand religion as a set of constructs learned in cultural and linguistic contexts. Therefore, he asserts, no common religious experience is found around the world. Rather, because the very structure of our experience relies upon the language we have learned, the structures of our understanding, and the cultural context which will allow us to express this, we cannot have any experience which is not first shaped. He means more than just our language and the way we express an experience is shaped by our context; more radically, the whole symbolic structure that encapsulates our thought shapes our experience. For him, there is no 'pure' experience. For us to be consciously aware of an experience 'it is in some fashion symbolized', which means it is formed by our brains and modes of understanding before being relayed into our mind and becomes part of the patterns that exist there.[21] An experience we are not aware of is not an experience, and for it to become an experience it must enter our pre-existing structures for being and understanding. The fallacy of the 'experiential-expressive' model lies, for him, just in this, that he believes it says we can have 'private experiences', that is something just inside our head unrelated to anything else, which may then be related directly to a 'transcendent reality' as a common core found in various religions. Lindbeck argues we cannot have an experience that is not shaped by our potential for experiencing/understanding – and this potential is what, from birth then into childhood and adulthood, is given by our socio-culturo-linguistic milieu. As he puts it: 'It is conceptually confused to talk of symbolizations (and therefore experiences) that are purely private.'[22] We can only experience those things which we have the language to express, and this language, the symbolization system on which it is based, has its 'origin in interpersonal relations and social interactions'.[23]

This line of thought means that, for Lindbeck, to be 'a Christian involves learning the story of Israel and of Jesus well enough to interpret

21 Lindbeck, *Nature*, pp. 37–8.
22 Lindbeck, *Nature*, pp. 37–8.
23 Lindbeck, *Nature*, p. 38.

and experience oneself and one's world in its terms'.[24] Therefore, for him, the Christian experience must be different from the Buddhist, Hindu, Muslim, Jewish, or any other experience. Quite simply: 'Adherents of different religions do not diversely thematize the same experience; rather they have different experiences.'[25] In his terms then, every tradition is its own cultural-linguistic worldview, which is quite different from that of any other. Therefore, we are wrong to speak of a common set of things called 'religions'. Every religion is seen as a unique and distinct set of cultural-linguistic constituents.

We can see that the particularist argument sees itself in tune with contemporary metatheory in religious studies in disputing the term 'religion'. However, I will advance a critique of this below.

Tradition-specific

Post-liberal theology agues that Christianity should look within itself and speak from its own set of resources. For instance, Lindbeck's 'cultural-linguistic' model leads to what has been termed 'a sociological sectarianism combined with a catholic ecclesiology',[26] which suggests that only within the Church do we find the experiences that inform the Christian worldview. Therefore the self-expression and development of that tradition can, legitimately, only be an inward examination of Christian resources. Likewise, Hans Frei develops notions of narrative to understand theology, where: 'Theology . . . is by and large an exploration of the meaning of first-level Christian assertions.'[27] The Radical Orthodoxy project suggests the same idea.[28] Therefore a

---

24 Lindbeck, *Nature*, p. 34.

25 Lindbeck, *Nature*, pp. 39–40.

26 deHart, Paul J., *The Trial of the Witness: The Rise and Decline of Postliberal Theology*, Oxford: Blackwell Publishing, 2006, p. 58.

27 Frei, Hans W., 1992, *Types of Christian Theology*, New Haven and London: Yale University Press, p. 81.

28 Milbank speaks of an 'internal Christian discourse' (Milbank, John, 2000, 'The Programme of Radical Orthodoxy', in Hemming, Paul (ed.), *Radical Orthodoxy? A Catholic Enquiry*, Aldershot: Ashgate, p. 37.

strong contemporary theological tradition seeks to develop an internal dialogue, using church traditions, fathers, Gospels, etc., without heed to an external secular or liberal world, or to other sources and claims to truth. This has implications for the theology of religions in the following ways:

1 Understanding the purpose of other religions, from a Christian perspective, does not require consideration of the facts, teachings or nature of other traditions.

2 This understanding of other religions can only be the result of reflection upon the internal dynamics of previous Christian meditations upon what it has said about other religions, and Christianity's own inherent self-understanding.

3 There is no space for: a) integrating a comparative approach; b) exploring multiple religious belonging; or, c) inculturation for Christians in the context of another culture-socio-religio-philosophical system.

We should consider the implications of this standpoint. It attacks the basis of, for instance, John Hick's advocacy of pluralisms, which is derived, in part, from experiences of, and meetings with, religious Others. This basis is utterly illegitimate for those who come from the particularist camp. Not only is it seen as unsound theologically, but also methodologically. The diversity of experience, understood as contrasting 'cultural-linguistic' systems, means:

The datum that all religions recommend something which can be called 'love' towards that which is taken to be most important ('God') is a banality as uninteresting as the fact that all languages are (or were) spoken. The significant things are the distinctive patterns of story, belief, ritual, and behaviour that give 'love' and 'God' their specific and sometimes contradictory meanings.[29]

---

29 Lindbeck, *Nature*, p. 42.

What, for Hick, may be similar ideas of saintliness are, for Lindbeck, nothing of the sort:

> Buddhist compassion, Christian love and – if I may cite a quasi-religious phenomenon – French Revolutionary *fraternité* are not diverse modifications of a single human awareness, emotion, attitude or sentiment, but are radically (i.e. from the root) distinct ways of experiencing and being orientated towards self, neighbour, and cosmos.[30]

That is to say, in relation to any term, such as 'love', its activity must be seen 'within a religion', which means a particular set of concepts, attitudes, etc., and it is this whole context that 'thereby shapes reality'[31] for adherents. Any surface similarity, it is claimed, masks a deeper contextual difference. For particularists, pluralisms are flawed in at least two ways:

1 Theologically: they respond to a set of cultural circumstances outside the Christian tradition.[32]
2 Methodologically: they seek to integrate different religious worldviews, which is seen as fundamentally untenable.

To develop this second point further we may turn to Griffiths, who states:

> It seems reasonable to say that Greek Orthodoxy and Gelug Tibetan Buddhism are different religions just because it is performatively impossible to belong to both at once – in much the same way that it is performatively impossible simultaneously to be a sumo wrestler and a

30 Lindbeck, *Nature*, p. 40.
31 Lindbeck, *Nature*, p. 114.
32 For Lindbeck the liberal traditions are problematic (see, deHart, pp. 58ff), while, for Milbank, they represent a heresy against the Christian tradition itself (see, especially, Milbank, John, 1989, *Theology and Social Theory*, Oxford: Blackwell).

balance-beam gymnast, or natively to live in the house of English and the house of Japanese.[33]

His claim is that as religions are of divergent kinds, we simply cannot develop a theological system or understanding that argues all are heading to the same end, or, in the context of tradition-specific theology, we cannot develop a theology that finds a sympathetic voice or parallel methods of expression in another religious tradition. Such a view argues against any form of seriously inculturated theology – that is to say, one that builds on indigenous cultural-social-religious-philosophical principles.[34] This is not to suggest all thinkers of a particularist stamp hold this view, but it is a problematic issue within the system.

Holy Spirit

The particularist standpoint does not, in most cases, favour exclusivist attitudes, as the Holy Spirit may be at work in other religions. This is best understood in relation to inclusivisms. D'Costa argues that two major problems occur in inclusivisms' understanding of the Holy Spirit. First, he claims inclusivisms assert that salvation in non-Christian religions is possible because the Holy Spirit is active within them. Second, inclusivist thinkers speak as if they knew where the Holy Spirit acted within other faiths.[35] I believe that he is not entirely correct on the first point

---

33 Griffiths, *Problems*, p. 13.

34 A case is argued by Stephen Williams that Hindu *bhakti* and Buddhism, in particular, cannot reconceptualize an indigenous theology, although he does admit some points of contact with aspects of *Advaita* (Williams, Stephen, 1997, 'The Trinity and "Other Religions"', in Vanhoozer, Kevin (ed.), *The Trinity in a Pluralistic Age: Theological Essays on Culture and Religion*, Cambridge: Eerdmans, pp. 26–40, see esp. pp. 35–6). Such an attitude supposes that the historical accident that saw Christian doctrines become formulated along the lines of particular Greco-Roman philosophical traditions are the be all and end all on the matter, and that no other expression is adequate.

35 D'Costa, Gavin, 2000, *The Meeting of Religions and the Trinity*, London: Continuum, pp. 22–4. When D'Costa speaks of inclusivisms he seems to have in

as many inclusivists believe that salvation is not available through other religions; we have seen the distinction between John Nicol Farquhar and Karl Rahner in this regard; arguably, for both, salvation does not come through other religions as such, but only through the Christian path.[36] However, on the second claim he seems correct. While inclusivisms are not of one type, and so not as easily bracketed as particularist critiques suggest, inclusivists tend to claim to know the 'good' and 'bad' elements of other religions. As a paradigmatic inclusivist, Farquhar makes an excellent example. A brief overview of the chapter subheadings of his major work of fulfilment theology *The Crown of Hinduism* reveals the way he believes that he locates where the Hindu tradition does, or does not, provide stepping stones to Christian faith. For instance: in Chapter II ('The Hindu Family'), his final section title is 'Christ's principles form the natural crown of the Hindu family'; discussing image veneration and worship (Chapter VIII, 'The Work of Men's Hands') his penultimate section is, 'The religious needs which inspire Hindu idolatry', suggesting he knows its spiritual function, which, for him, is met in Christ, so his final section is, 'Christ, the image of God, satisfies these aspirations and needs in spiritual ways'.[37] Therefore, for Farquhar at least, an inclusivist

mind, primarily, Karl Rahner and his 'anonymous Christian' model.

36 The inclusivist styles of Farquhar and Rahner are discussed in the section on inclusivism in Chapter 1. Whether salvation comes through other religions for Rahner is a matter of debate; typically it may be said that he sees salvation 'mediated' through them. I therefore tend to interpret him as seeing 'salvation' as something Christian; however, Schmidt-Leukel has indicated to me that his understanding is more generous and 'mystical'.

37 Farquhar, John Nicol, 1930 [1913], *The Crown of Hinduism*, London: Humphrey Milford/Oxford University Press. It may be noted here that I have taken a certain liberty in using Farquhar's thought for, as I have argued previously, his understanding of Hinduism is quite negative, and therefore it is not clear that he actually sees the Holy Spirit working in Hinduism in any active sense (Hedges, Paul, 2000, *Preparation and Fulfilment: A History and Study of Fulfilment Theology in Modern British Thought in the Indian Context*, Bern: Peter Lang, pp. 334–40). However, the general idea that inclusivist-style figures believe they know the spiritual aspirations underlying other faiths, and therefore their good and bad areas, and hence where the Holy Spirit may be said to be working within them, if it is, applies as much to Farquhar as to most others within the tradition.

approach suggests it can neatly characterize those aspects of other religions with the potential to be fulfilled.

I would suggest, in relation to D'Costa's argument that, to my mind, the most telling critique against an inclusivist approach is that it forms the other religion into the pattern of one's own, thereby denying its inherent integrity. This seems disregarded in D'Costa, who, particularly in his most recent work, suggests that it is the theological worry of how salvation occurs in and through other religions that is the most serious concern.[38]

We can contrast the particularist position to the inclusivist in four ways:

1   Knitter tells us they 'don't offer any clear-cut, sure-fire directions'.[39] Therefore, in contradistinction to knowing where the Holy Spirit operates, the particularist will not say what parts of other religions are endorsed.

2   If religions are individual and unique 'cultural-linguistic' systems, particularity would not endorse parts, because it 'violates the rule according to which each tradition has to be treated as a totality; one cannot affirm only some aspects of another tradition'.[40] If a religion is an internally self-referring 'cultural-linguistic' network then, the argument goes, it can only make sense in its entirety.

3   D'Costa, at least, is worried about the implications of saying the Spirit is working in other faiths because, as he points out, 'It is clear that the Spirit cannot be dissociated from Christ',[41] for, in Christian theology, the work of the Spirit is intimately tied in with the work of Christ. Therefore, saying the Spirit can be found in

---

38 See D'Costa, Gavin, 2009, *Christianity and World Religions: Disputed Questions in the Theology of Religions*, Chichester: Wiley-Blackwell, pp. 19–25.

39 Knitter, Paul F., 2002, *Introducing Theologies of Religions*, Maryknoll: Orbis, p. 218.

40 Kärkkäinen, Veli-Matti, 2004, *Trinity and Religious Pluralism*, Aldershot: Ashgate, p. 78, referring to D'Costa, *Meeting*, pp. 22–3.

41 D'Costa, *Meeting*, p. 110.

other religions means acknowledging that Christ is found within them, which is not for him an easy step. If Christ were present, then they too would be loci for salvation.

4 We get a sense that other religions have some value and significance, for they exist in this world alongside us, which would equate to an inclusivist position. This answer, however, is hedged around by the lack of 'clear-cut, sure-fire directions' that Knitter spoke of, where that meaning is not specified. DiNoia tells us:

> other religions are to be valued by Christians, not because they are channels of grace or means of salvation for their adherents, but because they play a real but as yet perhaps not fully specifiable role in the divine plan to which the Christian community bears witness.[42]

Particularities: exclusivist and inclusivist modes

It is implied in the fourth point above that, in reply to Stanley Samartha's fundamental question, 'Can it be the will of God that many religions should continue in the world?',[43] particularity gives a favourable answer. This, despite its claim that we do not know the role or place of other religions, but there is believed to be some purpose or value within them as part of God's overall plan. Therefore, despite his difficulties, D'Costa acknowledges that the Holy Spirit is, he believes, present somehow in other religions, and that an engagement with other religions in the form of interreligious prayer is possible, but he does not know whether this will allow us to find the 'mystery of God afresh', or whether it will 'be an act of irreverent infidelity', and so he asks for prayers for those engaged in this endeavour 'for the sake of Christ'.[44] An open attitude is

42 DiNoia, J. A., 1992, *The Diversity of Religions: A Christian Perspective*, Washington DC: The Catholic University of America Press, p. 91.

43 Samartha, Stanley, 1991, *One Christ – Many Religions*, Maryknoll: Orbis, p. 79.

44 D'Costa, *Meeting*, p. 166.

found among most particularist-style thinkers, such as Griffiths, DiNoia, and the borderline figure of S. Mark Heim. However, some particularists believe Christianity has nothing to learn from other religions, notably Milbank, who thinks that the only true Christian approach is to convert the religious Other and to approach them with 'mutual suspicion'.[45] It is worth noting that some theorists in the area dispute the idea that there is a fourth category to be added to the classical threefold typology, and Alan Race is an example of this, who suggests that particularists are simply exclusivists or inclusivists in post-modern guise.[46] However, whatever position we take it is worth noting that particularists adopt positions that are both relatively 'open' and 'closed' to the religious Other.

Salvation

As DiNoia suggested above, the particularist does not see other religions as sources of salvation. For particularists, other traditions are entirely different types of entity from Christianity, they are not all 'religions' aimed at a similar direction: 'salvation'. We shall unpack this in due course, but, for the moment, we should note one logical outcome. As Lindbeck argued, being Christian was about learning the internal language and symbolic system of Christianity, such that you could live and inhabit it. Therefore, only through this root can you come to salvation, but if damnation, the opposite alternative is understood as the rejection of this, then, for Lindbeck at least, this is not possible for people outside the Christian framework:

> there is no damnation – just as there is no salvation – outside the church. One must, in other words, learn the language of faith before one can know enough about its message knowingly to reject it and thus be lost.[47]

---

45 Milbank, 'End', p. 190.
46 Alan Race has suggested this to me on a number of occasions.
47 Lindbeck, *Nature*, p. 59.

Some particularist thinkers have therefore suggested that, in a similar way to Rahner, either a post-mortem meeting with Christ, or a purgatorial cleansing is needed.[48] Others no doubt prefer to leave this as an open question.

Fundamentally attacking other options in the theology of religions, particularity suggests the notion that all religions are aiming at something which can, unproblematically, be termed 'salvation' is false. If every religion is its own self-referring 'cultural-linguistic' system then the idea that all are aiming at the same goal is incoherent. This they would suggest is not just true theoretically, but also empirically, given the diversity and range of afterlife options. For instance, something such as the following may commonly be stated: Hindus wish to achieve *moksha*, Christians to attain heaven, Buddhists seek nirvana; the first is annihilation of the self in the absolute, the second is theistically orientated, while the last is the negation of self, expressed as *anatman*. This conception is particularly stressed by McGrath who has argued that each religion offers its own particular version of what is loosely translated into English by the term 'salvation' and, moreover, that this translation is part of the problem, hiding a vast diversity of viewpoints and worldviews. Each tradition he argues offers its own 'salvation', or rather, final end. These are diverse, but recognizing that diversity is both intrareligious (within religions) as well as interreligious (between religions) he argues that all Christian perspectives are united, and distinguished from all others, because they are based in New Testament notions of salvation about the life, death and resurrection of Jesus Christ, or occur 'in and through Christ'.[49] As such, he argues, it is pointless to say every religion is moving towards a similar salvific goal; instead, each has a very different sense of what man's ultimate destiny entails. Furthermore, for McGrath, this sense of difference

---

48 The former is favoured by the Protestant Lindbeck (Lindbeck, George, 1992, *The Church in a Postliberal Age*, Buckley, J. (ed.), London: SCM Press, p. 83), while the Catholic DiNoia opts for the latter (*Diversity*). Interestingly, D'Costa classifies both as 'universal-access exclusivists' (*Christianity*, pp. 30–1).

49 McGrath, 'Particularist', pp. 163 and 171.

is embodied not just in doctrine but also in liturgical practice, such that he says it would be hard, if not impossible, to graft Buddhist notions of salvation onto a Christian liturgy.[50] This idea is inherent in Griffiths' notion that it would be 'performatively impossible' to belong to two distinct traditions. DiNoia offers a further analysis by considering the stated ideal models of the spiritual life in the Catholic Christian and Theravada Buddhist traditions. He suggests the way to reach them, and the goals envisaged, cannot be equated.[51] Therefore, particularists argue, alteric models of the religious life signify diverse and contrary goals in transcendent terms. To assume, with the Hickean pluralist, that all religions are centred around the Real which represents a common end goal for life is, they suggest, to run contrary to the available evidence. Any supposedly common words, as Lindbeck suggests, tell us nothing, for each operates within a very different system, and encourages, as DiNoia suggests, diverse ideals and ends.

Of course, if we accept this notion of salvific differences, then ontological questions arise: what ends are the various religions aiming at? If the no 'clear-cut, sure-fire' approach is that which marks out particularity then we can expect no answer; however, someone with affinities to particularity, S. Mark Heim, does offer us an answer. Heim, unlike those who are generally included within the particularity camp, does not eschew inclusivism, indeed, he readily identifies himself under this nomenclature.[52] He suggests the Christian God can be related to in a variety of ways, and this is what is happening in other religions, where both personal and impersonal understandings of the Triune God are conceived.[53] With regard to 'salvation', Heim suggests that the varied religious ends are actually attainable. He therefore changes the term 'salvation' to 'salvations', suggesting that 'these different ends might

50 McGrath, 'Particularist', p. 171.
51 DiNoia, *Problems*, pp. 45–6.
52 Heim, S. Mark, 2001, *The Depth of the Riches: A Trinitarian Theology of Religious Ends*, Grand Rapids: Eerdmans, p. 8.
53 Heim, *Depth*, p. 245ff.

PAUL HEDGES

factually co-exist as ontologically and eschatologically distinct states'.[54] For him, the Christian concept, attainment of the beatific vision, is the highest 'salvation', the 'salvation' of different religions being of an ontologically lower level.

Post-modernism[55]

Perhaps, Heim fails to be a particularist by being insufficiently postmodern. That is, he falls short of Lyotard's expression of post-modernism as the end of meta-narratives, by expounding his own meta-narrative that places every religion under the mastery of Christianity. Certainly, a number of thinkers within the particularist matrix explicitly see their ideas as grounded in a post-modern milieu that transcends the modern

54 Schmidt-Leukel, 'Pluralisms', p. 98. Indeed, the plural term, 'salvations', has been first the title of an article and then a book by him arguing for this position (Heim, S. Mark, 'Salvations: A More Pluralistic Hypothesis', *Modern Theology* 10, 4 (1994); 1995, *Salvations: Truth and Difference in Religion*, Maryknoll: Orbis Books), while his book *Depth* 'provides the metaphysical basis for his multiple ends theory' (Schmidt-Leukel, 'Pluralisms', p. 98; see also Cheetham, David, 2008, 'Inclusivisms: Honouring Faithfulness and Openness', in Hedges and Race, *SCM Core Text Christian Approaches*, pp. 76–7).

55 'Post-modern' is notoriously hard to pin down. For definitions and analysis, Lakeland, Paul, 1997, *Postmodernity: Christian Identity in a Fragmented Age*, Minneapolis: Fortress Press, is a good starting place, especially when thinking about these ideas in a religious context. From a post-modern perspective, Vanhoozer's Introduction in *The Cambridge Companion to Postmodern Theology* is worth consulting. However, particularly insightful and useful are Lyon, David, 1994, *Postmodernity*, Buckingham: Open University Press, Tester, Keith, 1993, *The Life and Times of Post-modernity*, London: Routledge, and Clarke, J. J., 1997, *Oriental Enlightenment*, London: Routledge. It is worth noting that I have chosen to use the hyphenated form, which helps emphasize its dependence upon modernity (Tester), as well as distancing my usage from the 'fundamentalist' postmoderns who see it as a radical alternative to modernity – something I will expand upon in the critique. For a classic statement of post-modernism see Lyotard, Jean-Francois, 1992 [1979], *The Postmodern Condition: A Report on the Condition of Knowledge*, Manchester: Manchester University Press.

cultural and intellectual framework.[56] 'Post-modern' is a highly contested term, so we must give some account of it, emphasizing its employment in particularist thinkers rather than giving a comprehensive account.

Post-modernism is a term that, although widely used, remains disputed with almost every commentator having their own definition. Part of the trouble comes from the fact that post-modern philosophy (hereafter post-modernism) and post-modern culture (hereafter post-modernity) are not often clearly distinguished. The former we will discuss below. The latter is a complex set of relations in contemporary Western society, such as multiculturalism, communication technology, and consumerism, which affect the way we live. In this sense, we may all (in the Western context I am speaking from) be said to live within post-modernity, even if we have not embraced post-modernism. It is, however, not a simple divide because post-modernism arises from the situation of post-modernity and, partly at least, it describes (one way of being within) this situation.

While notoriously difficult to define, it is nevertheless possible to identify various ideas commonly associated with post-modernism:

1   It is rooted in dissatisfaction with the modern world, especially the rational tradition of the Enlightenment (project), exemplified by Immanuel Kant and Friedrich Hegel. It seeks to reconstitute knowledge, or, at least, to challenge traditional forms of knowledge.

---

56 See Milbank, J., 1990, 'The End of Dialogue', in D'Costa, G. (ed.), *Christian Uniqueness Reconsidered*, Maryknoll: Orbis, pp. 174–90 (on Milbank's relationship to post-modernism, see Hedges, Paul, 2010 (forthcoming), 'Is John Milbank's Radical Orthodoxy a Form of Liberal Theology? A Rhetorical Counter', *Heythrop Journal*; McGrath, A., 1996, 'A Particularist View: A Post-Enlightenment Approach', in Okholm, D. L. and Phillips, T. R. (eds), *Four Views on Salvation in a Pluralistic World*, Grand Rapids: Zondervan, pp. 151–80; and D'Costa, *Meeting*, pp. 3–4 (more recently, though, he has distanced himself from a post-modern stance; see D'Costa, *Christianity* – a work still marked, though, by a particularist mode).

2   Jean-Francois Lyotard's suspicion of meta-narratives – totalizing theories, which subsume the local and particular to universal concepts – because any interpretative framework must come from somewhere and have inbuilt presuppositions. Instead, we can only have local, or petite, narratives.

3   Michel Foucault's arguments on the way knowledge and power are entwined; to define something, is, in some way, to claim control over it, to interpret it in *your* way.

4   Jacques Derrida's challenge to conventional linguistic usage and understanding. He is especially famous for saying everything is text, which he glossed elsewhere by saying everything is context, that is to say, all we have is given to us through language, there is no external referent point. Everything we say, know and experience is embedded within our given and inherited conceptual systems.

Post-modernism also has various themes associated with it:

1   Respect for the 'Other', a term taken from Emmanuel Levinas. As such, it decries the way in which the marginalized or repressed (or exotic) are either ignored or packaged and controlled by an elite (for example Western, male, powerful, academic), and seeks to give them their own voice(s).[57]

2   Heteroglossy, which comes from Mikhail Bakhtin. This implies a multiplicity of voices, as opposed to monoglossy, or a single voice or narrative.

3   Indeterminacy, where the stress is upon partial and unfinished understandings, where knowledge is always becoming and never fulfilled, against the notion of final knowledge and full understandings, which are held to be part of the ideology of modernity, and is a particular argument levelled against pluralisms.

---

57 Worth noting are the borderlines between post-modernism and other traditions, such as feminism, which in seeking to represent one repressed voice can be seen as post-modern, but which has deep disagreements with post-modernism.

4   Denial of fixed essences, that is to say, everything is seen as being a complex and changing set of relationships, in contrast to
modernity's (claimed) 'essentialism', which tries to define the
true and unchanging nature of things.

To complete our definition of it, we must also mention a philosopher
often associated with the so-called post-modern linguistic turn, Ludwig
Wittgenstein. This linguistic turn can briefly be glossed as a change of
focus from understanding things, that is assuming we are discussing
the essence of things, to understanding what we say about things, that
is recognizing that language shapes all we do. His concept of language
games is used explicitly by Lindbeck and McGrath, and implicitly by
others. This suggests that any 'cultural-linguistic' system (in Lindbeck's
terminology) is its own unique language game with particular rules, and
therefore incommensurate with other 'cultural-linguistic' systems which
have their own language games.[58]

The importance of post-modernism to several features of particularity discussed so far can be unpacked. The critique of the category of
religion attacks Enlightenment meta-narratives, while also considering
Foucault's critique of the way the term seeks to exert power over the
systems. The emphasis upon tradition-specific usages is also related,
where we move from meta-narratives to local narratives, which do not
encapsulate all things, but, instead, talk only from one position. Also, the
offering of no 'clear-cut, sure-fire directions' can be said to represent a
post-modern indeterminacy. Another important aspect of the particularist agenda is respect for the Other, which leads into one of its principal
critiques of pluralisms, that it is exclusivist:

I want to suggest that there is no such thing as pluralism because all
pluralists are committed to holding some form of truth criteria and by

---

58 I have expounded upon the use and relevance of Wittgenstein to particu-
larity elsewhere (see Hedges, Paul, 'Particularities'; 'The Inter-Relationships of
Religions: some critical reflections on the concept of particularity', *World Faiths
Encounter* 32 (July 2002), pp. 3ff., 3–13).

virtue of this, anything that falls foul of such criteria is excluded from counting as truth (in doctrine and in practice).[59]

This post-modern context gives rise to three central charges against pluralisms:

1   Guilty of false terminology, for it is not, as pluralism implies, open to a plurality of choices, but rather restrictive.
2   Guilty of a meta-narrative, of presuming to know the way we can speak of all others.
3   Guilty of a colonialist Western agenda of seeking to impose a liberal framework upon the way we understand religions.

We have addressed these issues in previous chapters, and it is not clear that these charges can be clearly upheld against any nuanced pluralist stance. Here, I will briefly outline some key points of defence. Pluralisms are seen to be part of a liberal Western Enlightenment worldview,[60] presenting a meta-narrative, a grand overarching theory into which all other datum may be placed. Therefore, the charge is made that whereas every religion presents its own worldview, pluralisms actually seek to replace these with its own worldview. Thus, while an Advaita Vedantin may tell us her/his impersonal Brahman is the absolute truth, and the theistic *bhakta* would tell us her/his personal deity is the absolute truth, the claim is that pluralisms subsume both, and all other religious truth claims, to its own story, that they are both ways of articulating the 'Real' which can be described in both personal and impersonal terms and that neither is better nor worse.

Particularists are alive to the charge that they may be guilty of a similar arrogance because of their commitment to the truth of the Christian tradition. A response is found in D'Costa (quoted earlier) that it was a

59 D'Costa, Gavin, 'The Impossibility of a Pluralist View of Religions', *Religious Studies* 32 (1996), pp. 223–32, pp. 225–6.
60 As D'Costa puts it, '*Christian* pluralism is in fact Enlightenment modernity' (*Meeting*, p. 1).

category mistake to say revelation is superior to other religions.[61] Christianity is simply playing a different language game, therefore it is meaningless to say that Christianity is better than Buddhism, Hinduism, or Islam – it is like trying to decide under the rules of chess the outcome of a game of baseball or cricket. It simply makes no sense. As Gerard Loughlin has expressed it, 'the Christian story resists mastery by being the prayerful tale of one who comes in the form of a servant and who will return as a friend'.[62] Christianity does not assert its truth over and against the Other – though we must bear in mind that here Loughlin, and others, are discussing an idealized Christianity, rather than the historical contingency of the Church embodied in history which clearly has most often done the opposite of resisting mastery. However, if we accept, for the moment, this idealized picture, we can comprehend their position. If no comparison is possible, we then understand McGrath's comment that, 'It is no criticism of Buddhism to suggest that it does not offer a specifically Christian salvation.'[63] It is through faithfulness to the Christian message that particularists see themselves avoiding oppression of other traditions. Indeed, D'Costa tells us that interpreting other religions through a Christian lens is not oppressive quite simply because it is truthful.[64]

Orthodoxy

Talking from within the Christian tradition is not just another postmodern petite, or local, narrative, rather the return to Christian tradition draws from the theological heritage of particularities. This includes such figures as Karl Barth, Hendrick Kraemer and Hans Urs von Balthasar. Barth is, of course, the central figure in Neo-orthodoxy, a forerunner of

---

61 D'Costa, Gavin, 'Roundtable', p. 246.

62 Loughlin, Gerard, 1996, *Telling God's Story: Bible, Church and Narrative Theology*, Cambridge: Cambridge University Press, p. 24.

63 McGrath, 'A Particularist View', p. 174.

64 D'Costa, *Christianity*, p. 91. His exact words are: 'Only from this [Christian] theological narrative can other religions be truly understood, simply because Christianity is true.'

post-liberalism.[65] As well as being a central academic prop for 'conservative' Christianity and critic of liberalism, he has two particular ideas that
feed through to particularity: a return to biblical narrative as central in
theology; and, the contrast between revelation and religion. While influential for Protestants a similar reaction against liberalism and an emphasis upon biblical narrative is found in Barth's friend and Roman Catholic
theologian, Hans Urs von Balthasar.[66]

For particularities the basic models to comprehend the religious
Other are the Trinity and the person of Christ, understood in traditional
formulae. It is, in particular, those things which are seen as coming from
revelation, rather than anything that may belong to religion in general

---

65 Some post-liberal figures would stress an independence from him, but
there seems a clear line from Barth to Lindbeck and Frei and onwards to Milbank,
which links up Neo-orthodoxy with the main post-liberal schools and thinkers.

66 He co-founded the journal *Communio*, with Cardinal Joseph Ratzinger,
now Pope Benedict XVI, to form a counter to the journal *Concilium*, associated
with Karl Rahner and Hans Küng, both, of course, inclusivist thinkers. After leav-
ing the Society of Jesus, Balthasar was marginalized in the Church, and it was
only after Vatican II, where he was the only major Catholic theologian not invited,
that he came back into the fold of the Church as his conservative voice found
sympathy with John Paul II and, as noted above, Ratzinger. The former named
him as a Cardinal, though Balthasar died a few days before the ceremony in 1988.
Theologically, he was a friend and admirer of Karl Barth and, despite differences,
he, like Barth, emphasized God's own story, and the return to a biblical worldview – although this oversimplifies the range and complexity of his theology, as
does the term conservative, for he was, in many ways, a highly original theological
thinker. While largely ignored by academic theology until recently, his influence
through *Communio* and his relationship with the previous and current popes have
made him a significant influence in Roman Catholic circles, and increasingly to a
wider audience. However, while an influence on particularity, Balthasar's theology of religions is of an inclusivist character: '[T]he idea of the Bodhisattva, analo-
gously related but ultimately inadequate, forms a sort of spiritual background to
the "thought of substitution which realizes its perfection in the Cross of Christ"'
(Gawronski, Raymond, 1995, *Word and Silence: Hans Urs von Balthasar and the
Spiritual Encounter between East and West*, Grand Rapids: William B. Eerdmans,
p. 187, quoting Hans Urs von Balthasar, *Epilog*, Einsiedeln: Johannes Verlag, 1987,
pp. 55–6). However, he also recognized the very severe differences between Buddhism and Christianity (ibid., see pp. 21–4 and 186–7).

that is stressed. Milbank makes this case when arguing that while certain aspects of the Christian worldview may have roots in a generic Indo-European theism, even a Triadic theism, the Christian Trinitarian formula is unique.[67] Indeed, the place of the Trinity in relating to other religions is considered of exceptional and intrinsic importance for the Christian, as Vanhoozer states: 'The Trinity . . . is . . . the transcendental condition for interreligious dialogue, the ontological condition that permits us to take the other in all seriousness, without fear, and without violence.'[68]

This concept is critical to particularity, and others express a similar idea, for instance, D'Costa who claims that the Trinity allows a more 'tolerant' and 'open' approach to different religions. Its significance means we should spend time considering it. D'Costa provides a good statement in three key points into which he unpacks a considerable amount of the particularist worldview:

My argument is that such a notion of revelation actually upsets the apple cart in at least three ways. First, the Trinitarian doctrine of God, properly understood, refuses closure in history, such that it is only through engagement with other religions in history that the church comes to a fuller confession and witness to the truth, which it never possesses.[69]

This first statement makes sense within the context of Loughlin's words, quoted earlier, that Christianity avoids 'mastery' by being a provisional project. As such, as Lindbeck, Milbank and others would agree: orthodoxy is an ongoing project.[70] D'Costa, explicitly, says that Christianity will learn

67 Milbank, 'End', p. 188.

68 Vanhoozer, Kevin J., 1997, 'Does the Trinity Belong in a Theology of Religions?', in Vanhoozer, Kevin (ed.), *The Trinity in a Pluralistic Age*, Cambridge: Eerdmans, p. 71. I have elsewhere expounded more fully upon this particular statement as it is an excellent expression of the particularist agenda (See, Hedges, 'Particularities', pp. 17 and 28).

69 D'Costa, 'Roundtable', p. 246; see also, D'Costa, *Meeting*, p. 9.

70 Milbank, John, 2000, 'The Project of Radical Orthodoxy', in Hemming, L. P. (ed.), *Radical Orthodoxy? A Catholic Enquiry*, Aldershot: Ashgate Publishing, p. 44: 'orthodoxy . . . [is] a project always to be completed . . .'

from its encounter with different religions. This creates a tension with the commitment to internal Christian resources; however, we should remember that particularity is not a unified school of thought. Yet, such a tension seems built in, and we see it reflected in D'Costa's thought, because, as we have seen, while he endorses interreligious prayer he claims not to know whether this is permissible exploration or faithlessness. Therefore it seems highly problematic for him to say so clearly here that Christianity will develop from its encounter with different religions![71] We develop this below. However, we now address his second point:

> Second, terms that pluralists always use such as 'openness', 'equality' and 'tolerance' are more coherently specified within this Trinitarian approach which does not mythologize or deny the claims that other religions make, but is willing to engage with them robustly, respectfully, and patiently . . . [72]

This is a riposte to the pluralist and, to a lesser extent, the inclusivist, suggesting they 'mythologize' or 'deny' different religious claims (fitting the religious Other within their own system). In contrast, he suggests, being Trinitarian, and respectful of the truths of Christian doctrine, the particularist can come to different religions 'robustly, respectfully, and patiently'. It may not be clear how this is done, but D'Costa seeks to explicate a way that this is possible. Although he says the finality of revelation is in the resurrection of Jesus, the comprehension of this is still an ongoing matter:

> However, by saying *a priori* that there is no new revelation apart from Christ, one is neither circumscribing nor restricting the reality of the

---

71 There often seems to be a tension within D'Costa who evidently wants to adopt an open and receptive stance to the religious Other, but finds his post-liberal theology problematic (as seen in *Meeting*). In his most recent work, where he labels himself an exclusivist, seemingly in response to more exclusive trends within some recent Vatican statements we find his openness to the religious Other in conflict with his Catholic retrenchment (*Christianity*).

72 D'Costa, 'Roundtable', p. 246.

Holy Spirit's universal and particular activity, or limiting it exclusively to previous practices and understandings within the living tradition.[73]

There is still more to be known, while, for D'Costa and other particularists, the activity and location of the Spirit is unknown. This must be considered in a tradition-specific context:

> The statement that there is no new revelation is a claim that all truth, in whatever form, will serve to make Christ known more fully to Christians – (and to the world?), *without understanding* what this will mean in advance in practice and theory.[74]

D'Costa argues that because his position respects different religions as total systems in their own right, and not as something to be placed in relation to Christianity, then his discourse is simply about the internal disclosure of Christian truth. That is, the different religion is respected as a complete system in its own right, and therefore when we encounter the religious Other there is a possibility of open and responsive encounter without any predetermined assessment of how that Other will fit within my system. This relates to D'Costa's third point:

> Third, I try to demonstrate that far from being 'conservative' (admittedly a rather useless label), my approach justifies the practice of interfaith prayer, while resolutely refusing to imagine that the same 'God' is unproblematically presupposed, or that the 'Other' must relativize her belief. I argue that when Christians take their own trinitarian Christianity seriously, but critically, they are confronted with the reality of difference, and are not led to assimilate or domesticate.[75]

---

73 D'Costa, *Meeting*, p. 129.
74 D'Costa, *Meeting*, p. 129.
75 D'Costa, 'Roundtable', p. 246.

Particularists assert that we simply do not know that, in different religions, anything similar is going on. The same God is not 'unproblematically presupposed', and therefore we do not simply 'assimilate' or 'domesticate' by saying, 'Ah yes, such and such a part of religion X relates to this part of our religion, and now we know what your truths are and how they fit.' Instead, what I believe D'Costa is suggesting is that interreligious prayer with the religious Other may open up new realms of understanding and experience which will transform and transcend what we know of Christ. However, this is not done by taking over parts of the Other into our system, but as part of the internal integrity of Christian theology as a self-reflective programme upon the Christian understanding of the whole created order which surrounds us.[76] Moreover, it is a reflection upon Christian orthodoxy, on what is known of the Trinitarian God through tradition, and what is known of God through the person, life and death of Jesus of Nazareth as the Christ of the Christian community.[77]

Assessing the particularist standpoint[78]

The particularist position is deeply problematic in relation to what I have said about the nature of theology and religion in Chapters 1 and

---

76 We may see this as having affinities to Scriptural Reasoning, which also sees itself (at least in some forms) as an internal reflection on Christianity.

77 As opposed to reflection upon him as the Jewish Messiah, or a historical figure in the context of his life and times as, possibly, a Galilean rabbi and reformer of Second Temple Judaism (see, for instance, Sanders, E. P., 1985, *Jesus and Judaism*, London: SCM Press, Maccoby, Hyam, 2003, *Jesus the Pharisee*, London: SCM Press, Vermes, Geza, 2003, *Jesus in his Jewish Context* (among many works), London: SCM Press, and, Borg, Marcus, 1991, *Jesus: A New Vision*, London: HarperCollins).

78 Much of the following critique is found, though often in a different form, in Hedges, Paul, 2008, 'Particularities: Tradition-Specific Post-modern Perspectives', in Hedges and Race (eds), *SCM Core Text Christian Approaches*, pp. 112–35.

2. Nevertheless, aspects resonate with themes we have suggested are important. Moreover, we must offer a thorough and critical assessment as it is an increasingly prevalent viewpoint (theologically and ecclesiologically) which many believe offers the most sophisticated theological and methodological response to the religious Other. However, this is not so, as we will see. In our critique we will follow the same headings that we used to classify the particularist standpoint: Religion; Tradition-Specific; Holy Spirit; Salvation; Post-modernism; and Orthodoxy.

To begin, we should note the fundamental problem is its extreme radical difference (based in post-modern alterity). Asserting utter difference, like asserting utter similarity, is widely criticized, for instance, in the political and cultural arena. Cultural theorist David Morley argues: 'Just as deconstruction and post-structuralism warn us against the universalization of totality, so . . . we must avoid universalizing difference', while he argues we cannot follow Lyotard in claiming that unity is terror, or that the imposition of structure is terroristic.[79] I believe his words can be well applied to our context too.

Religion

The particularist critique of religion draws upon critiques found within religious studies and the social sciences. However, it neither avoids the problematic modern constructions of religion, nor provides a satisfactory account for a number of reasons. First, while particularists are correct that many pluralist conceptions of 'religion' reinforce certain unitary and Western understandings, the notion of the relationship of religions is not just a modern Western one. Religious traditions have related to one another throughout history (see Chapter 2). Moreover, particularity remains stuck within the monolithic construction of religion that it is

---

79 Morley, David, 2000, *Home Territories: Media, Mobility and Identity*, London and New York: Routledge, p. 251. He cites H. Fern Haber, 1994, *Beyond Postmodern Politics*, London: Routledge, as a key source for his ideas and argument in this regard.

supposedly attacking,[80] and fails to make, on the whole, any sophisticated response to critiques of such problematic divisions as 'secular' and 'religious' spheres. To use Fletcher's terminology, it employs the 'container construct' concept of religion as blocks of clearly demarcated meaning and identity.

The particularist understanding of 'religion' is, moreover, based around outmoded and discredited notions of cultural islands, which do not reflect the actuality of religious traditions throughout history. The notion of closed 'cultural islands' suggests each 'religion' is the product of a specific culture, its own 'cultural-linguistic' framework, whereas a vast amount of cross-fertilization between cultures and religions exists throughout history. Examples include the common heritage of Islam, Judaism and Christianity, which is cultural, social and theological (not suggesting, however, that these are discrete domains), while they have all borrowed from Zoroastrianism.[81] Clearly each is not a hermetically enclosed and self-referring system. This ideological position will be addressed further in the next section.

---

80 See: Fletcher, Jeannine Hill, 2008, 'Religious Pluralism and Modern Religious Identity', *Theological Studies*, 69, pp. 394–411, pp. 402 (her position is argued at length in Fletcher, Jeannine Hill, 2005, *Monopoly on Salvation? A Feminist Approach to Religious Pluralism*, London: Continuum, Chapter 3); Kwok, Pui-lan, 2005, *Postcolonial Imagination and Feminist Theology*, London: SCM, p. 201, who says in taking his definition of religion from Clifford Geertz, Lindbeck fails to see its Christian rather than neutral basis; and, Nicholson, Hugh 2007, 'Comparative Theology After Liberalism', *Modern Theology*, 23:2, p. 238, who link Talal Asad's critique of Geertz to Lindbeck. For two recent examples of the way post-liberal style theologians critique modernist versions of religion, but remain trapped within it, see, first D'Costa, Gavin, 2009, *Christianity and World Religions: Disputed Questions in the Theology of Religions*, Chichester: Wiley-Blackwell. In Chapters 3 and 4 he examines debates around modernity's construction of religion and alternative views, but then throughout the rest of the book uses 'religion' in a distinctly 'modern' fashion. The same may be said of Nicholson ('Comparative Theology'), who in an otherwise excellent and insightful paper begins with the critique of 'religion' by Masuzawa, McCutcheon and others as a critique of 'liberalism' but then continues to use 'religion' as an uncontested monolithic term.

81 Hedges, 'Particularities', pp. 123–4.

We address the critique of a common religious experience, discussed above as a part of the particularist understanding of religion, in the next section.

Tradition-specific

Fletcher persuasively argues that tradition-specific theologies assume 'an imaginative landscape where nations contain cultures, and cultures contain religion, and a singular religion contains an identity', embedded in a problematic tribalism.[82] Theological identity in the context of Inter-cultural Theology radically destabilizes these false post-liberal premises (see Chapter 1). There is no monolithic 'Christian tradition' that exists, either within itself or apart from other cultures and identities; something our contemporary context is making increasingly clear, where the 'conscious mixing of traditions and crossing of boundaries highlights the ways in which the rest, now so obviously visible in the West, have always been part of the West'.[83]

We must also specifically address the cultural-linguistic framework, for particularists could concede that there is no pure Christian identity apart from all others, but argue that the formulation of traditions occurs within particular cultural-linguistic systems that shapes and forms identities within them, such that we, in effect, have come to exist within closed religious worlds. This returns to the issue of religious experience, to which we respond in two ways: theoretical, and mystical-spiritual/empirical.

I will attend to the theoretical question first showing the problem inherent in Lindbeck's analogy of love, which extends by analogy to religious experience.[84] First, his claim is that Buddhist, Christian or other religious languages of compassion (*karuna*) or love (*agape*) are based in utterly different linguistic-cultural systems and so cannot be compared.

---

82 Fletcher, 'Religious Pluralism', pp. 407 and 403.

83 Featherstone, Mike, 1995, *Undoing Culture: Globalization, Postmodernism and Identity*, London: Sage Publications, p. 11.

84 For a more detailed exposition of the following argument see Hedges, 'Particularities', pp. 122–3 and 126.

However, it is quite clear that the concept 'love' can be translated cross-culturally, otherwise in what way could Shakespeare's play *Romeo and Juliet* be translated and appreciated in such diverse places as Austria and El Salvador, let alone Japan and Malaysia? Clearly, Ockham's Razor[85] would lead us to suggest there is a similar, if not identical, human experience of love. Moreover, if we replace Lindbeck's neutral concept of 'love' with the more weighted concept of 'pain' we immediately see the problems. Are we to say because the various terms we translate into 'pain' in English are different across cultures that Africans, Australian Aborigines or others have no concept of pain, or have a concept radically different from our own? Clearly, this is not a discourse we, or I believe Lindbeck, would endorse.

As to the mystical/spiritual and empirical question, there is a considerable body of literature debating whether a common band of mystical experience can exist across cultures.[86] In part the debate is between those who see mystical events as mediated by their cultural context and those who see them as 'pure consciousness events'. The best approach, to my mind, is summed up by John Keenan who draws on both:

> pure consciousness events do occur, but I think that they can play no role in any philosophy or theology of religious plurality. Being pure

---

85 A theological, philosophical and scientific analytic tool that insists we do not multiply concepts/entities unnecessarily.

86 This is well represented by the works of Katz, Stephen T. (ed.), 1983, *Mysticism and Religious Traditions*, Oxford: Oxford University Press (who argues against the identifiability of mystical experiences) and Forman, Robert K. C., 1999, *Mysticism, Mind, Consciousness*, Albany: State University of New York Press (who argues for the identifiability of mystical experiences). Also, vital in this debate is the work of Grace Jantzen who has shown how the term 'mystical' has utterly different understandings at different stages of the Christian tradition, and thereby destabilizes the idea of a unified mystical tradition (Jantzen, Grace, 1995, *Power, Gender and Christian Mysticism*, Cambridge: Cambridge University Press). Space does not permit me to deal specifically with Jantzen's particular arguments, but suffice it to say despite the different uses and understandings of what the 'mystical' may be there is an undercurrent of, for want of a better word, 'mystical' or 'spiritual' experiences across many traditions which will be our focus here.

from thought, they are unavailable for thinkers . . . We have available only subsequent descriptions, and those certainly are not the pure experience.[87]

As someone steeped in both Christian and Mahayana Buddhist spiritualities it may be suggested that Keenan is better placed than Lindbeck, or most other particularists, to speak on the relation of comparative mystical experiences. Moreover, empirically, it seems undeniable that a crossover between Christian and other mystical traditions and experiences occurs: figures such as Thomas Merton, Abhistikananda and Bede Griffiths are well-known examples.[88] Moreover, the growth of inter-monastic dialogue shows how contemplatives of different traditions can relate to each other within the dialogue of experience.[89] We may suggest that the speculations of post-liberalism are untenable in relation to not just theory, but also the practice of the Christian life at its deepest levels.

While some Christian theologians, or others, on the basis of (superficial) textual and descriptive differences insist that, for instance, Buddhist emptiness and the fullness of the Christian deity are incompatible, or that identifying personal and impersonal conceptions of the absolute are

87 Keenan, John, with Smith, Buster G., Davis, Lansing and Copp, Sydney, 2009, *Grounding Our Faith in a Pluralist World – with a little help from Nāgārjuna*, Eugene, OR: Wipf and Stock, p. 38. He refers, in a note (17), to Louis Roy's 2003, *Mystical Consciousness: Western Perspectives and Dialogue with Japanese Thinkers*, Albany: State University of New York Press, and 2001, *Transcendent Experiences: Phenomenology and Critique*, Toronto: University of Toronto Press.

88 For more on this topic see the section on 'multiple religious belonging' in Chapter 2.

89 See: Coff, Pascaline, 1989, 'One Heart – Monastic Experience and Interreligious Dialogue', in Bryant, M. Darrol and Flinn, Frank (eds), *Interreligious Dialogue: Voices from a New Frontier*, New York: Paragon House, pp. 207–10; Bryant, Darrol M., 2009, 'Meeting at Snowmass', quoted in Race, Alan (ed.), 'Interfaith Dialogue', in Hedges and Race (eds), *SCM Reader: Christian Approaches*, pp. 87–99; Monastic Interreligious Dialogue website, http://monasticdialog.com/index.php.

contradictory, there are strong counter arguments.[90] As Francis Clooney has argued, dismissing Advaita Vedanta as a monistic philosophy and therefore unrelated to Christian theological notions of God is to commit a gross orientalist misreading.[91] Certainly, many Christians have had experiences that would equate personal and impersonal understandings of God, something that is not philosophically untenable (Chapter 3); the case of Frances S. Adeney discussed by Schmidt-Leukel is one example.[92] Moreover, we see crossovers between traditions in many instances, and Judith Berling notes that just as some Christians do Zen meditation there are also Protestants who engage in Benedictine traditions as well – if we go back but one or two hundred years, a short time in religious history, we would find this latter considered as illegitimate a border crossing as the former.[93] It would be good to reflect on Diana Eck's understanding of such border crossings:

> When I 'recognize' God's presence in a Hindu temple or in the life of a Hindu, it is because, through the complex of God, Christ, and Spirit, I have a sense of what God's presence is like. Recognition means that we have seen it somewhere before. I would even say that it is Christ who enables Christians – in fact, challenges us – to recognize God especially where we don't expect to do so and where it is not easy to do so.[94]

---

90 See, for example, O'Leary, Joseph Stephen, 1996, *Religious Pluralism and Christian Truth*, Edinburgh: University of Edinburgh Press, esp. Chapters 5 and 6.

91 Clooney, Francis X., 1990, 'Vedanta, Theology and Modernity: A Case Study in Theology's New Conversation with the World's Religions', *Theological Studies* 51, pp. 268–85, pp. 274–8.

92 See Schmidt-Leukel, Perry, 2009, *Transformation by Integration: How Inter-faith Encounter Changes Christianity*, London: SCM, pp. 187–90; this is best read in the context of the whole chapter, pp. 173–93.

93 Berling, *A Pilgrim*, p. 36. See also Chapter 1 on ecumenism.

94 Eck, Diana, 1993, *Encountering God: A Spiritual Journey from Bozeman to Banaras*, Boston: Beacon Press, p. 79. To further consider the way Christ challenges us to see God in the religious Other, see Chapter 3 herein.

This talk of 'recognition' is significant. If, as we have suggested (see Chapter 2), religions have 'recognized' one another throughout history as discourses of a similar nature then we may also be led to see a similarity of experience. This certainly is the case of countless Christians throughout history who have entered into interreligious encounter with religious Others.[95] Notably, the four theorists/theologians we have just mentioned (Clooney, Schmidt-Leukel, Berling and Eck) are all experts in religious traditions beyond simply their own Christian tradition, the first two also being deeply accomplished theologians as well.

It could be counter argued that our claim is 'liberal' (Schleiermacherean) by seeing doctrine as subservient to experience. However, experience has a primary place in the Christian tradition: it was the Easter experience as an extraordinary and challenging event that shaped the disciples' understanding of Jesus; it is often claimed that at the end of his life Aquinas had a spiritual experience which led him to see his theological writings as 'so much straw'; Hesychasm, formed through the new experiences of Symeon the New Theologian and Gregory Palamas, helped forge an understanding of continuing revelation through the Spirit

---

95 Beyond the names of the famous figures who have lived between religious worlds it has also been true of many Thomas Christians in India for two millennia and seems to have been the case for the Nestorian Christians in China. Also, if I may be permitted to speak from personal experience, my own modest religious experience (the descent or indwelling of the Holy Spirit to use Christian language) is something I have 'recognized' in the writings of Zen masters, Meister Eckhart, and Hindu *kundalini* experiences. For those who have 'known' the way religious worlds meet and slide into one another it is possible, although somewhat rhetorical, to dismiss those who see religious experiences as instances of alterity as 'knowlessmen' whose learning is simply that of paper and books, but without the experiential aspect of Christian understanding and being. (I am indebted to Terry Pratchett for the term 'knowlessmen', found in his book *Guards! Guards!* (1989, Discworld Series 8, London: Gollancz) – I recognize the gender prejudice within the term, but have kept it in the male genitive as, I would suggest, it is mainly men who would uphold this position, feminist perspectives, perhaps, being more open to seeing the unity of religious experiences (see Chapter 5)). However, I do not wish to argue that experience trumps all else.

within the Orthodox Church.[96] Evidently seeing experience as primary in shaping belief is not a modern invention.

Finally, the boundaries of tradition-specific approaches are broached by what Knitter terms 'religious friends', wherein difference is not erased but we learn to speak across divides between us. This shows the permeability of boundaries.[97] The issue of interreligious friendship, with similar conclusions, is also addressed by Schmidt-Leukel.[98] It is also something we find in women's dialogue and stressed in feminist theology of religions (see Chapter 5). Such relationships often lead beyond fixed identity and confessional boundaries.

Holy Spirit

The Holy Spirit is invoked by particularists to acknowledge the value of different religions without prescribing their nature or role. However, this is not without problems. Many recent inclusivist thinkers have developed pneumatological (Spirit) theologies of religion which means it is far from distinct (not, of course, a problem in itself).[99] However, as D'Costa argues, Spirit and Logos cannot be clearly demarcated, hence any pneumatology will either recognize the presence of the Christ in different religions (suggesting they have their own salvific value, which particularists deny) or else problematically separate these two aspects of the Trinity. Also, in and of itself, positing that the Spirit rather than the Logos is at

---

96 On the significance of the Easter experience see Borg, Marcus, 1991, *Jesus: A New Vision: Spirit, Culture, and the Life of Discipleship*, San Francisco, CA: Harper One; on Hesychasm, see Maloney, George, S. J., 1980, 'Introduction', in Symeon the New Theologian (trans. C. J. deCatanzaro), *The Discourses*, New York: Paulist Press, pp. 1–36. See also, Jong, Pieter de, 1989, 'Transformation through Interreligious Dialogue', in Bryant and Flinn, *Interreligious*, pp. 79–88, p. 86.

97 Knitter, Paul F., 2005, 'Is the Pluralist Model a Western Imposition? A Response in Five Voices', in Knitter, Paul F. (ed.), *The Myth of Religious Superiority: A Multifaith Exploration*, Maryknoll, NY: Orbis, pp. 28–42, pp. 38–40.

98 Schmidt-Leukel, *Transformation*, pp. 43–5.

99 See Cheetham, 'Inclusivisms', pp. 75–6.

work in the religious Other does not let us know how to dialogue with, or relate to, them. For instance, D'Costa says his own standpoint:

> allows the religions to be viewed as a complex and dynamic process, which may be judged to be pure idolatry, the best thinking and imagination of human persons in a particular context, a movement inspired by the Holy Spirit and moving toward Christ, a moment when the kingdom of God becomes inchoate in history, a context which has produced wonderful holy and just people, and a mixture of all of these and more . . .[100]

This leaves us with nothing concrete to understand different religions – surely it matters whether they are entirely idolatrous or inspired by the Spirit? Moreover, his suggestion that they are 'complex and dynamic' and may be 'a mixture' of many things does not help us deal with the problematic nature of religious identity. Indeed, for D'Costa, religions still operate as monolithic entities which can be set up and viewed in opposition, or occasional co-operation. This, as we have seen, is a spectre that haunts particularist notions. However, the trope of the Spirit may be a useful tool for Christians to create an internally coherent understanding of different religions.

Salvation

Particularity is clearly right that the internal dialogues of every religion are not saying exactly the same thing about 'salvation'. Nor could we expect, through some translation process, to create a coherent and consistent system of afterlife or salvation expectations. However, this would also be the case within the various Christian systems, as Daphne Hampson has shown.[101] We are faced not just with diverse systems

---

100 D'Costa, *Christianity*, p. 211.
101 Hampson, Daphne, 2001, *Christian Contradictions: The Structures of Lutheran and Catholic Thought*, Cambridge: Cambridge University Press.

interreligiously, but also intrareligiously. For instance in relation to Christian notions of salvation and the afterlife we will find, in various traditions, notions of an intermediate state (after death and before the eschaton) where, in Abraham's Bosom, we await heaven, or in Hades, we await hell, or we may need some form of purging, or just sleep till the Second Coming. Meanwhile some teach all will be saved, others that most will be damned to hell. Clearly these cannot all happen and, on a doctrinal level, are utterly incompatible. Two main responses can be made to reconcile these:

1   Theologically speaking our ultimate end is unknown, and these are just human conceptualizations, therefore differences are superficial.

2   All Christian notions are united by being 'in Christ'.

However, the first faces the very real objection that we could say the same about the differences between religions, a point developed below. Before that we must give attention to the problematic phrase of being 'in Christ'.

The phrase, 'in Christ', is often evoked as a catchall ecumenical position to show the distinction of Christian and other positions.[102] However, to take an extreme position we could say the phrase is meaningless and entirely contextually derived. Today, it is widely used to draw all Christians together; however, in the context of the phrase *'extra ecclesia nulla salus'* its purpose would be to divide Christians. The mutual anathemas between the Roman Catholic and Orthodox churches excommunicated other Christians, declaring some to be 'in Christ' and others not

---

102 For instance see Williams, Rowan, 2006, 'Christian Identity and Religious Plurality', Plenary Session Paper from the World Council of Churches Assembly, Porto Alegre, available at, http://www.oikoumene.org/en/resources/documents/assembly/porto-alegre-2006/2-plenary-presentations/christian-identity-religious-plurality/rowan-williams-presentation.html, accessed 4 August 2009.

'in Christ'.[103] Likewise, in the schisms between Rome and Protestants, or over Chalcedon, the same split was made: some Christians are 'in Christ', other Christians are not 'in Christ'. Still today, some groups that claim Christian identity, notably the Jehovah's Witnesses and Mormons, are seen not to be part of the Christian Church by most other Christians and so not 'in Christ'. Meanwhile, some churches, especially a number of evangelical Protestant ones, would exclude Roman Catholics, Copts, Orthodox or many other Protestants from being 'in Christ'. The claims and decisions about who is and is not 'in Christ' is not in the realm of some supernatural, uncontested, neutral space, but part of the human dynamics that construct all theological formulae. Moreover, the very real differences of conceptualization of what being 'in Christ' might mean make it difficult to see how any unity can be attained. Between a very Protestant suggestion that we have a personal relationship as a friend with Jesus, and the Orthodox notion of our becoming into the likeness of God through deification we see a vast gulf. Indeed, such differences can lead to claims that the others are heretics or not actually 'in Christ'. To draw an analogy, Jews, Muslims and Christians all accept as their deity the God of Abraham, hence their common designation as 'Abrahamic religions'. However, vast differences emerge in discussions over whether they worship the same God, and certainly it is clear that, in many ways, each tradition has vastly different conceptualizations of this same deity, which is not to downplay the many commonalities either. Indeed, each sees their salvation as being in relationship to this deity: are Jews,

---

103 It may be objected that excommunication is a matter of church polity, simply stating we are no longer in communion with these people, not that they are not Christians. Indeed, in purely abstract theological terms this may be so; however, the actual practice and rhetoric surrounding the matter worked to place these others in the category of the damned or heathens (although periods of rapprochement did still exist). A comparable case would be to say that in 'pure' Christian theological terms all people have equality before God; however, slavery and the killing of other human beings (whether it be indigenous peoples from outside the cultural area or religious Others) has been justified and supported by the Church at many times. Certainly, the idea that wrong belief or denominational allegiance equates to damnation, thereby justifying violence against other Christians, has a long tradition in wars that have claimed religious justification.

Muslims and Christians united by being in salvation through the God of Abraham? My point is simply that there is some arbitrariness about where we draw the boundaries of who is 'in Christ' and who isn't. Indeed, if we accept the Logos Christology that inspires Karl Rahner's 'anonymous Christian' concept and is proclaimed in the prologue of John's Gospel (see Chapters 1 and 3) we find that those who can be spoken of as 'in Christ' form a much wider circle (something inherent in seeing the Spirit operative in different religions). We are therefore stuck with the very human question of who decides who is and who is not 'in Christ'? Now, clearly, the question is not, as I suggested in an extreme interpretation, 'meaningless and entirely contextually derived'. There obviously are traditions of interpretation, but we face very real problems when we draw boundaries (see Chapter 1).

More problems arise when we consider the factors that have shaped the Christian notion of 'salvation'. First, the Christian afterlife was shaped by Jewish and Hellenistic ideas, while the Jewish ideas of Jesus' day had been shaped through Zoroastrian influences gained in the days of the Babylonian exile. As such, any idea of a pure 'Christian' notion of 'salvation' unrelated to other religious traditions is simply absurd.[104] Indeed, we know that the early church was strongly shaped by other

---

104 The borrowing of Zoroastrian notions of resurrection, heaven, hell, as well as messianic motifs is clearly recognized in mainstream historical and biblical research. While some recent works of a reactionary nature have argued against this, for instance, saying that the introduction of these ideas at the time of the Babylonian captivity is a natural outworking of demands for justice found in previous texts, or that there is no direct proof of borrowing (as though the author of Isaiah, for instance, would say, 'look everyone this a Babylonian idea which I'm adding in here, see it makes much more sense of our Israelite traditions doesn't it?'), the arguments are tendentious, subjective (we have to assume that this is a natural outworking), and unable to answer the basic objection about why it happened at the same time that a very strong external influence was occurring, so even if it was an internal development, there is at least an external shaping that must have occurred. The arguments for Zoroastrian and other influences on Jewish ideas are set out in McDannell, Colleen and Lang, Bernhard, 1990, *Heaven: A History*, New Haven and London: Yale University Press, Chapter 1; counter arguments against Zoroastrian influence are found in Johnston, Philip S., 2002, *Shades of Sheol: Death and Afterlife in the Old Testament*, Leicester: Apollos, Chapter 10.

mystery/salvation religions of the time, with elements of Orphic and Mithraic influence being seen in the New Testament texts, in early Christian liturgical practice, and in early Christian art. The meaning, then, of being 'in Christ' is not simply a Christian meaning, but a Christian-in-relationship meaning (see Chapters 1 and 2).

We must also address the stereotyped and monolithic representations of religious traditions often employed.[105] According to Alister McGrath:

> The Rastafarian vision of a paradise in which blacks are served by menial whites, the Homeric notion of Tartaros, the old Norse concept of Valhalla, the Buddhist vision of *nirvana*, the Christian hope of resurrection to eternal life – are all obviously different.[106]

However, it is not clear that the various heavenly hopes (Islamic, Jewish, Zoroastrian, as well as Buddhist, Hindu, etc.) are any more incompatible than the variety of Christian ones. Again, why does McGrath not mention other religions who accept resurrection, such as Islam and Zoroastrianism?[107] Given what we have said above about the diversity of views within Christianity it may even be suggested that some views in different religions are more compatible with some Christian ones than very divergent Christian ones are with one another. However, a further claim is that many religions have vastly different conceptualizations. McGrath notes Christian resurrection and 'the Buddhist vision of *nirvana*' (presumably read as realizing *anatman*, no-self) as distinct. We could add the Hindu concept of *moksha* as another worldview often seen as distinct. Certainly,

---

105 For a further discussion of these issues see Hedges, 'Particularities', pp. 123–6.

106 McGrath, Alister E., 1996, 'A Particularist View: A Post-Enlightenment Approach', in Okholm, Dennis L. and Phillips, Timothy R. (eds), *Fours Views on Salvation in a Pluralistic World*, Grand Rapids: Zondervan, pp. 151–80, p. 171.

107 We may also note that McGrath's use of 'resurrection' as the Christian motif ignores the diversity of views that exists on this point, some seeing it as literally being bodies upstanding (following indications in John 20.24–29), others suggest that we have spiritual bodies (following Paul's use of terms for 'spiritual vision' to refer to Jesus' resurrection appearances and his language of spiritual bodies, for example 1 Cor. 15.3–8 and 15.42–54).

in many ways Buddhist nirvana, Hindu *moksha* and Christian resurrection all have an utterly different conceptual basis. However, two points need to be made. First, a careful and respectful reading of the traditions show areas of reconciliation and mutual enlightenment.[108] This is not to say that they are all the same, they clearly are not; however, it is not clear either that they must be antithetically opposed. Second, religions are not monolithic, with divergent perspectives in each. Contrasting *moksha* and a personal Christian heaven is not useful as most devotees within the Hindu family of religions belong to Vaishnavite bhakti traditions that may even decry *moksha* and seek a personal union with Vishnu (variously conceived), the supreme deity, in the afterlife.[109] Likewise, as many have observed, Pure Land Buddhist devotion has much in common with Christian devotion, which popularly envisages a heavenly end.[110] We must attend as much to intrareligious diversity as interreligious diversity.

While particularity is right that there is not a common experience of 'salvation', indeed, the term 'salvation' as a common catchall erases differences, we cannot say all the notions are, of necessity, more mutually contradictory than those found within religious traditions. Indeed, theologically and philosophically, many religions suggest their talk of salvation and the afterlife, especially final ends, are attempts to express

---

108 See Schmidt-Leukel, *Transformation*, Chapters 6 and 7, esp. pp. 113–18; and Thangaraj, M. Thomas, 'The Word Made Flesh: The Crucified Guru: An Indian Perspective', in Oduyoye, Mercy Amba and Vroom, Hendrik M. (eds), *One Gospel – Many Cultures: Case Studies and Reflections on Cross-Cultural Theology*, Amsterdam: Rodopi, pp. 107–27. Proposals for a polycentric pluralism would also suggest ways that could be mutually enhancing rather than contradictory. Our discussion of religious experience (above) as well as the philosophical problems raised against pluralism (Chapter 3) are also apposite here, and suggest that the ideas could be reconciled as different conceptualizations of a common theme (however, this raises the danger of reducing the real differences).

109 See Zaehner, R. C., 1990, *Hinduism*, Oxford: Oxford University Press, p. 145.

110 The classic work on this is Streeter, Burnett Hillman, 1932, *The Buddha and the Christ: An Exploration of the Meaning of the Universe and of the Purpose of Human Life*, London: Macmillan, pp. 103–10; see also, Lai, Pan-chiu, 2008, 'Chinese Religions: Negotiating Cultural and Religious Identities', in Hedges and Race (eds), *SCM Core Text Christian Approaches*, pp. 270–88, pp. 273–7.

the inexpressible in human language – if each is a human and culturally bounded expression then showing differences has little value in relation to showing how religions may relate to ultimacy.

Post-modernism[111]

Among particularists, McGrath, perhaps, most strongly emphasizes its post-Enlightenment nature against outmoded liberal/modernist theologies. Such a view takes what may be called a 'fundamentalist' interpretation of post-modernism in which the 'modern' world has been 'overcome' and so no longer needs to be addressed. Part of this claim is against the supposed single universal expounded by the modern Western world, yet alterity becomes an equally essentialist paradigm. I will explore this by considering how Vanhoozer employs a favourite post-modern adage; Borges' story of the way the animals were kept in the Chinese emperor's menagerie. In this story animals were classified according to those belonging to the emperor, embalmed, tame, strays, having just broken the water pitcher, that from a long way off look like flies. Such a classification system, he claims, is no 'less arbitrary' than the defining system of modern Western zoology; after all, he tells us, 'science' is merely the story told by white Western men.[112] However, certain problems underlie this:

1   As Eagleton has exposed, post-modernism often underpins an attempt to maintain control and is associated with certain Western

---

111 It should also be noted that a particularist-style approach need not be based in a post-modern framework. A particularist-style theology is also found in the work of the missionary A. G. Hogg long before the 'post-modern' era (see Hedges, *Preparation*, pp. 347–60). Moreover, D'Costa's most recent particularist manifesto appears intended to not be post-modern, reverting to a Roman Catholic confessionalism (D'Costa, *Christianity*), it does though still maintain some post-modern elements.

112 Vanhoozer, Kevin (2003), 'Theology and the condition of postmodernity: a report on knowledge (of God)', in Vanhoozer, K. (ed.), *The Cambridge Companion to Postmodern Theology*, Cambridge: Cambridge University Press, p. 15.

imperialist assumptions (we shall address this in due course).[113] For instance, claiming science is the story of 'white Western men' conveniently ignores the fact that non-Western men, not to mention women, also practise it, and is guilty, as Sula Suleri has pointed out, of reinforcing old binary distinctions between East and West.[114]

2   It ignores the history of the development of science, and the important role played by Islamic culture, as well as important knowledge and developments transported from such places as India and China along trade roots as far back as Roman times.[115]

3   The claim that 'Western' science is just one competing system among many is all very well as rarefied rhetoric. However, we may ask when the post-modern person is involved in a car crash will he go to the hospital organized on the conventional Western medical system, or the 'post-modern' one down the road, where the departments are organized in the 'no less arbitrary' alternative system of illnesses which occurred on a Tuesday, accidents which occurred while sitting on a chair, head injuries which can be cured by placing a piece of damp celery on them, and all other

113 Terry Eagleton, *The Illusions of Postmodernity*, Oxford: Blackwell, 1996, p. 124.

114 Suleri, Sara, *The Rhetoric of English India*, Chicago: University of Chicago Press, 1992, p. 13.

115 Science is by no means the preserve and territory of Europe, for much that we call 'our science' has roots in the Middle East and beyond. Islamic nations extended and passed on the learning of ancient Greece into modern Europe: 'Between AD 800 and 1450, the most important centers for the study of what we now call "the exact sciences" were located in the vast multinational Islamic world.' 'Introduction', in Hogendijk, Jan P. and Sabra, Abdelhamid I. (eds), *The Enterprise of Science in Islam: New Perspectives*, London: The MIT Press, 2003, p. vii, while see pp. vii–xix for a brief discussion of some aspects of the transmission of these sciences from Greek and India (another important centre for scientific and mathematical developments) to the West. On Chinese contributions see the pages noted above in Hogendijk and Sabra, as well as Shen, Fuwei, *Cultural Flow Between China and Outside World Throughout History* [sic], 'China Knowledge Series', Beijing, Foreign Languages Press, 1997, which details the trade routes and intellectual encounters of over 2,000 years.

problems which are solved by exorcism?[116] This may seem somewhat facetious, or a superficial argument, however, a distinctly
ironic tone is intended; such fundamentalist post-modern claims
are so manifestly no more than the blowing of hot air that they
should be treated with a certain contempt.[117]

Several more responses to 'fundamentalist' post-modernism that underlies particularities are in order. First, far from being more respectful of the
'Other', post-modernism can hide or efface them as clearly as modern
approaches – as seen with Vanhoozer's arguments above (see also below
on power issues). Second, post-modern fundamentalism which seemed
popular when post-modernism was a new fad has been largely displaced
with a recognition that post-modernism may best be seen as a new stage
within modernity;[118] as David Tracy has put it: 'A thinker today can only
go through modernity, never around it, to post-modernity.'[119] It may be

---

116 It should be stressed that I am in no way implying that all alternative or
non-Western medical systems are ineffective, or, even, that exorcism does not
have its place, for I am not. Many such treatments have proven medical efficacy,
and others provide important supplements or correctives to the traditional Western system.

117 If Western science is just one system among others then let those who expound it throw away their computers, word-processing systems, central heating,
electric lights and everything else that they accept as an integral part of their lives
and live by an 'alternative' system; as has been noted, post-modernism is, in certain ways, just a philosophical expression of post-modernity 'being the cultural
logic of late capitalism' (see Jameson, F., 1991, *Postmodernism, or, The Cultural
Logic of Late Capitalism*, Durham, NC: Duke University Press).

118 Influential critics of post-modernism who take this view include the sociologist David Lyon (*Postmodernity*), the literary critics Keith Tester (*Life*)
and Terry Eagleton (*Illusions*), the intellectual historian J. J. Clarke (*Oriental*),
while the sociologist Ian Burkitt believes post-modernism's failure to consider
embodiment makes it captive to any essential modernist worldview (*Bodies of
Thought: Embodiment, Identity and Modernity* (London: Sage Publications, 1999),
pp. 129ff.).

119 Tracy, David, 1996, 'Preface', *Blessed Rage for Order: The New Pluralism
in Theology, with a New Preface*, Chicago: University of Chicago Press, p. xv.

suggested that what post-modernism brings is an extra edge to the modern hermeneutics of suspicion, which has allowed the modern world to become more clearly aware of its own presuppositions, whereby we acknowledge that every position is bound by time, language, culture and a host of other factors, without being left with total relativism.[120] Third, we are therefore not dealing with pluralisms as an outmoded product of modernity and particularities as a product of contemporary thinking. Certainly, pluralist views often display some problematic 'modernist' tropes (arguably epiphenomena rather than inherent[121]), yet the same is true for particularists, who employ 'religion' as bounded by 'modernist' notions. Finally, employing meta-narratives is another charge levelled against pluralisms, especially Hick's;[122] however, particularists also employ meta-narratives. For instance, in declaring the truth of the Christian story is non-oppressive by being based in revelation it simply repositions

---

120 It has been argued that it is an inevitable part of being human is that we make interpretive formulae, and building from basic concepts we can speak with some surety about certain things. This point is argued by David Ray Griffin and others within the post-modern process school, or reconstructivist post-modernism. See Griffin, D. R., 1998, 'Postmodern Theology and A/theology', in Griifin, D. R., Beardslee, W. A., and Holland, J., *Varieties of Postmodern Theology*, New York: State University of New York Press, pp. 40ff. He also expands here upon the useful notion of what he calls 'hard-core common sense notions' which he sees as a grounding against relativism (pp. 35–9). While not agreeing wholeheartedly with his notions and while, in no sense, a process theologian, I do believe that Griffin's Whiteheadian-inspired system provides an important and often overlooked alternative to the usual conservative–liberal, post-modern debates that dominate much theology.

121 They are addressed in places by pluralist theologians. See, for instance, Knitter, Paul F., 2005, 'Is the Pluralist Model a Western Imposition? A Response in Five Voices', in Knitter, Paul F. (ed.), *The Myth of Religious Superiority: A Multifaith Exploration*, Maryknoll, NY: Orbis, pp. 28–42, esp. pp. 28–33. See also Chapters 3 and 6 herein.

122 However, Hick could be seen, in some senses, as more post-modern than many particularist-style thinkers (see Hedges, Paul, 2004, 'A Post-modern Reading of John Hick's Pluralistic Hypothesis', *Interreligious Insight* 2:2, pp. 44–55).

the act of ontological violence, or meta-narrative assertion, to a higher transcendent level.[123]

Orthodoxy

The advocacy of a straightforward orthodoxy is problematic, especially in a contemporary ecumenical situation, where many Christians who would once have derided each other as heretics or schismatics now work in partnership and recognize the legitimacy of each other's beliefs and traditions (Chapter 1). Nevertheless, although we need open doors to a variety of beliefs as valid Christian ways of understanding, the issue still arises that we live within particular traditions. As we have seen, one problem for presenting a pluralist Christian approach has been the perception that it lies outside 'the Christian system' (Chapter 3). One answer to this, of course, is to help widen, in legitimate ways, the self-understanding of Christians as to the nature and boundaries of their tradition. However, I strongly suspect that the German Protestant theologian Reinhold Bernhardt is right in saying that:

It seems to me . . . that the religions will never move beyond a 'Ptolemaic' framework; they will have to engage each other in a never-ending dialogue of their 'mutually inclusive' viewpoints, each worked out from the standpoint of one's own tradition.[124]

Hence we may always need 'orthodox' and tradition-specific approaches; however, these, as was argued in Chapter 1, and has been implicit

---

123 Gavin Hyman has persuasively argued this case against similar moves in Milbank's theology (See Hyman, Gavin, 2001, *The Predicament of Postmodern Theology: Radical Orthodoxy or Nihilist Textualism*, London: Westminster John Knox Press, pp. 73–7). It is not clear how and why Christian claims of this kind work out against other religious claims to have 'revelation' or transcendent knowledge, etc. (see Hedges, 'John').

124 Bernhardt, Reinhold, 2005, 'The *Real* and the Trinitarian God', in Knitter (ed.), *Myth*, pp. 194–207, p. 206.

throughout this book (and I will argue more fully below), must be seen as broader and more open categories than is traditionally the case.[125] As such, particularist reliance on outdated, monolithic notions of 'orthodoxy' must be challenged.

Particularity, power and the religious Other

Having addressed the six categories by which we explored particularities, it would be useful to address the vexed question of power. As noted, the particularist system tends to support a dominant Western hegemonic

---

125 The current rise of conservative theological tendencies in Western scholarship makes the call for this more important than ever, with the current popularity of post-liberal and Radical Orthodox theologies being symptomatic. Meanwhile, there is a growth and normalization of evangelical and conservative apologetics in academic theology. For instance, Alister McGrath (2006, *Christianity: An Introduction,* 2nd edn, Oxford: Blackwell) suggests very early dates for the Gospels, with Mark being 'in the early 60s', Luke and Matthew both in the 70s, and John 'after 70', noting that their sources go back to the 30s, without any reference to alternative views, or even hinting that many think John may be well after AD 100, or any of the others at least ten years later than he suggests (pp. 84–90). Therefore students are introduced to these texts as though they were almost word-for-word representations of material dictated by Jesus' disciples from memory, telling us that the synoptic problem 'does not call their historical accuracy or theological reliability into question, but allows a deeper understanding of the formative period of the gospel traditions' (p. 92), a stance that clearly disagrees with the views of many contemporary biblical scholars, as seen in the mainstream introductory textbooks of Delbert Burkett (2002, *An Introduction to the New Testament and the Origins of Christianity*, Cambridge: Cambridge University Press, p. 244, who gives the mainstream scholarly dates for the Gospels as Mark *c.* 70, Matthew and Luke 80–100, John 80–110), and Bart D. Ehrman (2004, *The New Testament: A Historical Introduction to the Early Christian Writings*, 3rd edn, Oxford: Oxford University Press, pp. 61–5 and 89–90, who dates Mark 65–70, Matthew and Luke 80–85, and John 90–95). A symbol of the retrenchment of traditional beliefs as normative without regard to ecumenical problems, when we brand other Christians with the label of 'heretics' or 'faulty Christians' (are they 'in Christ'?) is the recent edited volume, *Heresies and How to Avoid Them: Why it Matters What Christians Believe* (Quash, Ben and Ward, Michael (eds), 2007, London: SPCK).

Christian supremacy.[126] In relation to this we should consider how, in her analysis of how tying religious identity to a cultural bounded system, Kwok Pui-lan has revealed a link to discourse on identity supremacy, which shifted in the nineteenth century from bloodline to culture as a justification for difference and racism.[127] Certainly, I am not accusing any of the figures mentioned of racism, and certainly many, such as D'Costa, are acutely aware of the issues around this. However, it must be recognized that the particularist position of tying religious superiority to a cultural-religious system has affinities to a number of disreputable practices; indeed, Kwok has shown how aspects of Lindbeck's language has deep affinities with US rhetoric linked to a colonial ideology.[128]

One issue worth noting is that the particularist is not averse to using their own terms to describe the religious Other. In this regard it is useful to mention Milbank, whose foray into the arena is perhaps notable for its misunderstanding of the issues, for which he is rightfully (if belatedly) criticized by D'Costa.[129] It is worth observing that critics have shown, as discussed above, that Milbank's supposed non-violent ontology is nothing of the sort.[130] This may suggest that where particularities are unsympathetic to different religions, they manifest an unreflective exclusivist style. While the whole system of particularity should not be tarred with the same brush, it does, as a whole, seek to maintain an isolated Christian discourse that cannot be touched by religious Others: by making 'alterity' a motif there is no place for connection or critique. Moreover, its claims of respect hide the fact that the religious Other is sidelined as

---

126 Hedges, 'Particularities', p. 129, especially the reference to Williams, Stephen, 1997, 'The Trinity and "Other Religions"', in Vanhoozer, Kevin (ed.), *The Trinity in a Pluralistic Age*, Grand Rapids: Eerdmans, pp. 35–6 (p. 135 fn. 70).

127 Kwok, *Postcolonial*, pp. 198–9.

128 Kwok, *Postcolonial*, pp. 199–200.

129 See D'Costa, *Christianity*, pp. 48–53 for his critique of Milbank, 'End'.

130 It may be noted that his claims that Augustinian Trinitarianism is superior to Vedantic conceptions is based upon assertion and orientalist misreading, an argument developed further in Hedges, Paul, 2011, 'Radical Orthodoxy and the Closed Western Theological Mind', in Isherwood, Lisa. et al. (eds), *The Poverty of Radical Orthodoxy* , Eugene, OR: Wipf and Stock.

inferior (lacking revelation) and so the respect claimed to be given to their whole system is little more than a patronizing tolerance.[131]

In response to such critiques, a particularist answer might be that the differences between themselves and those who claim to be 'neutral', 'secular' or 'liberal' is that they are open about their biases.[132] However, it is far from clear that this is the case, as indicated above. Moreover, Schreiter has argued that it is important to understand difference in such a way that it is not homogenized or isolated.[133] If pluralisms stand accused of colonial imposition by placing different religions under a Western meta-narrative by employing the trope of similarity, then, likewise, the particularist imposes their own meta-narrative of 'radical difference'. However, at least in principle, pluralisms, inspired by radical openness, allow their system to be critiqued by the Other, whereas particularities refuse dialogue or interchange in any meaningful way.

Conclusions

The particularist agenda clearly engages with a number of key arguments we have raised, such as the problematic category of 'religion'; however, it uses this as a tool to dismiss some expressions of pluralisms yet continues to employ the term in deeply problematic ways. Moreover, it constructs Christian theology, and religion as a whole, in terms of monolithic cultural islands by proclaiming the radical difference of all systems and cultures. This, as we have seen, is untenable. Nevertheless, it raises some important issues, such as the real differences between religious traditions as well as the need to speak from within a particular tradition. We will return to address what we can learn from its discourse of radical difference in relation to radical openness in Chapter 6. First, however, we must address another perspective on these issues.

---

131 For an extrapolation of these themes, see Hedges, 'Particularities', pp. 121, 127–30.

132 Nicholson, 'Comparative Theology', p. 237; this is also argued for at length by D'Costa, *Christian*, pp. 97–102.

133 Schreiter, Robert J., 2004, *The New Catholicity: Theology between the Global and the Local*, Maryknoll, NY: Orbis, p. 45.

5

Listening to the Sounds of Silence[1]
Feminist Challenges to, and Perspectives
on, the Regnant Discourse

Framing the questions

Introduction

Ursula King's axiom has become well established: feminism is 'a missing dimension of dialogue'.[2] Although uttered more than 15 years ago, recent studies in the areas suggest that King's words still hold true.[3] Despite the fact that many women are involved in dialogue, especially at grassroots level, they often experience themselves sidelined by male-dominated hierarchical institutions and 'masculine' constructions of encounter. So we have to ask a range of questions:

1   Fundamentally, how can this be rectified?

---

1 The term and concept of silence is a common theme in various works on feminist theology in this area, while my title obviously plays on the well-known title of a Simon and Garfunkel song and album.

2 King, Ursula, 1998, 'Feminism: the missing dimension in the dialogue of religions', in May, John D'Arcy (ed.), *Pluralism and the Religions: The Theological and Political Dimensions*, London: Cassell, pp. 40–55, p. 43 (King's words were originally spoken at a conference in 1995).

3 See, for instance, Egnell, Helene, 2006, *Other Voices: A Study of Christian Feminist Approaches to Religious Plurality East and West*, Uppsala: Studia Missionalia Svecana, Chapters 3 and 7, O'Neill, Maura, 2007, *Mending a Torn World: Women in Interreligious dialogue*, Maryknoll, NY: Orbis, and Tetlow, Ruth, 2005, 'The missing dimension: Women and inter faith encounter in Birmingham', *Current Dialogue* 46.

2   What, if anything, is distinctive about the feminist approach (that is, what is the missing dimension)?

3   How can this approach (actually approaches, as we will see) be integrated into the theology of religions and interreligious dialogue?

In this chapter we will address ourselves primarily to question 2, and elsewhere in the book to question 3, although the method for this will be explained here. Whether question 1 can be in any way adequately tackled in a work like this is debatable, but it is a contribution.

I would like to begin with a story – this seems appropriate as the Swedish missiologist and Lutheran pastor Helene Egnell sees the act of sharing stories as distinctive in women's dialogue. I was drawn to consider this area after one conference, where, as a co-organizer, I looked at the main conference room with a couple of male colleagues and we thought this will do, and off we marched. Later, part of the female contingent was missing and going off to search I discovered them rearranging the room. The seating structure, which had consisted of the main speakers placed in a U-shape at one end of the room a fair distance from the audience, had been 'softened' to bring the two groups closer and to face each other in a less intimidating manner. Therefore, a few days later, in introducing Egnell's paper, on feminist contributions to dialogue, I suggested that the experience of all those at the conference had been influenced by a 'feminine dimension'. After her paper, a straightforward controversy developed: the feminist theologians considered themselves to be advocating a particular and distinct position; however, quite a number of senior male theologians of religions (the patriarchs of the tradition) denied that there was a distinctive feminist voice, for them the feminist approach simply endorsed pluralisms. These events led me to investigate whether feminist theologians have a distinct and significant contribution, and subsequently to write this chapter.

A few caveats are needed here. First, one danger would be to say that the feminist contribution was in 'soft' areas (ethics, relationships, chair arrangement, etc.) as opposed to 'hard' areas (doctrine, typologies, ideas, etc.). To address this, on the one hand, feminist writers have made specific 'hard' contributions; on the other, the language of 'soft' and 'hard' is itself problematic. It: a) suggests the 'soft' areas are less important; and b) encourages a sense of these problematic (patriarchal) binary oppositions. Second, feminist contributions are diverse, and some of them may differ little from what we find in certain male theologians. For instance, Marjorie Suchocki suggests: 'A Feminist perspective . . . suggests that one must radically affirm religious pluralism.'[4] Yet, Fletcher argues some women embrace pluralisms while others have sought to go beyond them.[5] It is primarily to this area, where women suggest they are offering a new perspective that I address myself, yet here even Egnell acknowledges things can sound very similar.[6] Third, while this chapter reflects a quest of understanding to investigate what, if anything, is the feminist voice in interreligious dialogue and the theology of religions, I realize that, in one sense, it is a precarious task, even presumptuous,[7] for a man to write around what the feminist approach is (an act of patriarchal power relations in constructing the voice of the other?). However, to not do so would be to relegate it to a marginalized discourse of 'contextual' theology (an even worse act of patriarchal power relations?).

Women's experiences

To ask why women may have a significant contribution to this debate, we may begin with an assessment of women's position in the Christian tradition:

---

4 Suchocki, Marjorie H., 1988, 'In Search of Justice: Religious Pluralism From a Feminist Perspective', in Hick, John and Knitter, Paul F. (eds), *The Myth of Christian Uniqueness*, London: SCM, pp. 149–61, p. 149.

5 Fletcher, Jeannine Hill, 2008, 'Feminisms: Syncretism, Symbiosis, Synergetic Dance', in Hedges, Paul and Race, Alan (eds), *SCM Core Text Christian Approaches to Other Faiths*, London: SCM, pp. 136–54, pp. 144–51.

6 Egnell, *Other*, p. 303.

7 The term 'presumptuous' was my original, Egnell suggested 'a precarious task' as a better alternative – I have chosen to keep both (Egnell, Helen, personal email correspondence with author).

Living in a social world characterized by patriarchy and a religious tradition whose theological questions and answers have been provided almost exclusively by men, Christian women have a double experience of otherness that is critical to understanding their theological perspective. Women come at the theological act with a sense of disjunction, knowing that the realities of God and Christ, spirit and grace are central to their identities. Yet they are also aware that the language the tradition offers as an expression of these realities misses the mark, is not their own, and has excluded and distorted them.[8]

There is quite a lot to unpack within this quotation and, in certain ways, it is key to what feminist theology has to offer as distinctive. Obviously, women speak in a world where the major terms are not their own. This may seem to some banal or commonplace, but let us just briefly consider a few ways in which 'male' language has shaped the world and, within it, the place and experience of women, which does not lie so much in the direct meanings of words, but in their connotations. Several words in English (no doubt some parallels apply across different linguistic-cultural systems) have direct equivalents between male and female alternatives, for example: master, mistress; governor, governess; priest, priestess; wizard, witch. Now, on a direct level each is just an analogue of the other, but when we look further at connotations and general usage we see other things: master – strong and powerful, in charge; mistress – a polite term for a wife (as in, rather archaically, 'the mistress of the house is home', that is, the (dominant) master is out), but a married man's lover is its normative usage today; governor – conjures up images of a powerful male figure greatly respected; governess – usually refers to a female

---

8 McCarthy, Kate, 1996, 'Women's Experience as a Hermeneutical Key to a Christian Theology of Religions', *Studies in Interreligious Dialogue* 6.2, pp. 163–73, p. 165 (this is reprinted in Fletcher, Jeannine Hill, 2009, 'Feminisms', in Hedges, Paul and Race, Alan (eds), *SCM Reader: Christian Approaches to Other Faiths*, London: SCM, pp. 71–85, pp. 75–85. For a good overview of women in Christianity and feminist theology see Young, Pamela Dickey, 2004, 'Women in Christianity', in Anderson, Leona M. and Young, Pamela Dickey (eds), *Women and Religious Traditions*, Oxford: Oxford University Press, pp. 160–86.

teacher in a private house, but carrying a sense of stern, and conjuring up images of a repressed old spinster; priest and priestess – the use of the latter term as a mark of insult towards female priests in recent Anglican debates on the ordination of women surely says enough (Christians, of course, have female priests, not priestesses!); wizard and witch – contrasts a strong male image with that of an evil old crone. Such language shows that the way in which the world is perceived through our everyday habits of speech creates a place in which women may come to see themselves as outside the dominant modes of discourse, and placed such that they cannot speak of themselves in central positions. Women are therefore an 'other' in the culture – and, indeed, until very recently, this applied more broadly, they would learn about a history of men inventing things, discovering things, and ruling things, with very few exceptions and, still today, the discourse of male ascendancy is taught to children ('boys don't cry', 'those are girls' toys' (dolls, cooking sets, etc.)).

Before assessing what feminist theology may contribute it is worth looking further at the context of the female experience and ways of understanding this.

Gender construction and deconstruction

I will begin this section with another story, this time from Egnell's own experience. In 1986, she attended a field study in South East Asia with nine other students (five men and five women altogether) in mission studies:

> On one occasion, we visited a Hindu temple in Kuala Lumpur, Malaysia. At the end of the *puja*, the priest invited us to come forward and receive ashes on our foreheads along with the worshippers. Four of us – all women – stepped forward, while the others retreated.[9]

This led, she tells us, to a discussion on 'the significance of gender in this incident'. This, I think, indicates part of the problem: the way that

---

9 Egnell, *Other*, p. 11.

the debate is set up (to look for gender differences – on this see below), an analysis which accords with Egnell's own interpretation. Here, we should think of the way that feminist debates have developed and been constructed both in culture and in the specifically theological frames of discourse. We may, perhaps, do this best by beginning with what has been termed the various waves of discourse on both gender and feminism. We may regard each as being three in number; they also share some common themes and have similar time frames for development, though they are not, by any means, identical.[10]

The first wave of gender discourse, which is closely linked with first-wave feminism or Liberal Feminism, is seen as beginning with the Enlightenment worldview and women demanding equality with men. Based on the notion that all people share a common rationality, and so having links with the Enlightenment demands for the emancipation of Jews and other marginal groups, it basically defined humanity along intellectual lines. Its concern is with justice and equality and it believes that minds can obtain the truth, and that bodies, and therefore their differences, are essentially not important. Its standpoint on relations between the genders was one of equality.

Various reasons were found to be dissatisfied with this first wave. For one thing it was not thought to represent a female perspective, which engages more with embodiment (a term that recurs, and is discussed below), whereas this is seen by some as a very masculine (rational and detached) standpoint. Moreover, it did not seem to fully question the ways in which discourses on men and women create the problems. Second-wave gender discourse, or Gender Constructionism, argued that women are not born they are made. Here, the systems that enforce male

10 For an introduction to these themes see: for a brief overview, Rampton, Martha, 2008, 'The Three Waves of Feminism', *Pacific: The Magazine of Pacific University*, available at, http://www.pacificu.edu/magazine/2008/fall/echoes/feminism.cfm, accessed 8 September 2009; for a longer account, Krolokke, Charlotte and Sorensen, Anne Scott, 2005, *Gender Communication Theories and Analyses: From Silence to Performance*, London: Sage, Chapter 1, 'Three Waves of Feminism: From Suffragettes to Grrls'; and Burkitt, Ian, 1999, *Bodies of Thought: Embodiment, Identity and Modernity*, London: Sage, Chapter 5.

and female gender roles were brought into question and the structures of society that support this: for instance, ideas that women are soft, caring, nurturing and gentle was seen as something society imposed upon certain people to make 'the female gender';[11] likewise, boys, when young, were seen to be constructed by being given toys of soldiers, cars, tanks, etc. Like, Liberal Feminism, it wanted to say that there is no distinction between men and women, and in radical forms, especially associated with Judith Butler, was seen to deny the very notion of gender at all as a natural fact: both men and women were created through societal pressure and the discourses of culture that had over many centuries, even millennia, enforced these views.[12] In terms of second-wave feminism, we may say that arising from this were notions of women as better than men, which blamed a domineering patriarchy for the problems of society – men are aggressive, greedy and oppressive.[13] This links in with second-wave gender discourse which sees patriarchal society as creating linear and oppressive straitjackets making boxes which people needed to fit into. In both, patriarchy was the problem, an enemy which needed to be overcome, and men had to learn to change.

Again, dissatisfaction was felt with these options. Obviously, on a simple biological level there are differently sexed bodies, while it seemed to deny that women had their own important contribution to make – if we are all the same. Also, while engaging embodiment, unlike Liberal Feminism, it undermined it by seeing it as a construct, and so subverted physicality to an abstract level of social construction. Further, the debates

---

11 It is useful to note the distinction commonly made between 'sex' which refers to the biological embodiment and male and female bodies, and 'gender' which refers to the behavioural patterns attributed to male and female.

12 See Butler, Judith, 1990, *Gender Trouble: Feminism and the Subversion of Identity*, London: Routledge, see pp. 139–40, and 1993, *Bodies that Matter: On the Discursive Limits of 'Sex'*, London: Routledge, see pp. 5–11; her work is discussed in Burkitt, *Bodies*, pp. 90–8.

13 Such an approach is even found in some forms of feminist theology; see Ruether, Rosemary Radford, 'The Emergence of Christian Feminist Theology', in Parsons, Susan Frank (ed.), *The Cambridge Companion to Feminist Theology*, Cambridge: Cambridge University Press, pp. 3–22, p. 3; see also therein fn. 1, p. 18.

drew sharp battle lines between the sexes which many see as unhelpful. This leads us to third-wave gender discourse, closely linked with third-wave feminism, or the contemporary phenomenon of Naturalist Feminism, which sees men and women as equal but different. While some differences of opinion exist, the following represent some key aspects of the debate:

1   A recognition that men and women are not fundamentally the same in every aspect, but, perhaps, complementary (although not in a binary sense of having well-matched ways of doing things, that is, emotional–rational, etc.).

2   For women, therefore, freedom is not to become like men, or even better than men, but rather to realize who or what you are and being valued for this, and happy to inhabit this space.

3   There is also a recognition that 'women' (or men) is not a homogenous category, rather women's experience comes in many forms. In particular, third-wave feminism was the point at which white Western feminists realized that there was not a common 'essence' of 'womanness' that they spoke for, but that skin colour, social factors, etc. make a variety of experiences, and that our identities are complex things.

To expand on these three points. While third-wave gender discourse can see the traits of men and women as being complementary, associated with this move is a recognition that we shouldn't simply see this as binary opposites. Taking on some insights from Gender Construction, it is recognized that both men and women are shaped by their societies, but more than this: all people are individuals. It is not simply the case that all men are very 'masculine', while all women are very 'feminine'. The creation of a discourse that certain things are male or female, masculine or feminine is seen itself as part of the problem. This is the case, especially where, as can happen, stark dichotomies are drawn:

On the face of it, my informants construct men and women as two completely different kinds of human being. Women are emotional, caring, peace loving, down-to-earth and practical. Men are rational, theoretical, calculating and prone to be violent.[14]

This is too stark: we have no doubt all experienced that some women are rational, calculating or prone to violence, and men can be emotional and peace loving. However, there is no doubt that we live in societies that shape our expectations of men and women in different ways. Exactly what differentiates the genders is far beyond the scope of this paper, but the notions raised in third-wave feminism and contemporary gender theories seem to make sense of my understandings as well as those of Egnell. If I briefly spell this out: men and women do have differences, but not in clearly distinct ways, although culture can lead to certain gender traits being emphasized. Moreover, the hybridity of our identities means each individual is shaped differently (see the related discussion in Chapter 1).[15] In this respect it is interesting to note that a comprehensive survey of literature on gender differences between cultures found that differences between men and women were more or less pronounced in different situations, as well as between cultures.[16] In particular, gender differences are more pronounced in Western societies than in Asian or African, while they are more apparent in inter-gender situations than intra-gender situations. It was therefore concluded: 'The cross-cultural evidence reviewed suggests that women and men are not mainly similar or different, they can be both.'[17] This suggests that there are no essential differences between men and women but that as social actors different roles will operate; how much of this is due to the physiology of differently sexed bodies and how much to the gender that is laid over this by

---

14 Egnell, *Other*, p. 88.

15 The hybridty of identity is a theme in some recent feminist theology; see Fletcher, Jeannine Hill, 2003, 'Shifting Identity: The Contribution of Feminist Thought to Theologies of Religious Pluralism', *Journal of Feminist Studies in Religion* 19, pp. 5–24, esp. pp. 16–19.

16 Guimond, Serge, 2008, 'Psychological Similarities and Differences between Women and Men across Cultures', *Social and Personality Psychology Compass* 2:1, pp. 494–510.

17 Guimond, 'Psychological', p. 501.

culture and society is hard to determine. Again, we must not forget the way particular circumstances will affect this for any individual. So the question arises: how are we to see this in relation to theology, and how will this lead us to find (and look for) a feminist contribution to the theology of religions and interreligious dialogue?

Feminist theology

In terms of feminist theology, there are clearly certain aspects that have been developed within it, and are tied into the different waves of feminism.[18] Therefore, we will find various strands of thought in feminist theology, which is not a unified tradition. We do, though, find some principal trends in feminist theology:

1 'Herstory' theology, the recovering and reclaiming of the role and ideas of women in theological history.
2 Challenging the way the dominant discourse is constructed, so it has an 'inherent critique' of what is often termed the 'male and masculine hegemony' of 'Western epistemology'.[19]
3 Employment of standpoint epistemology, which suggests that our worldview and interpretative structures are created from our particular social and cultural location, which includes gender.

Relating this to traditional theology, it is undeniable that mainstream, or 'malestream'[20] theology has been an activity undertaken by men for

---

18 See Ruether, 'Emergence'.

19 Fletcher, Jeannine Hill, 2006, 'Women's Voices in Interreligious Dialogue', *Studies in Interreligious Dialogue* 16:1, pp. 1–22, pp. 6–7, quoting Sefcovic, Enid M. and Bifano, Diane Theresa, 2004, 'Creating a Rhetorical Home for Feminists in the "Master's House" of the Academy: Toward a Gendered Taxonomy of Form and Content', *Women and Language* 27, pp. 53–63, p. 53.

20 The term 'malestream' is used by Egnell to describe the fact that in many societies with male domination the ideas express essentially male-centred notions, and often suggest the concerns are universal whereas they may be more connected to those of men alone (*Other*, p. 28). The term was coined by Elisabeth Schüssler Fiorenza.

men, and that the role and contribution of women has been neglected. Theology has, moreover, been strongly shaped by certain patriarchal norms and expectations, that is primarily 'male' concerns have been addressed, and women have been given positions which are often lower or subordinate. Here, though, we should be careful: in relation to our third-wave opinions, we could say that theology has been largely rational, anti-body, concerned with domination and power structures, etc. Such characteristics are, in part, undoubtedly true, but to categorize this as a uniquely 'male' way of doing theology is to deny individuality. Are there not rational female theologians, and women who are abusive of power relations? Once we say one style of theology, rational and dualistic, is male, and another style, caring and empathetic, is female we have created a discourse of power, duality and fixed identities, which some feminist theology (as a discipline), at its worst, may tend to do. However, we must also not deny that there are differences between the ways men and women may typically approach problems, but, I believe, we are on dangerous territory if we see some areas or approaches being solely the preserve of a 'male' or 'female' theology. Indeed, feminist theology has taken much inspiration from certain styles of theology pioneered and done mainly, but not exclusively, by men, notably liberation and process theology. As such, Egnell suggests we should not see the contributions as being specifically 'female' or from 'women' but as areas raised in 'feminist theology' as a discipline.[21]

Even if we follow Egnell's suggestion to focus on feminist theology alone we are faced with certain questions. How do we, or should we, distinguish theology done by women from feminist theology? Does a theology that includes female experience, but written by a man, count as feminist theology? Does a single reference or claim to being female or feminist in a work that is otherwise 'malestream' make something feminist theology? Is believing in women's equality enough to make one a feminist? I do not intend to try and offer a definition of what is feminist theology – there are certainly many interpretations which would make it too difficult a task to undertake. It is, though, worth mentioning some

21 Egnell, *Other*, p. 27.

definitions developed by Enid Sefcovic and Diane Bifano that Fletcher explores. According to their taxonomy, academic work can have one of two styles:

masculine style: argumentative and objective, the disengaged expert is distanced from the subjects of research and discussion;
feminine style: dialogic and open-ended, recognizing and valuing the way personal experience informs the research and data.[22]

While it can have one of three types of content:

traditional content: focuses on male actors and includes masculine biases that take male experience and perspectives as the norm for 'the religion';
female-focused content: includes the experience of women in the religious tradition in recognition that gender impacts one's experience in a religious tradition;
feminist content: includes a systematic analysis of the ways in which religious traditions function as structures of oppression.

In using this to survey activities within the 2004 Parliament of the World's Religions, Fletcher observed that 'both women and men participate in interreligious dialogues in ways that cross over in these gendered categories'.[23] Moreover, to suggest that women who engage in 'argumentative and objective' styles of work are doing things which are 'masculine' and therefore not properly 'feminine' is both contrary to what we have said about third-wave gender discourse and feminism, as well as being deeply disempowering to women who work in this way.[24] Certainly some feminist theologians will seek to use concepts from traditional theology as a better alternative to new concepts advanced by other feminist

---

22 Fletcher, 'Women's', pp. 7–8. See also Egnell, *Other*, pp. 27–8.
23 Fletcher, 'Women's', p. 8.
24 This latter point was suggested to me by Rose Drew (personal email correspondence with author).

theologians which may be said to be based in female experience.[25] Also, there is a hierarchical implication that we should distinguish 'female-focused' from 'feminist' content which strikes me as antithetical to much of what feminist thought wishes to do. Indeed, as expressed, the 'feminist content' category could be read as a liberationist style which is not limited to feminist theology.

Given the above, we will not seek to distinguish 'male' from 'female' approaches, but, following Egnell, to seek for a feminist contribution. We will interpret this somewhat broadly by looking at those who write explicitly as feminists, or else when women are doing things, or writing, *qua* women. Within this we will include both of what are termed above 'female-focused' and 'feminist' approaches as it is difficult to clearly disentangle them, and as Fletcher notes things 'cross over' the categories. We cannot create a clearly bounded and defined 'feminist' category which does not cross over into women's experience and female perspectives in broader ways.

Seeking the feminist contribution[26]

To help clarify the issues we will use five broad categories, which, I hope, will be thought to do justice to the ideas, rather than placing them within an alien 'malestream' conceptualization:

1   Bottom up.
2   Renewal.

---

25 For instance, queer and feminist theologian Elizabeth Stuart defends traditional concepts of reincarnation against the eco-feminist notion of 'recycling' as afterlife (see Stuart, Elizabeth, 2001, 'Elizabeth Stuart Phelps: A Good Woman Doing Bad Theology', *Feminist Theology* 9, pp. 70–82, pp. 79–82.

26 This discussion is heavily indebted to Helene Egnell's comprehensive and insightful study of the feminist theology of religions, *Other*, which has both provided evidence to support my hunches as to feminism's contribution, and raised areas I had not considered. I will also use a number of other surveys, alongside contributions from particular feminist theologians.

3   Multiple interstices and boundary crossing.

4   Disputing 'malestream' concepts.

5   Forms of encounter.

This fivefold categorization does not separate ideas exclusively, as concepts in each category inform and permeate the others; in many cases, notions could have been classed in other categories. I will also point out areas which I do not think are exclusively, even primarily, the preserve of feminist theology; I do not do this in a spirit of critique, but to help clarify the issues.

Bottom up

In dialogue and theology we see a base in *women's experience*.[27] This means it may start in different places from men's experience, for instance, the home rather than the seminary.[28] Clearly, women will see traditions in different ways and bring different perspectives. We should not buy into some of the extreme essentializations built around this, such as: 'Men talk about religion – women live it.'[29] Although, I would not also deny what may seem stereotyped experiences, such as: 'there is greater acceptance of emotions in [an] all-women group: "when you are cleaning up after a women's dialogue meeting you're cleaning up all these tissues . . . "'[30] Reflecting that there are differences we can concur with McCarthy's statement of what may be the obvious, but which we need to fully understand the implications of: 'One thing that can be said about women without fear of overgeneralizing is that they are not men.'[31]

Also women may reflect a *different locus* based on 'neighbourhoods, NGOs, women's centres'.[32] This may reflect a more localized and bottom-up tendency. Some of this may not be unique to women, but male

---

27 Egnell, *Other*, p. 39.

28 Egnell, *Other*, p. 87.

29 Egnell, *Other*, p. 77.

30 Egnell, *Other*, p. 76, quoting an interview with Diane D'Souza.

31 McCarthy, 'Women's', p. 165.

32 Egnell, *Other*, p. 95.

contributors may not pay enough attention to it (although my experience of local interreligious activity suggests that there are many men engaged at this level; however, an empirical study would be needed to say any more).

There is also a third characteristic to this bottom-up focus, which is what Egnell terms 'religion as practiced'.[33] This relates to what has been termed the 'little' tradition as opposed to the 'great' tradition, that is to say, the workings out of religion and its practice in homes, cultural norms and the like, as opposed to the (supposedly) pure, doctrinal and elite formulations ('religion as prescribed'). In as far as most religious traditions have tended to have a hierarchy composed solely of, or at least dominated by, men, Egnell's characterization holds true. However, we must not neglect the fact that many men, especially minority groups, belong to traditions that are 'little', perhaps even being, in formal terms, 'guilty' of 'heresy' or 'syncretic tendencies'. As such, I do not think we should see this as exclusively female terrain; nevertheless, in terms of interreligious dialogue and the theology of religions, it is certainly the case that male theologians have normally spoken of and from assumptions of the 'great' tradition, while feminist theology highlights this other area.

Renewal

In common with feminist theology, a focus in the feminist theology of religions is *reclaiming traditions*.[34] This obviously relates to women's experience, and the writing of Christian 'herstory'. Relating to our first chapter on the nature of theology, we should see this as related to Christian identity and what it means to be a Christian in the light of the female experience, the implications of which for the theology of religions will be developed under our next category. However, one emphasis on renewal, in terms of putting things aright, is the *emphasis on ethics and praxis* as the fundamental of women's dialogue. Fletcher sees this in the

---

33 Egnell, *Other*, p. 42.
34 Egnell, *Other*, p. 151.

light of 'women's well-being' as a criterion.[35] Generally, though, it is suggested that women believe dialogue should be based in people's lives, and the relationship of religion to other aspects of society should be foregrounded.[36] In particular, this often means ethical concerns related to Human Rights, ecology and other areas. This is not to say that these issues do not arise in male theologians, and Egnell readily admits that this same focus is seen in the pluralism of Paul Knitter, who also privileges justice over dogma.[37] However, a distinctive claim is that by grounding their theologizing in women's experience with an ethical slant, feminist theology of religions *resists relativism*, by having clear embodied principles as its basis.[38] Therefore pluralism/diversity (radical openness to the religious Other) and universals (ethical absolutes) are claimed to be kept in balance in a feminist approach (we address this issue in Chapter 7).

Egnell argues that a factor found only in women's dialogue is *'life'*.[39] To be 'life-affirming' she suggests is seen as a criterion of 'true religion', and she quotes the Christian social worker and Dalit activist Annie Namala on this:

Any religion/faith of the individual or community that does not have a practical programme to reach out to, relate to, love and support another person/other groups has no real religion/faith. [. . .] So can we then claim what religion ought to be – Life was before religion and religion is meant to strengthen this life.[40]

---

35 Fletcher, 'Feminisms', p. 152. Fletcher notes that 'most feminist theologians' now expand this to '"the well-being of women and others" (or the well being of all, including non-human life)' (personal email correspondence with author).

36 Egnell, *Other*, see pp. 80, 89, 151.

37 Egnell, *Other*, p. 293. See on this, Knitter, Paul, 1995, *One Earth Many Religions: Multifaith Dialogue and Global Responsibility*, Maryknoll, NY: Orbis.

38 Fletcher, 'Feminisms', pp. 142–3.

39 Egnell, *Other Voices*, p. 331.

40 Namala, Annie, 2002, *Doing Interreligious*, unpublished report from the Women's Interreligious Journey, Henry Martyn Institute, from a copy in Helene Egnell's archive, quoted in Egnell, *Other*, p. 71.

Whether we see this as a concern from feminist theology may be disputed. I know few male theologians or participants in the area who would say they don't have an interest in the praxis/ethical underpinnings, and I doubt any would be against the principle of 'life' (though some may wish it to be defined more vigorously!). Yet, it is certainly the case that it has a higher priority in the writings of most feminist theologians than in most male theologians; indeed, my experience of my students is that the female ones are more inclined to be involved in interreligious action, while the men prefer to discuss theory and doctrine. We could certainly see a stronger emphasis, if nothing else, being brought by feminist theology.

Interconnectedness is something Egnell often discusses alongside relationality (included in our fifth category); however, I would see them as somewhat distinct, though interrelated.[41] While relationality is primarily about intra-human connections, interconnectedness implies a concern for all things and ecology, and so is bound up with eco-feminism in the work of such figures as Kathleen Coyle, Ruether and Anne Primavesi.[42] This is certainly an area that is not often connected into the theology of religions, but has a place in some interreligious dialogue encounters. If we take the suggestion that women's concerns are often sidelined, we may see the ecology agenda being sidelined at the expense of the centrality of ideas such as salvation and doctrine (this may also help promote the dialogue of action, see Chapter 2).[43]

Building out of all of this and more, there is also a concern with the development of *women's spiritualities*.[44] This is an element that McCarthy takes as one of three key ones, and which she says is 'an embodied

41 Egnell, *Other*, pp. 295ff.

42 Egnell, *Other*, p. 297.

43 This point was suggested by Sara Singha: 'the idea behind eco-feminism would be so helpful in furthering interreligious dialogue with marginalized peoples of different faiths' (personal email correspondence with author). She has also observed that Sallie McFague's work on God's Body would also fit in with the examples of Coyle, Ruether and Primavesi listed above.

44 For an excellent selection of texts on this theme see King, Ursula (ed.), 1996, *Feminist Theology from the Third World: A Reader*, London: SPCK.

spirituality'.[45] An embodied spirituality, found in much literature, suggests that women tend to see things less in terms of the abstract and philosophical and more in terms lived through their physicality.[46]

Multiple interstices and boundary crossing

One of the best definitions of what is distinctive about the feminist theology of religions was given by Joke Lambelin who suggested that in bringing together a web of *multiple interstices* of identity and approaches we find the feminist contribution, where complex identities become basic.[47] McCarthy also suggests the multiple social locations from which women come is key, which we will come to below. I think the term 'interstices' is a very important one, implying the cracks and boundaries between identities, suggesting both liminality and boundary crossing, a theme picked up by Egnell. This relates to 'religion as practised', where women may wish to break out of the boxes constructed by male hierarchical institutions which may not fit their experience.[48] This theme will be developed in further categories.

The sense of *multiple social locations* is emphasized by McCarthy.[49] Using the example of American relational theologian and Episcopalian Carter Heyward, a lesbian priest, she says that, in terms of their 'plurality of social location', women are always aware they occupy several different positions (here, the confused/problematic identity of being, within a Christian tradition, a woman, a priest and a lesbian). This challenges the absolutist, universalist tendencies often found in the dominant

---

45 McCarthy, 'Women's Experience', p. 132.

46 For more specifically on this, see the collection of papers in Althaus-Reid, Marcella and Isherwood, Lisa (eds), 2008, *Controversies in Body Theology*, London: SCM.

47 Lambelin, Joke, 'Voicing Silence. Towards an inclusive-feminist theology of interreligious encounter', ESITIS Conference, Salzburg, Austria, 16 April 2009; the definition was in answer to a question. At the time of giving this paper she was a PhD student at the University of Leuven, Belgium.

48 On some aspects of this see Egnell, *Other*, pp. 89, 109, 151.

49 McCarthy, 'Women's', p. 165.

male theological discourse, for such an identity realizes, by its very being, that it does not exist as part of a single unitary narrative.[50] However,
McCarthy's citing of a lesbian priest raises the issue that this same 'plurality of social location' can exist within the male experience, with the
direct analogue being a gay priest.[51] Moreover, the experience of the 'plurality of social location' may equally apply to a male working-class priest,
and those who are ethnically outsiders, while a growing literature on the
theology of disability is pointing to the way a variety of people and their
experience is excluded from mainstream discourse.[52] McCarthy indeed
addresses the post-colonial context, looking at a range of leading (female) theologians from outside the West, such as Mercy Amba Oduyoye
(Africa), Chung Hyun Kyung (Korea) and Ivone Gebara (Brazil), suggesting that the 'otherness and multiple social locations of women's experience as represented by Heyward, Oduyoye and Chung are foundations,
I believe, for a new kind of affirmation of religious difference'.[53] However,
we have already suggested that Heyward's experience and insights are
not unique to feminist approaches, while the post-colonial context is not
a distinctly female one. Indeed, on this McCarthy claims:

> From the outer edges where women stand, exclusive truth claims tend
> to ring false, both because women are sensitive to the distortions such
> claims have wrought on those who lack power and because women's
> own experience has attuned them to the complex multiplicity of hu-
> man experience.[54]

---

50 McCarthy, 'Women's', pp. 165–6.

51 This is not to say that gay and lesbian theologies are identical, but they do
share common characteristics, certainly in as far as they exist as counter trends to
the mainstream; see Stuart, Elizabeth, 2002, *Gay and Lesbian Theologies: Repeti-
tion with Critical Difference*, Aldershot: Ashgate.

52 There is a growing literature around Disabled theologies; see, for instance:
Eiesland, Nancy, 1994, *The Disabled God: Toward a Liberatory Theology of Dis-
ability*, Nashville, TN: Abingdon Press; Lewis, Hannah, 2007, *Deaf Liberation
Theology*, Aldershot: Ashgate; and Hull, John M., 2001, *In the Beginning There
Was Darkness: A Blind Person's Conversations with the Bible*, London: SCM.

53 McCarthy, 'Women's', p. 167.

54 McCarthy, 'Women's', p. 167.

When we look at the insights found in the theologians McCarthy cites we can either look to other liberation theologies, or else to other theologians working within the cultures from which they come. For example, McCarthy quotes Chung:

> They [female Asian theologians] claim their identity as both Asian and Christian. They take themselves seriously . . . Recently Asian women theologians have started to look into Asian myth, folktales, songs, poems, proverbs, and religious teachings from Hinduism, Buddhism, Islam, Taoism, shamanism, tribal religions, Confucianism, and Christianity for their theological resources.[55]

Of course, many male Asian theologians are also seeking to live out their experience as both 'Asian and Christian' and they too look to the resources of indigenous traditions, with examples such as Brahmabandhab Upadhyay, C. S. Song and Peter Phan.[56] Now, I do not wish to claim that what the Asian female theologians say is the same as what the Asian male

---

55 Chung, Hyun Kyung, 1990, *Struggle to Be the Sun Again: Introducing Asian Women's Theology*, Maryknoll, NY: Orbis Books, p. 108, cited in McCarthy, 'Women's Experience', p. 166. Chung goes on to say that these resources help women realize the inadequacies and oppressive nature of 'normative' theology (Chung, *Struggle*, p. 109).

56 On some of the contemporary issues see Thangaraj, M. Thomas, 2008, 'Religious pluralist, dialogue and Asian Christian responses', in Kim, Sebastian C. H. (ed.), *Christian Theology in Asia*, Cambridge: Cambridge University Press, pp. 157–78, and on historical precedents, Hedges, Paul, 2001, *Preparation and Fulfilment: A History and Study of Fulfilment Theology in Modern British Thought in the Indian Context*, Berne: Peter Lang, esp. Chapter 4. The definitive work on Upadhyay is Lipner, Julius, 1999, *Brahmabandhab Upadhyay: The Life and Thought of a Revolutionary*, Delhi: Oxford University Press. Song's theology is well represented in his work, Song, Choan-Seng, 1982, *The Compassionate God: An Exercise in the Theology of Transposition*, London: SCM, while an excellent example of his story theology is 1993, 'Oh, Jesus, Here with Us!', in Sugirtharajah, R. S. (ed.), *Asian Faces of Jesus*, London: SCM, pp. 131–48. Phan's most notable work to date is Phan, Peter, 2004, *Being Religious Interreligiously: Asian Perspectives on Interfaith Dialogue*, Maryknoll, NY: Orbis.

theologians say. However, all experience multiple locations. Moreover, each of these figures is a distinctive voice – what no two female theologians say is the same, just as what no two male theologians say is the same.

The above relates to what many have picked up as a key feature: *marginality*. Because women have often not been included in the creation of the elite traditions which have prescribed official versions of identity, some women have a sense of exclusion based on this, and it is a key feature in the approach of the feminist theology of religions.[57] Again, this is not an exclusively feminist issue: women do not speak as the only oppressed or marginal voice in the debate, more or less all non-white, non-Western peoples of both genders can do this (though women may, in such cases, be doubly marginalized), but we find this also of the poor (including the white Western male), the disabled, and others. Indeed, in creating a voice for a certain group it has been shown that feminism can, as a middle-class Western perspective, serve to oppress or marginalize other groups of women, an issue addressed by such figures as Chung and Kwok Pui-lan:[58] women are just as capable of creating 'patriarchal' power structures that oppress and silence others as men! I do not wish to deny, though, that feminist theology can make a contribution here, although, it can sometimes add to the problem. To explain this, I will address some, admittedly rather uncharacteristic, remarks made by Egnell. In offering a critique of Michael Barnes, Egnell notes that both he and many of the figures he admires are 'highly educated', 'white', 'European' and 'male', which suggests they cannot fully engage with the position of women or Dalits or other excluded peoples.[59] However, I could observe that many of these tags also apply to Helene herself, and this may, by

---

57 See Egnell, *Other*, pp. 80, 104, 153, and throughout.

58 This is an important issue picked up in Egnell's work, which rightly brings out the critique offered by Asian women to male Asian theologians, male Western theologians, and Western feminist theologians (*Other*, Chapter 6). See also Kwok, Pui-lan, 2002, 'Feminist theology as intercultural discourse', in Parsons (ed.), *The Cambridge Companion*, pp. 23–39, pp. 28–33.

59 Egnell, *Other*, p. 314.

extension, be seen as suggesting that she cannot draw a parallel between herself as a dominant European white female and Dalits or other Third World oppressed minorities. Indeed, in suggesting who can and cannot relate to them, her words could be taken as an act of the kind of Western middle-class feminism that she rightly critiques throughout her work – although she is generally acutely sensitive to such issues. However, as noted, this cursory and genderist dismissal of Barnes is uncharacteristic. It should also be read in relation to where, just a few pages before, she had suggested it as a caricature of feminist theology to say that white Western males are always 'evil',[60] especially as she almost immediately goes on to say: 'If Barnes joined company with feminist theologians to explore this broken middle, the outcome could be very exciting.'[61] I think Egnell has just gone somewhat over the edge with the rhetoric in one instance. Thus she does not deny that the writing of mainstream theology by mainstream theologians is opposed in essence to an understanding of marginality and marginal issues.[62]

One last area that comes from women's boundary crossing is *syncretism*.[63] Perhaps best associated with Chung, the notion of syncretism for her is a positive value, in which she hopes that 'Asian women's theology [can] . . . move away from the doctrinal purity of Christian theology and risk *the survival-liberation centred syncretism*'.[64] Yet syncretism is a theme found also in male theologians, such as Perry Schmidt-Leukel, within the Western context (see Chapter 6). However, it is, perhaps, more especially an Asian concern (but is also widely found in other non-European/North American contexts), seen through the activities of

---

60 Egnell, *Other*, p. 299.

61 Egnell, *Other*, p. 316.

62 If what Egnell implied in the dismissal of Barnes were correct it would be impossible for me to even attempt to write this chapter in any adequate way, as a theologian who exists among a privileged class in several ways; indeed I could even add, for my own case, 'Anglo-Saxon', 'straight', 'adult' and 'academic' to my list of 'sins'.

63 Egnell, *Other*, p. 41.

64 Chung, *Struggle*, p. 113.

centuries of work by (male) theologians to interculturate their faith.[65] We may therefore ask whether this is a distinctively feminist theme, about which I would raise two points. First, I would not wish to suggest that, perhaps, on the whole, women are not more open to this. Perhaps the interstices that build female experience make syncretism more amenable to feminist theology than 'malestream' theology? I remain open on this question, though perhaps non-Western feminist theology is a particularly potent site for such encounter.[66] Indeed, we must observe that the fear of loss of identity that can occur in syncretism is addressed as a theme for women in dialogue by Maura O'Neill.[67] Second, in at least one instance, male and feminist theologians may approach the issue in different ways (though this is not to suggest that male and female (even feminist) theologians may not employ either approach). In Schmidt-Leukel the concern is decidedly 'malestream', to produce a philosophical argument to show in rational terms that syncretism is not an offence to Christian integrity. Contrariwise, Egnell offers a reading of syncretism in political terms showing the way that the discourse is structured from above to remove syncretism as a viable option.[68] While not wishing to deny the power or intellectual integrity of Schmidt-Leukel's defence, in some senses it may be suggested that Egnell's discussion is more sophisticated, taking the discussion to a level beyond that of Schmidt-Leukel by showing how and why syncretism is made a problem rather than showing why, within the system, it is not a problem. In some ways (though we must keep in mind

---

65 For instance, Hindu converts to Christianity like Krishna Mohun Banerjea (see: Hedges, *Preparation*, pp. 144–9; Aleaz, K. P. (2008), 'Hinduism: We Are No Longer "Frogs in the Well"', in Hedges and Race (eds), *SCM Core Text Christian Approaches*, pp. 212–33, pp. 214–15; and, Banerjea, Krishna Mohan, 2009, 'The Relation between Christianity and Hinduism', in Aleaz, K. P. and Hedges, Paul (ed.), 'Hinduism', in Hedges, Paul and Race, Alan (eds), *SCM Reader: Christian Approaches*, pp. 150–7).

66 The controversy that surrounded Kwok Pui-lan's (in)famous WCC presentation in 1991 is perhaps a case in point.

67 O'Neill, *Mending*, pp. 104–5; on the issue see Schmidt-Leukel, *Transformation*, pp. 75–7.

68 See Schmidt-Leukel's 'qualified defence of syncretism' (*Transformation*, pp. 77–89) in relation to Egnell's introduction to the topic (*Other*, pp. 41–2).

our desire not to draw black and white dichotomies) this may be said to
typify 'malestream' and feminist theological responses.[69]

Disputing 'malestream' concepts

This category has already been implicitly, if not explicitly, anticipated in
some of our preceding discussions and is particularly associated with
O'Neill and her book *Women Speaking, Women Listening: Women in
Interreligious Dialogue*, which Egnell describes as 'the first book on
feminism and interreligious dialogue'.[70] Egnell suggests that women's
experience emphasizes the *'messy' and 'ambiguous' nature of religion*.[71]
Important expressions of this are Fletcher's suggestion that male discourse creates and maintains a sense of 'the religions' as monolithic categories, whereby 'the Christian' approach to, for instance, 'Islam' can
be summed up in such-and-such a way,[72] and Kwok's emphasis upon a
'multilayered, fluid and open' approach to religions.[73]

Other issues are that *men's dialogue is cerebral, women's dialogue is
practice*.[74] Again, it is suggested that *women raise different questions* in

---

69 One of Schmidt-Leukel's former doctoral students Rose Drew (personal
email correspondence with author), has brought to my attention one of the grey
areas that surround these discussions, for although his approach may be said to
typify a 'malestream' approach here, his argument for syncretism is, in another
sense, distinctly 'feminist' in that it seeks to disrupt the established boundaries
of religion (and so has strong affinities with the work of Fletcher, Kwok, etc.).
Could we classify his work in this regard, using Sefovic and Bifano's typology, as
'masculine-style' with 'feminist content' (he uses women as examples of syncretism so also has 'female-focused content')?

70 Egnell, *Other*, p. 274.

71 Egnell, *Other*, where these terms or the idea frequently arises, for example
pp. 63, 89, 123, 151.

72 Fletcher, *Monopoly on Salvation*; for a discussion see Chapter 2 herein.

73 Kwok, Pui-lan, 1995, *Discovering the Bible in the Non-biblical World*,
Maryknoll, NY: Orbis, p. 26. See also her, 2005, *Postcolonial Imagination and
Feminist Theology*, London, SCM. Her ideas are discussed herein in Chapters 2
and 6.

74 Egnell, *Other*, p. 93.

interreligious dialogue such as violence, health, prostitution, peace, minorities, migrant women workers,[75] which contrasts with less interest on such issues as doctrine and salvation. Also a *critique of masculine propositions* occurs, such as Hick's notion that we should move from self-centredness to reality-centredness for instance, which O'Neill sees as problematic because for some women it is not selfishness but self-abnegation that is the concern that it is felt needs to be addressed.[76] That is to say, pride or ego-centrism is seen to be a very 'masculine' issue, and shows the way notions of sin have been constructed by men; by way of contrast, O'Neil suggests, that in negating themselves we see another example of 'sinful' behaviour – hence what needs to be overcome is different. McCarthy also sees some general concerns within feminist theology relating to the theology of religions, such as the critique of God-talk, Christology and salvation.[77] We should also relate here the notion we have raised above, that some feminist theologians argue that pluralism is enmeshed in relativism and so seek to go beyond it. Further Egnell concludes that *men miss the point* even when they try to take account of women's concerns, or just take them on in token form without any concrete sign of change.[78]

Otheredness is our final element; one deeply related to marginality.[79] As suggested, women's sense of being on the margins of traditions is not unique. However, the female experience is unique. Even if we decide there is no distinctively feminist perspective, something which only

---

75 Egnell, *Other*, p. 104.

76 O'Neill, Maura, 1990, *Women Speaking, Women Listening: Women in Interreligious dialogue*, Maryknoll, NY: Orbis, pp. 27–8. See also the discussion of this in Egnell, *Other*, pp. 274ff. See also Chapter 3.

77 Fletcher, 'Feminisms', pp. 138ff. On questions of Christology between Western and Asian feminist theologians and also Fletcher's discussion of salvation see Egnell, *Other Voices*, pp. 222ff. and 333f.

78 See Egnell, *Other*, Chapter 8, which deals with the way male theologians have addressed and used feminist concerns and the general silence of women's voices.

79 Rather than using the term 'marginal', McCarthy refers to 'the experience of otherness' ('Women's', p. 165).

women can do is speak for themselves.[80] This, in itself, resists a male telling or conceptualization.

Forms of encounter

In this last category we address ways in which women may be seen to conduct interreligious dialogue differently. First, the stress is on *relationships*, getting to know the other rather than simply comparing concepts and ideas between traditions.[81] Connected to this is the notion we have mentioned already of *story telling*.[82] Related to the previous point, it is about getting to know the other through their stories. In explaining people's life journeys a greater appreciation and empathy is engendered, which is seen as preferable to discussing abstract ideas and concepts. Also, Egnell suggests that an *empathetic methodology* is found within feminism, that seeks to avoid 'epistemological violence' and 'achieve empathy' with the objects of research, thereby turning 'objects into subjects and co-researchers'.[83] This has much in common, it seems, with what may be termed 'post-modern' approaches. It has also been suggested that some women's dialogues have been marked by greater sensitivity and less formal structures.[84] Finally, although not a theme discussed by Egnell, it seems implicit in some of her work and has been discussed by other feminist theologians, though not in an interreligious context, that there is the notion of *embodiment*, which we have seen raised by McCarthy. While much (Western) theology has focused upon the spiritual and a dualistic separation of mind and body, women, it is suggested,

---

80 This was another response raised by Lambelin, 'Voicing', and I thank her for this insight.

81 This is another theme that occurs again and again in Egnell's analysis of women's dialogue movements and experiences (*Other*, for example pp. 35, 64, 70, 89, 151).

82 Egnell, *Other*, pp. 64, and 323.

83 Egnell, *Other*, p. 20. She specifically cites Bong, Sharon A., 2004, 'Asian Postcolonial and Feminist Methodology: Ethics as a Recognition of Limits', in King, U. and Beattie, T. (eds), *Gender, Religion and Diversity: Cross-cultural Perspectives*, London, New York: Continuum, pp. 238–49, pp. 241–2.

84 See Egnell, *Other*, p. 126.

are often more attuned to the physicality of their being and their sur-
roundings. I draw the reading back to my opening remarks, on the way
women reshaped the seating area. Is this an act that comes from women's
experience or feminist theory? Certainly feminist theology challenges the
disembodied nature of theology and philosophy (which was reflected in
first-wave feminism and gender discourse). Moreover, it is an area where
Western theology can learn from dialogue with other traditions; for instance, Daoism's stress upon the body as the locus of spiritual experience contrasts sharply with much that we know and believe in the West.[85]
In part we may see this, then, as a critique of a particular formation of
Western thinking and culture rather than a specifically 'masculine' aspect. This raises an issue which we have not really considered, the question of how much feminist discourse is a critique of specifically Western,
even modern Western, concepts, rather than anything else. It is an issue
we do not, though, have space to explore.[86]

---

85 Schipper, Kristofer, 1993 (1982), *The Daoist Body*, Berkeley: University
of California Press. My sense that this is an important correlation is confirmed
by the same point being raised, explicitly tied into feminist concerns, by Judith
Berling, 1997, *A Pilgrim in Chinese Culture: Negotiating Religious Diversity*, Eugene, OR: Wipf and Stock, pp. 126–9.

86 It would be fairly easy to suggest that the modern Western and Enlightenment emphasis upon reason has helped assert a worldview in which mind and body
are divorced (for a compelling account of the way such dualism is a recent innovation and not part of the earlier Christian heritage see Stuart, Elizabeth, 1998, 'A
Difficult Relationship: Christianity and the Body', in Isherwood, Lisa and Stuart,
Elizabeth, *Introducing Body Theology*, Sheffield: Sheffield Academic Press, pp.
52–77). However, there are certainly many precursors in Western thought, Pla-
tonism certainly being one of the most significant, and I would not therefore like
to suggest this is just a critique of Enlightenment thinking (see Akashe-Böhme,
Farideh, 2002, 'The Western Understanding of the Body as a Global Perspective',
in Ammicht-Quinn, Regina and Tamez, Elsa (eds), *The Body and Religion, Concilium* 2002/2, London: SCM, pp. 97–101). For more on religion and embodiment
see: Coakley, Sarah (ed.), 1997, *Religion and the Body*, Cambridge: Cambridge
University Press; Braun, Christina von, 'The Cultural Coding of the Male and
Female Body', in Ammicht-Quinn and Tamez (eds), *Body*, pp. 29–40; Turner,
Bryan S., *The Body and Society: Explorations in Social Theory*, 3rd edn, London:
Sage, Chapters 3 and 5; Burkitt, *Bodies*; and Isherwood and Stuart, *Introducing*.

Conclusions

It seems no single element can be said to be 'the feminist contribution'; indeed, as feminist theologians variously raise a variety of points it is problematic to see any single one as being alone suitable for elevation to this level. However, there are certainly elements that come from feminist theology that are significant and important contributions, which would include Fletcher's and Kwok's insights on the nature of 'religion', alongside the stress on 'life' and 'praxis'. However, where we see the feminist contribution most particularly is, we may suggest, in Lambelin's and McCarthy's notions that it is in bringing together a whole web of different nexus points, or interstices, that we will see feminism's particular contribution. This brings together aspects that may be said to come from women's experience as marginal voices and specific aspects of feminist theory.

A discussion of how these play out in the larger field are found throughout this book. Therefore, we will conclude this chapter with a series of thoughts about possible criticisms I will face in my use of this material, the situation of feminist theology, and comments for future developments.

Possible criticisms: 'malestream' appropriation?

While many challenges may arise to the issues addressed in this chapter, perhaps the most important may come from feminist theologians worried about 'malestream' appropriation. Egnell has explicitly addressed the way men have tried, and failed, to integrate feminist theology or women's issues into the theology of religions before.[87] These problems include tokenism and a failure to understand the issues/concerns. In response to such charges, in integrating feminist theological concerns into this work I think, indeed hope, that I have learned and developed as a theologian in the experience. If, as has been suggested, there are areas where feminist theology provides a useful corrective to much 'malestream' theology then it is not enough to simply take some key ideas, but to be challenged

---

87 Egnell, *Other*, Chapter 8.

at a deeper and more profound level. It is hoped this will not be seen as simply appropriating ideas or issues from feminist theology and inserting them in strategically useful ways into a work of 'malestream' theology. As Egnell claims: 'Though themes current in feminist thought do appear in malestream theologies of religion, the feminist challenge has not to a great extent been taken seriously.'[88] This work may not entirely escape such a charge: it addresses what could be seen as deeply androcentric concerns, while the whole text is addressed to theoretical rather than practical issues, and so may be said to typify 'malestream' theology. In defence, first, we can note an issue Egnell raises, which is that feminist theology cannot neglect 'religion as prescribed', which suggests the need to marry concerns between the 'malestream' and feminist areas, not simply erasing the former.[89] Therefore, an attempt has been made to integrate aspects of feminist theology into the debate, not simply as 'feminist' approaches but as part of the overall theological discussion (an issue addressed further below). Second, while this work is theory and not action centred, Egnell suggests that a similar gap exists between feminist theology of religions and women's dialogue, and says the former may 'provide a bridge across the gap between praxis and theoria'.[90] In bringing these issues into the wider debate a hope is to link to this bridge. Though perhaps one of Egnell's critiques of Barnes' work also applies to this: I do not *do* what I am talking about?[91] Third, if my work differs from that of feminist theologians then this should not surprise us, nor even be a bad thing. If men and women theologians are different (yet capable of being complementary?), as contemporary gender theory suggests, then what is important is that their ideas are brought into dialogue. After all, this is not a work in the feminist theology of religions, but the contribution of a particular theologian and reflects issues that seem important on my theological journey as it currently stands: as such we would expect it to voice issues that may be seen as belonging both to 'malestream' theology as

---

88 Egnell, *Other*, p. 310.
89 Egnell, *Other*, p. 333.
90 Egnell, *Other*, p. 306.
91 Egnell, *Other*, p. 313.

well as those raised in feminist theology, as well as other places. I would suggest this is a stance that has resonances within feminist theology.

Feminist theology and the theology of religions

Having addressed some challenges that I might face from feminist theology, we will raise two challenges to feminist theology. First, feminist theology must take the challenges raised by other religions more seriously. O'Neill has observed, in relation to the 'malestream' theology of religions: 'To what avail will religious people communicate with the "other" of other faiths when they have not yet learned to communicate with the "other" [i.e. women] of their own faith?'[92] Here she suggests that although much effort is made to look to the religious Other, some 'Others' closer to home are not included. Yet, the same challenge, almost in reverse, arises for feminist theology. As feminist theologians of religion have noted, mainstream feminist theology, despite its claimed concerns for the 'Other' and seeking new sources, sidelines and excludes non-Christians religious Others.[93]

The second challenge is about feminist theology as a 'contextual' theology. This relates partly to my use of this material in this book, where the work of feminist theologians is raised throughout not as specifically 'feminist' issues but as issues raised by particular theologians. There is a tension, indeed a danger, in 'feminist theology', for by writing itself as such it labels itself into a box which can be perceived to be of, from, and for a particular interest group, yet, if not labelled as such, may fail to raise

92 O'Neill, Maura, 1993, 'A Model of the Relationship Between Religions Based on Feminist Theory', in Kellenberger, J. (ed.), *Inter-religious Models and Criteria*, New York: St Martin's Press, pp. 41-2, quoted in Egnell, *Other*, pp. 283-4.

93 See Egnell, *Other*, p. 176, and Fletcher, 'Feminisms', p. 152, though the problem is most prominently addressed by Gross, Rita M., 2002, 'Feminist theology as theology of religions', in Parsons (ed.), *The Cambridge Companion*, pp. 60-78. See in this respect Mahmood, Sabha, 2005, *Politics of Piety: The Islamic Revival and the Feminist Subject*, Princeton, NJ: Princeton University Press, who discusses the way some non-Christian feminism, principally Islamic, is not considered feminist enough by Western feminists (my thanks to Sara Singha for this reference).

or highlight the issues with which it deals – we leave this as an issue for feminist theologians to deal with.[94]

Issues and hopes for the future

To some extent both the theology of religions and feminist theology are seen in the mainstream theological discourse as marginal concerns suited to those who may have an interest, but essentially unnecessary for 'proper' Christian theological reflection. Both have a role to play in subverting what appears to be this quite false and unhelpful attitude. Here, we should pay attention not so much to the 'malestream' nature of the discourse, rather its imperialist Western presuppositions (see Chapter 1). If we acknowledge how our traditions create exclusion through their imperialist hegemonic principles, then we can usefully employ Elisabeth Schüssler Fiorenza's term 'kyriarchy', which implies the rule of a lord, stressing not just women's domination but that found through ethnicity, class, economics or other factors.[95]

Finally, to end on a hopeful note, while it is certainly true that women are active in grassroots interreligious projects but are less represented at 'higher' positions, this may be changing. At least within academic discourse, a good proportion, if not the majority, of the young and upcoming students in the theology of religions are female – how many will be converted through to senior positions waits to be seen – which suggests things may be changing. Yet, there is still a gap, so we therefore continually need to seek ways to voice this silence.

---

94 This is a danger recognized by Egnell (*Other*, p. 170). As a general point, all voices should shape theology: male, female, black, white, yellow, brown, olive, rich, poor, free, transgendered, oppressed, etc., for whatever else we feel about Saint Paul he was surely right that such categories do not exist in the theological/ Christian realm (Gal. 3.28). I am, of course, aware that Paul's passage has been read by some feminist theologians as problematic by creating a realm of spiritual equality that ignores the very real problems of physical/social inequality, and certainly it has had this usage. However, as with all scripture much depends on interpretation, and is not, I suggest, inherently oppressive, but could be reclaimed or reused to overcome oppression.

95 See Egnell, *Other*, p. 28.

6

The Plurality and Particularity
of Religions
Beyond the Impasse?

Outline

Here, we bring together our discussions, starting with the pluralist and particularist impasse, which will lead us on to consider various areas for developing interreligious dialogue and the theology of religions. The final section will pick up two terms 'mutuality' and 'fulfilment', employing them to suggest ways forward.

Groundwork for the theology of religions and interreligious dialogue

In considering ways forward for the theology of religions and interreligious dialogue we must build upon various resources. We will consider how we can move beyond the impasse, before picking up several themes: the biblical concept of hospitality; syncretism; and hybridity. We will end this section with a reflection on Intercultural Theology, Comparative Theology and Interreligious Theology.

Religious pluralisms and particularities

If, as we suggested at the outset, there is an impasse between particularist and pluralist worldviews, we are, hopefully, now at a stage where we can start to reconcile these standpoints and move onwards. For this we must take on board three key facts:

1   Both positions have something very important to say. As I have argued, we need to embrace the radical openness that underlies the pluralist approach. At the same time, we must respect the particularity of every religion in at least two ways: on the one hand, to recognize that very different things are being said; and, on the other, to recognize that we need to stand within a particular tradition if we are to talk from anywhere meaningful to others.

2   Both positions are flawed, as traditionally expressed. Pluralisms often suggest that on everything important religions agree, while matters of disagreement are of a second-order nature – we may have much to learn from these disagreements, perhaps more than we can learn from the commonalities.[1] Meanwhile, particularities' expounding of the extreme position of 'radical difference' is untenable on many grounds. As such, we shouldn't simply highlight 'alterity' as the key motif.

3   Both pluralisms and particularities misconstrue religion and religious identity. Religions are not closed monolithic blocks, and religious identities always have fluid edges marked by hybridity and multiplicity. Here we may find ourselves in agreement with Judith Berling, who, speaking as a theologian, but from the context of being a historian of religions, says she finds it necessary to resist the extremes of both particularity and relativism, for religions are neither fixed and closed units, nor are they all teaching the same with each possessing integral systems which cannot be conveniently ignored.[2] Therefore, while opposed to the stance

---

1 Jacob Neusner hypothesizes that areas of commonality, for instance reciprocity, will not be part of the central grammar and thinking of any religious system (Neusner, Jacob, 2008, 'The Golden Rule in Classical Judaism', in Neusner, Jacob and Chilton, Bruce (eds), *The Golden Rule: The Ethics of Reciprocity in World Religions*, London: Continuum, pp. 55–64, pp. 55–6).

2 Berling, Judith, 1997, *A Pilgrim in Chinese Culture: Negotiating Religious Diversity*, Eugene, OR: Wipf and Stock, p. 35. Being, like Berling, both a theologian and a scholar of religion myself, with a particular interest in the history of

of radical difference, she notes that a danger of pluralisms is that they often ignore the particularity of identity.[3]

We therefore find the need to balance both the pluralist and particularist standpoints. To this end we will work through a number of themes and concepts that will build on what we have said so far. In doing this we find that the motif of radical difference is untenable (Chapter 4) but that the motif of radical openness is the one that offers us options that can work while maintaining the integrity of the Christian worldview. This may mean, however, both that we must accept that certain traditional views of Christianity must be challenged (of it as a fixed, closed and exclusive monolithic system), but also that we must express the attitude of radical openness in ways other than the pluralist vision as it has been tradition-ally expounded. In what follows I will develop themes that explore ideas already expressed in this book and explore those, and others, along new avenues to take us past the impasse.

Open and closed Christian theologies

First, we must emphasize the problematic nature of a closed and secure Christian identity, which often has resort to a colonial Euro-centrism.[4] This often relies upon Christianity as a set of doctrines, beliefs and creeds created and maintained through acts of exclusion, imperial domi-nation and internal power politics. Such a theology and view of history is not based upon the pursuit of the truths of the gospel or the following of Jesus, but rather related to the socio-political factors that led Christian and Jewish identities to separate, the enmeshing of the Christian story in a variety of new discourses, especially its struggles from becoming

---

religions, I think Berling has hit upon a key point that is brought out when these two disciplines are thought of together.

3 Berling, *Pilgrim*, pp. 32–3.

4 Jeanrond, Werner, G., 2002, 'Belonging or Identity? Christian Faith in a Multi-Religious World', in Cornille, Catherine (ed.), *Many Mansions: Multiple Religious Belonging and Christian Identity*, Maryknoll, NY: Orbis, pp. 106–20, p. 108.

an outsider (marginal) to an insider (centralized and coterminous to the state) religion within the Roman Empire that required a reversal of many of its fundamental ideas and attitudes (see Chapter 1). Alongside this, in our contemporary period, we have come to understand religions as closed containers, a view that both fails to understand the nature of religious traditions and the history and identity of Christianity (see Chapter 2). However, we cannot, therefore, simply resort to a response that every individual must create their own hybrid identity in a free-flowing flux which lacks rules and established norms. As Robert Schreiter has argued, both integrated (fixed and immutable) and globalized (transient and flowing) concepts of culture, and therefore identity, have attractions and problems.[5] A Christian theology of religions or engagement in inter-religious dialogue therefore has to attend to a view of Christian identity as rooted in tradition, but a tradition that is not monolithic and has many legitimate strands and discourses, and is also open to future change and development. The Spirit blows where it wills (John 3.8) and is not bounded to the provisional opinions of men (for such it largely was who wrote the inherited rulebooks, see Chapter 5). We must therefore realize that to be Christian is to inhabit a radically open identity.

Biblical hospitality and the religious Other

To help found a Christian approach for radical openness to religious Others, we must also explore the scriptural foundations upon which we can build. To this end we will suggest the importance of a key biblical theme, hospitality.

The significance of this theme was largely under-recognized in biblical studies and Christian theology for a long time. However, a contextual reading of both the Hebrew Bible and New Testament requires it to be kept as a prominent theme. Coming from a desert background, especially among nomadic societies, hospitality was not just prized as an abstract virtue but as an essential element of survival. To fail to give hospitality to

---

5 Schreiter, Robert J., 2004 [1997], *The New Catholicity: Theology between the Global and the Local*, Maryknoll, NY: Orbis, Chapter 3.

the stranger was the worst sin imaginable.[6] The paradigmatic instance is Abraham's hospitality to three strangers (Gen. 18.1–8), known traditionally as 'The Hospitality of Abraham',[7] but it is commanded in various places (for example, Exod. 23.9; Lev. 19.33–34; Deut. 10.17–19), and often demonstrated or praised (for example, Gen. 19.1–8; 2 Kings 4.8–11; 1 Sam. 25.8; Isa. 58.7). Illustrations in the New Testament would include as settings for Jesus' teaching (for example, Mark 1.29–34; Luke 7.36–50; Matt. 25.40), as a part of Jesus' teaching (for example, Luke 14.12–14; John 13.1–11), and it often appears as a cultural norm or is praised (for example, Acts 28.2; Matt. 10.40–42; Rom. 16.3; Heb. 13.1–2). Recently it has also assumed an important place within a number of contemporary theologies.[8]

---

6 Indeed, in this context a strong irony can be seen in the contemporary portrayal of homosexuality as the dividing line between true and false Christians, representing, it may be argued, the greatest sin in some rhetoric, where the sin of Sodom and Gomorrah is portrayed as homosexuality (via a traditional reading), whereas, in fact, a contextual reading shows that the 'sin' is actually a lack of hospitality (Gen. 18.16—19.28).

7 Perhaps, best exemplified through Andrei Rublev's famous icon. This work is discussed in relation to one of the paintings of the Indian artist Jyoti Sahi in an interreligious context in D'Costa, Gavin, 1998, 'The Christian Trinity: Paradigm for Pluralism?', in May, John D'Arcy (ed.), *Pluarlism and the Religions: The Theological and Political Dimensions*, London, Cassell, pp. 22–39. I disagree with D'Costa that the title of Rublev's icon 'The Hospitality of Abraham' is 'closed to any further signification' (p. 23) unlike 'The Old Testament Trinity' or 'The Trinity', as it is the trope of hospitality that is, arguably, most significant and is the one I will develop here.

8 See, for example, Stuart, Elizabeth, 1998, 'A Difficult Relationship: Christianity and the Body', in Stuart, Elizabeth and Isherwood, Lisa, *Introducing Body Theology*, Trowbridge: The Cromwell Press, pp. 52–77, pp. 57–62; Newman, Elizabeth, 2007, *Untamed Hospitality: Welcoming God and Other Strangers*, Grand Rapids, MI: Brazos Press; Bretherton, Luke, 2006, *Hospitality as Holiness: Christian Witness Amid Moral Diversity*, Aldershot: Ashgate; Pohl, Christine D., 1999, *Making Room: Recovering Hospitality as a Christian Tradition*, Grand Rapids, MI: Williams B. Eerdmans; and, Boersma, Hans, 2003, 'Irenaeus, Derrida and Hospitality: On the Eschatological Overcoming of Violence', *Modern Theology* 19:2, pp. 163–80.

Having established its centrality as a biblical concept, what might hospitality mean in an interreligious context?[9] First, we must be clear that hospitality is not a cosy concept about entertainment or making contacts. As Bruce Malina has shown, in the ancient Mediterranean world, it was about the transformation of the alien, or stranger, into a guest; even, it might be said, to make them part of one's own kinship group.[10] We see this radically in Jesus' own teachings where outsiders, those distanced from the mainstream, are welcomed and embraced (see our discussion of Jesus' radical openness in Chapter 3), whether this be social outcasts or religious Others. Indeed, as we saw with the encounter with the Canaanite woman in Matthew's Gospel, we find also, in the parallel story in Mark's Gospel, Jesus' notion of hospitality being challenged. Indeed, we should expect this challenge for Westermann has observed: 'The stranger comes from another world and has a message from it.'[11] Elizabeth Stuart, British Liberal Catholic theologian, expounds on this passage:

---

9 There are also some pointers to it in relation to interreligious dialogue. See Ustorf, Werner, 2008, 'The Cultural Origins of "Intercultural Theology"', *Mission Studies* 25, pp. 229–51, who suggests that following Derrida it may be useful (p. 246), and notes that it will be a theme at the World Council of Churches tenth assembly in 2013 (p. 239). See also the following paper on the WCC website: 2006, 'Religious plurality and Christian self-understanding', available at, http://www.oikoumene.org/fileadmin/files/wccassembly/documents/english/pb-14-religiousplurality.pdf, accessed 10 September 2009; it is also used in other contexts, see Winkler, Jim, 2007, 'The Radical Hospitality of Jesus', keynote address at California Pacific Annual Conference Immigration Event, California, 21 April 2007, available at, http://www.oikoumene.org/uploads/tx_wecdiscussion/The_Radical_Hospitality_of_ Jesus.pdf, accessed 10 September 2009. The Roman Catholic theologian of religions Michael Barnes also discusses hospitality as a key theme. However, I think the radical implications it holds, and which he at times veers towards, are not fully developed in his work – he always steps back from what he says to a more dogmatic presentation of denominational orthodoxy (Barnes, Michael, 2002, *Theology and the Dialogue of Religions*, Cambridge: Cambridge University Press, see, for instance, pp. 240–2).

10 Malina, Bruce, 1996, *The Social World of Jesus and the Gospels*, London: Routledge, pp. 228–35.

11 Westermann, Claus, 1986, *Genesis 12–36: A Commentary*, London: SPCK, p. 277, quoted in D'Costa, 'The Christian', p. 24.

In Mark's narrative the abolition of the purity laws [Mark 7.1–23] is followed by the story of the Syrophoenician woman (7.24–30). The structuring of the narrative is significant: after making a full-scale attack on the purity system Jesus has his theory tested by a Gentile woman. His reaction is shameful. But this woman, the fiercely protective mother, demands the hospitality that he has declared to be possible (albeit implicitly). '[B]e prepared for the coming of the Stranger, Be prepared for him who knows how to ask questions' warns T. S. Eliot in *Choruses from 'The Rock'* (Eliot 1963: 171). The Syrophoenician woman is the stranger who knows how to ask questions about Jesus' own praxis and in the process changes him, making him more hospitable.'[12]

Just as Durwood Foster said the discourse with the Canaanite woman (a Gentile) was an interreligious dialogue so too is this (see Chapter 3). Here, I would push Stuart and other Christians to test their notions of hospitality: who today is the stranger whom we must let challenge and transform us and our practice? I would argue that in our contemporary world situation we are called to hospitality with Buddhists, Jews, Muslims, Hindus, Pagans, Daoists, Confucians, Sikhs and others. The need for radical hospitality in an Asian Christian context has indeed been noted.[13] However, we still need to push at the borders of our understanding to ask what this hospitality might mean.

Hospitality cannot mean an inclusivist approach, where, in offering a limited openness, we take the religious Other into our system, and find a space for them. Such Constantinian imperialism is contrary to the spirit of the Jesus of the Gospels and the early Christian community. Jesus was a wandering preacher, an itinerant rabbi, dependent upon the hospitality of others, and the early church found itself as an alien in the world

---

12 Stuart, 'Difficult', p. 59.

13 Antone, Hope S., 2008, 'Book Review: Newman, Elizabeth, 2007, *Untamed Hospitality: Welcoming God and Other Strangers*, Grand Rapids, MI: Brazos Press', *The Ecumenical Review* 60:1–2, pp. 201–3, p. 203. Antone suggests that Newman's American Christian understanding of hospitality needs to be more radically extended.

which it was in, but not part of (John 17.16). To seek to dominate Others and to enclose them partakes of what may be called an ontology of violence as opposed to an ontology of peace. However, whereas some contemporary theologies seek to expound an ontology of peace as a way to claim their own superiority and ultimate victory, a Christian ontology of peace grounded in a biblical notion of hospitality will do the opposite.[14] To employ an extended quote from Rowan Williams, we must ask:

> not 'How do we convict them of error? How do we win the competition of ideas?' but, 'What do they actually see? And can what they see be a part of the world that I see?' These are questions that can only be answered by faithfulness – that is, by staying with the other. Our calling to faithfulness, remember, is an aspect of our own identity and integrity. To work patiently alongside people of other faiths is not an option invented by modern liberals who seek to relativize the radical singleness of Jesus Christ and what was made possible through him. It is a necessary part of being where he is; it is a dimension of 'liturgy', staying with the presence of God and the presence of God's creation (human and non-human) in prayer and love. If we are truly learning how to be in that relation with God and the world in which Jesus of Nazareth stood, we shall not turn away from those who see from another place.[15]

If we are to truly see from where other people stand and let ourselves be challenged in hospitality as Jesus was, we must accept fully the things they see, claims they make, and questions they ask. This is not, though,

---

14 Such an ontology of peace, suggested by Schreiter (*New*, p. 78), would stand in marked contrast to the proposal of Milbank associated with Radical Orthodoxy, which makes a transcendent, and inherently violent, claim for Christian superiority (see Hedges, Paul, 2010, 'Is John Milbank's Radical Orthodoxy a Form of Liberal Theology? A Rhetorical Counter', *Heythrop Journal* 15:5, pp. 795–818; we also discuss this theme in Chapter 4).

15 Williams, Rowan, 2006, 'Christian Identity and Religious Plurality', Plenary Session Paper from the World Council of Churches Assembly, Porto Alegre, available at, http://www.oikoumene.org/en/resources/documents/assembly/porto-alegre-2006/2-plenary-presentations/christian-identity-religious-plurality/rowan-williams-presentation.html, accessed 4 August 2009.

PAUL HEDGES

as a 'modern liberal' to 'relativize the radical singleness of Jesus Christ', for his uniqueness as a teacher and mediator of the divine is not in question – as we have noted it misconstrues what the pluralist stance should be to say that all religions teach the same thing or all offer some similar notion of salvation or the absolute. What Jesus taught, and the path to that through the Christian tradition, is not brought into question. However, we are deficient in hospitality when we claim that our root alone is supreme or that we have the best 'religion'; then we are no longer pilgrims and aliens in a strange land as Christians are called to be, but partakers in an imperialist Christianity that claims ownership, power, and control. Indeed, there are two avenues which we cannot take here:

1   The particularist-style root of claiming that we do not exercise dominion by invoking revelation because this only pushes the domination into an ontological sphere (see Chapter 4).
2   To claim that we have strict boundaries, about Christian integrity and truth which cannot be challenged, that dialogue/hospitality means everyone telling others about their own party line but not being willing to lose the monolithic and comfortable identities we claim (see Chapter 2).

What this means is, in some ways, quite radical, but as we have seen it is the path of radical openness that following Jesus requires: to be truly hospitable means not just to let the Other enter our world but to enter theirs too.[16] What that means in religious terms is also a challenge to us: our faiths and traditions remain relative and partial until they find their ultimate end, and it seems embracing other religious ends and ideas must share in that end.

I would, finally, like to attend to two particular New Testament passages in relation to 'The Hospitality of [Sarah and] Abraham'.[17] Our two

16 See Berling, *Pilgrim*, p. 130; she cites Ogletree, Thomas W., 1985, *Hospitality to the Stranger: Dimensions of Moral Understanding*, Philadelphia: Fortress Press, as a key source for her ideas.
17 D'Costa, 'Christian', rightly notes Sarah's 'double effacement . . . from representation and title', p. 26.

New Testament passages are Hebrews 13.2, 'Do not neglect to show hospitality to strangers, for thereby some have entertained angels unawares', and Matthew 25.40, 'And the King will answer them, "Truly, I say to you, as you did it to one of the least of these my brethren, you did it to me."' In the story in Genesis, three men come to Abraham's tent and are fed by him and Sarah, but it seems they do not truly realize their guests' true nature.[18] In our context, what could this mean? I suggest that an interreligious reading would lead us to show hospitality to the religious Other, who, as Westermann notes, 'comes from another world and has a message from it'. This message may, indeed, be one from angels, for in the strange (to us) religion we may find there the divine (to use a Christian term). If, as we have suggested, we find a sense of familiarity between religions and if we take the notion that 'you will know them by their fruits' (Matt. 17.16) seriously (see Chapters 2, 3 and 4) then, clearly, we owe hospitality to religious Others. This means to learn from their message, to honour them as guests, where host and guest become equals (and, indeed, recognizing that in their territory we are the guests and they the host). Are we to be judged on our hospitality to the religious Other in these terms? I would suggest it is a very real possibility.

Synthesis, symbiosis, syncretism[19]

Alongside syncretism, I have added two other terms to make a phrase first used, as far as I am aware, by Aloysius Pieris to address an interreligious context. However, whereas Pieris rejects, for his use, both syncretism, which he defines as a 'haphazard mixing', and synthesis, the

---

18 The story seems to imply they are God and two angels, but as this would be deeply problematic for the Judaeo-Christian tradition it is generally seen as three angels. The passage from Hebrews is a reference to this.

19 I take this phrase from Pieris, Aloysius, 1996, *Fire and Water: Basic Issues in Asian Buddhism and Christianity*, Maryknoll, NY: Orbis, p. 161. It is also used, in adapted form, as a subtitle to address feminist approaches in Fletcher, Jeannine Hill, 2008, 'Feminisms: Syncretism, Symbiosis, Synergetic Dance', in Hedges, Paul and Race, Alan (eds), *SCM Core Text Christian Approaches to Other Faiths*, London: SCM, pp. 136–54.

creation of a third religion which destroys the identity of each, there are positive usages for both terms. He does, though, endorse symbiosis, which he sees as the enrichment of each through their unique approaches. Here, I will not follow Pieris' definitions, instead keeping multiple meanings in mind, especially to accept the positive sides of these terms. For instance, although Picris disregards synthesis as a 'personal idiosyncrasy' that creates new traditions, we must not forget that many religions have been formed through just such a process. Arguably, Christianity is a synthesis of a missionary Jewish messianic sect with Greco-Roman mystery cults and religio-philosphic systems, while Sikhism could be said, through the Sant tradition, to be a synthesis of Hindu *bhakti* and Islamic Sufi traditions. It would be imprudent, therefore, to disavow such synthesis. Moreover, the experience of dual belonging of many today, while not necessarily seeking a new religion (indeed, many Christian dual belongers do not want to create a third religion, see Chapter 2) may result in such. On a less grand scale particular doctrines or teachings may benefit from a synthesis of different ideas (in a Hegelian sense).

Pieris' employment of symbiosis relates strongly to how we will use syncretism. In its general sense, symbiosis refers to a close relationship of mutual benefit or dependence, but, for Pieris and here, both benefit and dependence are intended. Diverse traditions must be brought together for mutual benefit; while religions are not closed systems but live in close relationship, always growing, learning and developing in dependence on one another (radical openness and radical difference). We will say more of this in the next section.

Syncretism can express the natural and inherent blending of religions. However, even the pick'n'mix approach of Pieris' definition, decried by many, should not be derided. In our contemporary context it marks out the religious life of many, and we should not disparage unnecessarily what may well be meaningful and uplifting voyages of spiritual discovery for those involved. Certainly, in as far as we are speaking from a Christian context such an approach is not one that would generally be endorsed. Nevertheless we should realize that all our religious lives are marked by some degree of syncretism. For a long time syncretism has had negative connotations, but recently a number of leading theologians have argued for its rehabilitation as a positive term in Christian theology and identity building.[20] Moreover, it is the most historically responsive way to understand Christian identity (Chapter 1), as well as that most in accord with what we can argue is the authentic integrity of the Christian system. As Timothy Light has argued: 'today's orthodoxy is the result of yesterday's mixing, and it has never been otherwise'.[21]

If we embrace a positive sense of syncretism we can follow Fletcher's suggestion that Christian theologians should embrace a dynamic Christian identity, and Schreiter's suggestion that theology must be universalizing not totalizing.[22] Fletcher speaks of the openness and flexibility needed to respond to our contemporary situation. Schreiter observes that we should delight in and extol the truths of our tradition (its universal aspect) without seeing our particular system as absolute and valid for all (the totalizing tendency). This can allow us to embrace a certain syncretism in relation to our religious identities. Historically, Christianity, that is our Christian identities and tradition, has been formed by syncretism, it has been shaped and formed in response to the religious worlds around it (see Chapter 1). Indeed, it is unavoidable, and 'Manuel Marzal

---

20 See: Jan Assmann for a discussion on usage (1996, 'Translating Gods: Religion as a Factor of Cultural (Un)Translatability', in Budick, Sanford and Iser, Wolfgang (eds), *The Translatability of Cultures: Figurations of the Space Between*, Stanford, CA: Stanford University Press, pp. 25–36, p. 33); Schreiter who has argued that the term has both positive and negative connotations both of which should be maintained (*New*, p. 63); Schmidt-Leukel who has offered a robust defence of the concept (Schmidt-Leukel, Perry, 2009, *Transformation by Integration: How Inter-faith Encounter Changes Christianity*, London: SCM, pp. 72–89); and Fletcher who has defended its contextual usage by Chung, Hyun Kyung ('Feminisms', pp. 148–50).

21 Light, Timothy, 2004, 'Orthosyncretism: An Account of Melding in Religion', in Leopold, Anita M. and Jensen, Jeppe S. (eds), *Syncretism in Religion: A Reader*, London: Equinox, pp. 325–47, p. 345, cited in Schmidt-Leukel, *Transformation*, p. 89.

22 Fletcher, Jeannine Hill, 2008, 'Religious Pluralism in an Era of Globalization: The Making of Modern Religious Identity', *Theological Studies*, 69, pp. 394–411, p. 411; Schreiter, *New*, p. 4.

has said that syncretism is the other face of inculturation';[23] we should
see that our Christian identity is bound up with the cultural context that
has shaped our particular Christian tradition. We should also be alert to
the power games we play when we apply the term 'syncretism' to that
we do not approve of: Mercy Amba Oduyoye has observed that Western missionaries charged Africans with syncretism when they lost control.[24] This point is relevant to us as we must realize that we should allow
legitimate syncretism of the Christian tradition today and not seek to
dominate other Christians, or ourselves, with fixed notions of Christian
identity based on monolithic, imperialist, Western forms of Christianity,
which were themselves products of syncretism.

However, we should see syncretism as evolution rather than revolu-
tion. Radical openness means we need permeable borders to our religious identity, but if we change too radically then, as we saw was a danger
with pluralisms, it can become detached from the religious constituency
that exists as its source. We must therefore walk between the poles of radical openness and particularity. Certainly, as we have seen, as generally
formulated, particularities disallow the syncretism of religious identity
which has been the natural heart blood of religion, for religions have always changed and adapted rather than being rigid and fixed, and therefore stagnant systems. While, we must not ignore the way we speak in
and from tradition-specific traditions we must allow for the fluidity of
systems, and openness to the religious Other. Meanwhile, feminist scholarship has kept us alert to a number of themes within this. This would
include the homogenizing way both pluralisms and particularities have
treated religions as composed primarily of elite traditions, and ignored
the little traditions, or religion as practised. Again, the complex web that
composes the interstices of our identity should be considered, against

23 Schreiter, *New*, p. 83, reference to Marzal, Manuel, 1991, *El rostro indio de
Dios*, Lima: Pontificia Universidad Catolica de Peru (English Translation: 1996,
The Indian Face of God in Latin America, Maryknoll, NY: Orbis).

24 Oduyoye, Mercy Amba, 2003, 'African Culture and the Gospel: Inculturation from an African Woman's Perspective', in Oduyoye, Mercy Amba and
Vroom, Hendrik (eds), *One Gospel – Many Cultures: Case Studies and Reflections
on Cross-Cultural Theology*, Amsterdam: Rodopi, pp. 39–62, p. 47.

monolithic or singular modes of identity construction. We must also be alert to the way our discourse is constructed from particular standpoints and thus can create a sense of distance from, or serve to 'other', those who do not participate in it. Certainly, as we have suggested, none of these is especially 'female' nor unique to feminist critique, but, nevertheless, they are issues highlighted more especially by feminist scholars in this area than by mainstream white Western male discourse (see Chapter 5).

One issue that also needs to be raised directly is the question of 'religion'. As we have seen, one of the great problems that bars development of both pluralist and particularist paradigms is a closed and monolithic construction of religion. Once we recognize the fluid and permeable boundaries of actual historical religious construction, including Christianity, we are free to embrace the positive connotations and implications of syncretism (see Chapter 2).

Hybridity

Another term used often in reference to identity construction is 'hybrid'. Especially for feminist writers in a post-colonial context, the term has been endorsed for speaking of hybrid religious identities.[25] The term hybrid when applied to humans has biological roots, where its meaning of 'a cross between two species' implied that the different races were different species.[26] However, the term has been extended by discourse around culture and post-colonial theory to have implications for how differences may meet: 'Hybridity thus makes difference into sameness, and sameness into difference, but in a way that makes the same no longer the same, the different no longer simply different'.[27]

This leads to themes we shall develop further in the next section. However, we should note two things here. First, as Fletcher suggests, the hybrid can be 'a way to think beyond the traditional theologies of

---

25 See Fletcher, 'Feminisms', pp. 149–50.

26 Young, Robert J. C., 1995, *Colonial Desire: Hybridity in Theory, Culture and Race*, London: Routledge, p. 8.

27 Young, *Colonial*, p. 26.

religious pluralism'.[28] In this we should be reminded of Chung's famous words:

> When people ask me what I am religiously, I say, 'My bowel is Sha-manist. My heart is Buddhist. My right brain, which defines my mood, is Confucian and Taoist. My left brain, which defines my public lan-guage, is Protestant Christian, and overall, my aura is eco-feminist.'[29]

While we may not all expect to become such diverse hybrids (for West-erners such options do not, on the whole, come naturally to us and there are dangers of appropriation in claiming diverse religious identities), it is nevertheless a striking comment on religious becoming. Rather than with Hick or many other traditional pluralists suggesting we must stay firmly within fixed and essentialist religious borders, we must recognize that we live in a world of more fluid religious identities.

Second, hybrid identities can subvert colonial power domination and, as used by Homi Bhabha, 'hybridity becomes the moment in which the discourse of colonial authority loses its uncial grip on meaning and finds itself open to the trace of the language of the other'.[30]

Intercultural Theology, Comparative Theology, Interreligious Theology

This discussion leads us to revisit Intercultural Theology, which stands against the hegemony of a universalizing theology, found especially in post-liberal traditions, which seek to portray and uphold a closed sys-tem. Rather, all theologies are contextual. Indeed, we may even say that the only true claims of any Christian theology is its own provisionality, while, at the same time, if it is true theology, it leads to God. This

---

28 Fletcher, 'Feminisms', p. 149.

29 Chung, Hyun Kyung, 1997, 'Seeking the Religious Roots of Pluralism', *Journal of Ecumenical Studies* 34:3, pp. 400–1, reprinted in Fletcher, Jeannine Hill, 2009, 'Feminisms', in Hedges, Paul and Race, Alan (eds), *SCM Reader: Christian Approaches to Other Faiths*, London: SCM, pp. 72–5.

30 Young, *Colonial*, p. 22.

may seem paradoxical, to assert both the relativity of a statement and proclaiming its ultimacy – its non-relativity in relationship to the utterly non-relative. However, such paradox must stand at the heart of all theology, and is affirmed in traditional theological thought, whether this be through Aquinas' notion of analogy, the tradition of the *via negativa* and *via positiva*, or, to start an interreligious conversation, the famous opening words of the standard recession of the *Dao De Jing*: 'The Way that can be followed is not the true Way, the Word that can be spoken is not the true Word.'[31] Moreover, our Intercultural Theology needs to be alert to the work of Comparative Theology, which will bring insights and challenges from other religions, which, in turn, will make our theology not just intercultural but also interreligious, but not thereby, as we have seen, surrendering Christian integrity. This may even lead to an Interreligious Theology that will not see its limits as bounded within its own tradition, but one that is open to insights from other religious traditions.

Mutuality and fulfilment

We will end this chapter with a reflection on two terms often used in interreligious contexts: 'mutuality' and 'fulfilment'. This will build upon various insights and suggestions we have encountered throughout this work.

The term 'mutual' is what Wolfgang Iser has called 'the dominant term' in intercultural hermeneutics.[32] While Knitter has suggested that a better term for pluralisms would be the 'mutuality model' as this stresses

---

31 '到可到非常到, 名可名非常名' (*DDJ* 1, lines 1–2, this is my own rendering, but relying upon other translations as a basis). The standard recession centres upon texts of the early centuries AD, especially that of Wang Bi, the 'originality' of which has been challenged by archaeological discoveries at Mawangdui and Guodian (for a brief overview of this see Littlejohn, Ronnie L., 2009, *Daoism: An Introduction*, London: I. B. Taurus, pp. 8–11).

32 This is his assessment of the papers that comprised the discussions and investigations that went to create the text Budick, Sanford and Iser, Wolfgang (eds), *The Translatability of Cultures: Figurations of the Space Between*, Stanford,

relationship as well as what each tradition may learn from the others.[33] If pluralisms suggest a static model, where we have a plurality of fixed religions each in relation to a central and defined (if only in its indefinablity) Real, then we may favour the term 'mutuality'. However, 'pluralisms' is so well established we must probably stick with it. If we do, however, we should do so in terms of the mutuality between faiths, that is their historical connections and contemporary interrelated dynamics. Also, we should bear in mind that different connotations, that include mutuality, are found when we speak or think of radical openness – a term which may help take us beyond the party boundaries and ideological constructs that currently haunts discussion of exclusivisms–inclusivisms–pluralisms–particularities.

The proposal is that we should not see religions as marked by radical difference, but as mutually related realms of cultural activity. Moreover, this mutuality means that each should learn and be inspired and changed by the others. At this stage we should make two points. First, our proposal is not that we should, therefore, seek to blend and merge religions together into a new global religion or seek to find a universal global/world theology to reshape Christianity. Each religion is shaped by its own historical and doctrinal context which is an important identity marker to those within it, as well as providing a way and means towards the spiritual goal it espouses. Second, notwithstanding the first point, each religion should understand both how it has been shaped through historical encounter and interaction with other religions (all are syncretic formations), and therefore, in the contemporary period, should be open to renewed learning and innovation. Indeed, because each religion is not a fixed and closed monolith, but a 'religion' in the sense of an area of cultural activity, this can lead even to radical change and challenge to the historical tradition. That is to say we must respect both the particularity

---

CA: Stanford University Press (Iser, Wolfgang, 1996, 'Coda to the Discussion', pp. 294–302, p. 300).

33 Knitter, Paul F., 2002, *Introducing Theologies of Religions*, Maryknoll, NY: Orbis, Part III.

and plurality of religions. This may lead into mutual religious belonging, structural syncretism, as well as more conservative adaptations.

It may be useful to offer an insight from outside the strictly religious sphere, from the more 'profane' world of political discussion. Here, according to the cultural theorist David Morley: 'Haber argues that "unity" (the requirement that a thing be at least minimally coherent enough to be identified and redescribed) does not necessitate "unicity" (the demand that we speak with one voice).'[34]

This quote sums up well the balance between particularity and plurality: unity (plurality) means things are 'at least minimally coherent' (particular), but does not demand 'unicity' (the destruction of voices).

I am not alone in this suggestion, and we can use the voices of some of those who have proposed similar ideas to take this forward. Ursula King has noted that we need 'mutual questioning and critique'.[35] Indeed, the idea that religions in dialogue should not just talk or exchange ideas as a matter of interest or information, but bring their own challenging truth claims to the table is also expressed by such figures as Paul Knitter and Hendrik Vroom.[36] In proposing this we would not want to go back to such nineteenth-century notions as that proposed by Frederick Maurice that each religion has one great controlling central idea which it has developed more fully and better than any other, and that a combination of these can be brought together to form the perfect religion (or, in Maurice's own terms, to help Christianity rediscover or explicate these

34 Morley, David, 2000, *Home Territories: Media, Mobility and Identity*, London and New York: Routledge, p. 252, ref. Haber, p. 120.

35 King, Ursula, 1998, 'Feminism: the missing dimension in the dialogue of religions', in May, John D'Arcy (ed.), *Pluralism and the Religions: The Theological and Political Dimensions*, London: Cassell, pp. 40–55, p. 41.

36 Knitter, Paul F., 2005, 'Is the Pluralist Model a Western Imposition? A Response in Five Voices', in Knitter, Paul F. (ed.), *The Myth of Religious Superiority: A Multifaith Exploration*, Maryknoll, NY: Orbis, pp. 28–42, p. 33, and Vroom, Hendrik M., 2003, 'Conclusion: Contextual Theology Revisited', in Oduyoye, Mercy Amba and Vroom, Hendrik M. (eds), *One Gospel – Many Cultures: Case Studies and Reflections on Cross-Cultural Theology*, Amsterdam: Rodopi, pp. 225–34, p. 227.

ideas which it inherently possesses to reach its own fulfilment).[37] However, every tradition no doubt has ideas which form a central focus which could act as a form of critique, or reforming paradigm (the term 'critique' carries, perhaps, too critical a connotation), for other traditions.

The idea of every religion learning and growing from its contact with others can mean a variety of things. For instance, the Indian theologian K. P. Aleaz suggests we may see God in Others and so use this to better understand the gospel.[38] This is important, because in as far as we are proposing a Christian paradigm the insights of religious Others must be brought in to help us reflect on our own internal resources. This is expressed by the German theologian Reinhardt Bernhardt under the catchphrase, an 'inclusivism of mutuality', where:

> Each bridgehead will be *inclusive* insofar as it starts on the side of one's own religion; but it will also be *mutual* since it will open one's own tradition to the challenging otherness of other religions.[39]

This brings us to our second motif word, 'fulfilment'. Here, again, we would not wish to adopt a nineteenth-century model of fulfilment which sees either one religion providing the answers to all others,[40] or sees a combination of all religions leading to the fulfilment of all in a universal religion. Neither must we endorse a unilateral model of fulfilment, but all must understand they can be fulfilled in contact with the Other.[41] Rather, by 'fulfilment' we would envisage an ongoing process of learning and inspiration, in a spirit of *mutual fulfilment*. This may lead to new, and

---

37 On Maurice's ideas see Hedges, Paul, 2001, *Preparation and Fulfilment: A History and Study of Fulfilment Theology in Modern British Thought in the Indian Context*, Studies in the Intercultural History of Christianity, Bern: Peter Lang, pp. 51–63.

38 Aleaz, K. P., 2005, 'Pluralism Calls for Pluralistic Inclusivism: An Indian Christian Experience', in Knitter (ed.), *Myth*, pp. 162–75, p. 171.

39 Bernhardt, Reinhardt, 2005, 'The *Real* and the Trinitarian God', in Knitter (ed.), *Myth*, pp. 194–207, p. 207.

40 For a study of this paradigm, see Hedges, *Preparation*.

41 Dupuis, Jacques, 2002, 'Christianity and Religions: Complementarity and Convergence', in Cornille (ed.), *Many*, pp. 61–75, p. 65.

unique, blends of two or more religions in 'dynamic interaction' as Aleaz suggests. However, as he points out this will be dynamic, not static, the aim is not to create a new fixed monolithic understanding of religion, but to understand religions without the 'modernist' pluralist/particularist motif of bounded and closed entities.[42] In part this will be the work of Comparative Religion, which, as Clooney has shown, will lead us to rethink our tradition, although in ways that mean more than simply rearranging the baggage of our tradition.[43] There are, of course, a range of suggestions already for what a Christianity inspired by, or interpreted in the light of, another religious tradition would look like.[44]

Mutual fulfilment: on not finding answers, just more difficult questions

Having expressed an ideal, we must think of the practicalities. What would the mutual fulfilment of religions mean? To some extent we can see this already. We know that some Christians practise Zen meditation as a way to develop a side of their tradition they find lacking, while the use of indigenous customs and symbols can be used to express Christian motifs, such as the famous example of the Trinity on the gateway of Shantivanam Ashram in India which uses the iconography of the *trimurti* (the so-called 'Hindu Trinity' of Vishnu, Shiva and Brahma).[45]

---

42 Aleaz, 'Pluralism', pp. 170–1.

43 A term used by Knitter for what Comparative Theology may entail (*Introducing*, p. 236).

44 See, for instance: Abhistikananda, 1974, *Saccidananda: A Christian Approach to Advaitic Experience*, Delhi: ISPCK; Sahajananda, John Martin, 2006, *Hindu Christ: Jesus' Message Through Eastern Eyes*, Winchester: O Books; Keenan, John P., 2009, *Grounding Our Faith in a Pluralist World – with a little help from Nāgārjuna*, Eugene, OR: Wipf and Stock; Hieromonk Damascene, 2004 [1999], *Christ: The Eternal Tao*, Platina, CA: Valaam Books; Griffiths, Bede, 1992 [1989], *A New Vision of Reality: Western Science, Eastern Mysticism and Christian Faith*, London: Fount; and Koyama, Kosuke, 1974, *Waterbuffalo Theology*, London: SCM.

45 On the use of indigenous imagery at Shantivanam, see Hedges, Paul, 2000, 'Architecture, Inculturation and Mission: The buildings of the Cambridge

The latter case raises the question of the localized aspect of this, what is often termed inculturation. To briefly address this specific case: how should Christianity be 'fulfilled' in the Indian context? Is it as simple as restating Christianity in Hindu terms to make it responsive to the local context? We should be aware that what we term 'Hinduism' is far from a single tradition, which will mean that there is not just one paradigm to challenge us but many, and we must also be aware of the differences between the north and south and other regional contexts.[46] Moreover, India is of course a multireligious nation, and so how should Islam, Buddhism, Jainism and Sikhism, to name some of the traditions found there, play into this? Indeed, when we ask this question we should realize that it raises very problematic questions about the power relations between these traditions and cultures. Perhaps the most important issue is the way that much Christian dialogue with the Hindu tradition has focused upon elite traditions and has neglected the way that little traditions, especially Dalits, may find themselves marginalized by this, especially given the history of oppression they have faced, and so we need to consider Dalit perspectives on religious plurality.[47] Alongside this we must consider how churches outside India would relate and be able to speak to Indic Christian churches. This brief overview of the situation of India shows a few of the complexities of the situation, which is complicated not just by the variety of theological/spiritual choices but also by the socio-political issues that are intimately bound up within it.

Mission to Delhi, and Their Meaning for the Church Today', *International Review of Mission*, LXXXIX, 353, pp. 180–9, pp. 184–5.

46 This is discussed ably in Barnes, *Theology*, (see especially Chapters 5, 6 and 8), as well as in Knitter, Paul F., 1995, *One Earth Many Religions: Multifaith Dialogue and Global Responsibility*, Maryknoll, NY: Orbis, pp. 157–72.

47 This is a largely understudied area, but see the reading by Singha, Sara, 2009, 'Dalit Theology: An Indian Christian Response to Religious Pluralism', in Hedges and Race (eds), *SCM Reader: Christian Approaches*, pp. 158–66. See also, Nirmal, Arvind P., 1994, 'Toward a Christian Dalit Theology', in Sugirtharajah, R. S. (ed.), *Frontiers in Asian Christian Theology: Emerging Trends*, Maryknoll, NY: Orbis, pp. 27–40, and Knitter, *One Earth*, pp. 167–9. It also receives attention in Collins, Paul M. , 2007, *Christian Inculturation in India: Liturgy, Worship and Society*, Aldershot: Ashgate.

We should, at this stage, return to the context of this work, which is within a Western (Anglican) ecumenical Christian framework. Here, we do not have an alternative indigenous religious tradition(s) that provides a cultural background for inculturation (the situation with indigenous peoples for North Americans, Australians and New Zealanders does, though, provide some context, while the revival of pagan and other traditions in Europe should not be neglected in dialogue). Moreover, the experience of cultural and religious diversity varies, with white Christians being just one community among others, if not a distinct minority, in some districts, but possessing an almost blanket uniformity in places. We are therefore faced with questions of the context and relevance of how we as Western Christians are faced with the challenge of mutual fulfilment in relation to other religions. It is not my intention to provide any easy answers to the questions which are raised here, nor to suggest a single or simple recipe for how the mutual fulfilment of religions could work. What I do suggest is that there is a need for religions to overcome the building of barriers, and embrace a radical openness to one another; however, this must be negotiated in a variety of ways within a variety of contexts. In whatever case it will require new and creative re-readings of tradition, what Kwok Pui-lan calls 'dialogical imagination'.[48]

Another issue that should be addressed is the different socio-economic experience of churches and how his would also play into the local context. In areas of deprivation and poverty a concern about how Shunyata may help us envisage the Trinity, or how reflections on the Dao could lead us to new insights in Christology may seem the most pedantic trivialities. However, perhaps an encounter with Islamic social ethics would provide insights in such a situation? Moreover, without wishing to gloss over difficulties or subsume very real social problems to an overarching spirituality, it should be observed that some of the areas of greatest socio-economic poverty are significantly religiously mixed, and in such places a meeting of religious traditions may help to alleviate some of the communal tensions. Indeed, given the nature of many of the local economic difficulties, we can see that these are tied to global economic

---

48 Kwok, *Postcolonial*, pp. 38–44.

factors and so, in some senses, as well as needing localized solutions, economic inequality and the structural inequalities of global capitalism would need to be addressed.[49]

We have come to these issues throughout this work with specifically Christian language and from an explicitly (Western) Christian context, though one grounded in an Intercultural Theology. This is necessary as we all come from somewhere, and we cannot simply start a dialogue or seek to learn with no grounding (here, of course, I speak to other Christians, but, I suggest, the same would apply to Muslims, Buddhists and others; a somewhat different context, of course, applies to the growing numbers of 'unchurched' or tradition-less people, yet they must also start in their place and work respectfully outwards from this). Against this context we must seriously consider the arguments we have outlined as imperative. To sum up the argument, a number of key issues should be highlighted, both reasons for adopting a stance of radical openness, but also implications from it:

1   We can argue that a radical openness to religious Others, and the notion of mutual fulfilment, is theologically justified through the biblical tradition of hospitality, and also by the Trinitarian notion of mutual communication and dance (perichoresis) which Christianity embraced in contrast to a unified image of deity.

2   By overcoming the dichotomy of plurality and particularity through understanding religions not as monolithic and bounded entities but as fluid traditions of interpretation within different cultural contexts, it becomes necessary that we should see them in active and dynamic dialogue and, indeed, we may even expect this to yield new insights and resources.

3   These insights mean that we must be driven beyond a theological and religious parochialism. Religiously, we must be cosmopolitans if we are to be true to the Christian principles I have

---

49 For a profound Christian meditation on these issues see Sung, Jung Mo, 2009, *Desire Market, Religion*, London: SCM.

suggested.[50] Therefore, we cannot stay within the limits of our tradition and look on other religions from the heights, adopting and adapting aspects of other religious traditions which we may deem useful to our purposes. As others have suggested we need an encounter of mutual learning. This means we must be prepared to be challenged at the heart and centre of our doctrines, just as we will seek to challenge others.

4   We cannot expect to still have a 'pure' Christian tapestry with some other religious embroidery at the edges, rather the very warp and weft of our traditions will be changed and altered creating a different picture. If we remain alert to what we have said about the way that religious traditions are created through the triumph of the politically powerful and the domination of empire, we need to accept the voices that come to us from the margins and Other places. If, as we have suggested, religions do relate in some measure, and if this is in relation to 'transcendence', we should expect *our* (those we, as humans, have created!) systems, *our* boundaries, and *our* fixed systems to be challenged! This involves, when we look to the religious realm, being ready to understand what being in relation to the transcendent means; the American theologian Carter Heyward gives us a fitting definition for this term: 'To transcend means, literally, to cross over. To bridge. To make connections. To burst free of particular locations.'[51]

5   It must be admitted that the kind of mutual fulfilment advocated here would be difficult for the major Christian institutional traditions as it would involve opening themselves to questioning, change and reform. However, as we have seen, the danger for individual theologians or Christians to break forth in this direction is that they will be divorced from the practice of their traditions, be seen as heretical, schismatic and syncretistic (in a negative

---

50 See Fletcher, 'Religious', pp. 409–10; she uses Appiah's concept of 'cosmopolitans' (she cites in this regard Appiah, Kwame Anthony, 2006, *Cosmopolitanism: Ethics in a World of Strangers*, New York: Norton, p. 57).

51 Heyward, Carter, 1984, *Our Passion for Justice: Images of Power, Sexuality and Liberation*, New York: Pilgrim Press, p. 245.

sense) and so may be unable, then, to have a more positive effect upon their denominational cohort. In relation to this quandary, communal responsibility and personal integrity need to be finely balanced and considered.

6   The need to bring radical openness and mutual fulfilment to the churches is a prophetic calling to lead people from the false idols of fixed doctrines, made by human hands, and the images of monolithic confessional identity set in stone: today, Jesus' teachings and Christian tradition should lead us to embrace different religions in a spirit of respect and openness. As was said of Moses: 'Our fathers refused to obey him, but thrust him aside . . . And they made a calf in those days, and offered a sacrifice to the idol and rejoiced in the works of their hands' (Acts 7.39 and 41). Are our traditions, denominations and doctrines our idols? We must ask whether we will be guided by the Spirit through Jesus' example of radical openness, who allowed the religious Other to challenge and expand his thinking, or the spirit of institutions and closed religiosity that ignores, represses and denies our religious neighbours. Indeed, we must ask ourselves in this context who are our religious neighbours (see Lev. 19.18; Matt. 5.43; Luke 10.25–37)?

Conclusions

We have come to an end with a set of difficult questions and hard decisions, rather than a clear and fixed system or plan which provides clear directions. Yet, we might expect nothing less. Moreover, many Christians will no doubt feel deeply disturbed by the propositions I have advanced, and many will no doubt feel it demands we give up too much of what is taken as clear and established Christian doctrine and identity. However, I have argued that this belongs to a false understanding of what Christianity is and should be. I would suggest that one aspect of good theology is that it should always take us beyond our comfort zone, and if this means being discomforted in our Christian identity, then this too is what is demanded of us. Maybe I ask too much, but what I think is clear is that we must move to develop our thought in relation to an Intercultural Theology and Comparative Theology, which will lead, I have suggested, to an Interreligious Theology. Little more need be said in conclusion, except that this would lead us on to ethical questions, an area to which we devote our final chapter.

7

By Way of Conclusion
Some Reflections on Religious Ethics in an Interreligious Global Context

Between the universal and particular

Our discussion of the issues so far has been in a mainly theoretical context, so we should conclude by offering some thoughts on the practical application of mutual fulfilment in relation to ethical thinking and action. Here, we need to pay attention to both the particularist and the pluralist perspectives, rather than see them as antithetical polar opposites. In relation to Human Rights, Sumner Twiss has argued that we are often split between the two poles of 'universalists' and 'particularists',[1] yet both camps have insights and important contributions to make, meaning we should seek a third way. Certain theorists make contributions along these lines in ways that accord with what I have suggested in the previous chapter. It would be useful to begin by reflecting on the thought of three thinkers which will help set out some guidelines. We begin with Bonaventura de Sousa Santos, according to whom:

> All cultures are relative, but cultural relativism, as a philosophical posture, is wrong. All cultures aspire to ultimate concerns and values, but cultural universalism, as a philosophical posture, is wrong.[2]

---

1 Twiss, Sumner, 1998, 'A Constructive Framework for Discussing Confucianism and Human Rights', in Tu, Weiming and Bary, Wm. Theodore de (eds), *Confucianism and Human Rights*, New York: Columbia University Press, pp. 27–53.

2 Santos, Boaventura de Sousa, 1999, 'Towards a Multicultural Conception of Human Rights', in Featherstone, Mike and Lash, Scott (eds), *Spaces of Culture: City, Nation, World*, London: Sage Publications Ltd, pp. 214–29, p. 221.

This clearly cuts across the two extremes of the particular and universal that Twiss spoke of, while being in accord with my suggestions about learning from the depths of every tradition without absolutizing what is in them or giving way to relativism. In this we will find the following words of Bryan Norden insightful:

> I am on the side of those who . . . recognize the significant disagreements that divide major thinkers and their cultural traditions, but believe in the possibility of constructive cross-cultural dialogue.[3]

This, again, recognizes what we have said about the way that a radical openness between traditions does not give way to a naive form of pluralism that insists that all religions are saying the same, but neither does it endorse the particularist agenda of cultural islands that can only speak within their own terms. Both of these figures are discussing ethical issues, but we will look to Wm. Theodore de Bary to express this in terms of directly ethical concerns:

> If, however, you view *human rights* as an evolving conception, expressing imperfectly the aspirations of many people, East and West, it may be that, learning from the experiences of others, one can arrive at a deeper understanding of human rights problems in different cultural settings.[4]

These three theorists, and the stance I am taking here, concur that while not wishing to claim that all religions or cultures say the same, or have identical ethical values, there is room for fruitful ethical conversation, as well as some basis for common ground. Paul Knitter also suggests we must find a way to seek a middle way between 'essentialism'

---

3 Norden, Bryan W. Van, 2003, 'Virtue Ethics and Confucianism', in Mou, Bo (ed.), *Comparative Approaches to Chinese Philosophy*, Aldershot: Ashgate, pp. 99–121, p. 117.

4 Bary, Wm. Theodore de, 'Neo-Confucianism and Human Rights', in Rouner, Leroy S. (ed.), *Human Rights and the World's Religions*, Notre Dame: University of Notre Dame Press, 1988, pp. 183–98, p. 184.

and 'relativism'.[5] However, to consider some of the problems this raises we will focus upon an area that has been hotly debated within and between religions in relation to Interreligious Dialogue, the concept of Global Ethics.[6]

What is global ethical thinking?

The concept of a Global Ethic accepts that we are now in a 'globalized' world (meaning, loosely, that cultures and societies live and interact as part of a whole system into which we are all, in various ways, tied), and within this wants to find the common ground, a bottom-line minimal consensus, upon which all religions can agree to come together on ethical demands. As a solidified concept and proposal it owes much to both Hans Küng and Leonard Swidler. The proposal of Küng is, though, the most widely known and cited, having been ratified as a 'Declaration Toward a Global Ethic' in 1993 at the (Second) Parliament of the World's Religions. Alan Race has summarized this based upon what he terms 'a standard cycle of religious commitment' as follows:

> there is a diagnosis of need (1), followed by a disclosure of fundamental awareness (2), which gives rise to a disciplined pathway of active change (3), and which in turn envisages the transformation of reality (4). At the heart of the Global Ethic lie the four Directives. They provide the bridge between the religious basis for ethical life

5 Knitter, Paul F., 1995, *One Earth, Many Religions: Multifaith Dialogue and Global Responsibility*, Maryknoll, NY: Orbis, p. 74.

6 An outline of this concept in relation to dialogue can be found in Race, Alan, 2008, 'Interfaith Dialogue: Religious Accountability Between Strangeness and Resonance', in Hedges, Paul and Race, Alan (eds), *SCM Core Text Christian Approaches to Other Faiths*, London: SCM, pp. 155–72, pp. 163–6. I have also discussed it in this context; see Hedges, Paul, 2008, 'Are Interfaith Dialogue and a Global Ethic Compatible? A Call for an Ethic to the Globe', *Journal for Faith, Spirituality and Social Change* 1:2, pp. 109–32. For another discussion on this in relation to interfaith issues see Knitter, *One Earth*, pp. 67–72.

and its practical outworking in dialogue and co-operation among the religions.[7]

The four directives, or commitments, are:

1   Non-violence and respect for life
2   Solidarity and a just economic order
3   Tolerance and a life of truthfulness
4   Equal rights and partnership between men and women[8]

Concerns about the Global Ethic

While these four points represent a series of basic assumptions that many may think are straightforward, a number of critics have pointed out problems. These have been summarized into five main points which I will briefly set out here.[9] It should be noted that some see these as fundamental problems that invalidate a Global Ethic, whereas I suggest they are 'concerns' which need to be met and considered in moving forward with a more nuanced investigation into interreligious ethical thinking in a global and postcolonial context.

Are we including the extremes? While endorsed at the World's Parliament of Religions, Küng's draft represents, it may be argued, a self-selecting, dialogue-inclined minority from the religions. Indeed, even at the Parliament, there was much argument and many refused to sign or ratify it; less than a quarter of all those present did so. Also, such a statement will be seen by many as a statement made by conciliatory scholars

---

7 Race, 'Interfaith', p. 163; for a diagrammatic presentation of the ethic, see p. 164.

8 Küng, Hans, 1993, 'Declaration Toward a Global Ethic', in Küng, Hans and Kuschel, Karl-Josef (eds), *A Global Ethic: The Declaration of the Parliament of the World's Religions*, London: SCM Press, pp. 23–4.

9 See Hedges, Paul, 2008, 'Concerns about the Global Ethic: A Sympathetic Critique and Suggestions for a New Direction', *Studies in Interreligious Dialogue* 18:1 (Fall), pp. 153–68, pp. 157–63. I will herein offer a brief outline of the case presented in this article, referencing it into the concerns and issues of this text.

and liberals within their own traditions who do not represent what they may consider a true representation of their faith. As such, rather than bringing religions together it may encourage some to react against it. As I have previously suggested:

> It may cause them ['radicals' or 'extremists'] to think that a GE means diluting the radical requirements of their faith to some lukewarm common standpoint. We do not have to go far to find 'extremes'. Forward quotes the words of the former Iranian President Ali Khamenei, 'When we want to find out what is right and wrong, we do not go to the United Nations; we go to the Holy Koran.' Forward continues with what he terms Khamenei's 'more colourful' language, 'For us the Universal Declaration of Human Rights is nothing but a collection of mumbo-jumbo by disciples of Satan.'[10]

This raises the question of what status a Global Ethic may have. Each religious tradition, even among those who accept it, will still need to draw on their own traditional resources for a 'thick' ethic, rather than the 'thin' and sketchy account given by any Global Ethic. This is not to deny, however, that useful work is clearly done where religions meet and talk together with an attitude of radical openness or, at least, a willingness to engage mutually in the dialogues of life or action (see Chapter 2).[11] However, we must be aware that openness can sometimes involve avoiding the tough questions and agendas that get raised, and we must address this.[12]

---

10 Hedges, 'Concerns', p. 157, citing Forward, Martin, 2001, *Inter-religious Dialogue: A Short Introduction*, Oxford: Oneworld, pp. 60–1, who quotes Mayer, A. E., 1999, *Islam and Human Rights*, London: Pinter, p. 34.

11 For an indication of the practicalities of these the British government's document *Face to Face and Side by Side: A Framework for Partnership in our Multi Faith Society* (Department for Communities and Local Government, 2008, Wetherby: Communities and Local Government Publications) is informative.

12 See for instance Allen, John L. Jr, 2003, 'Interfaith Dialogue: beyond "tea and cookies"', *National Catholic Reporter*, 19 September.

Are there common points to a Global Ethic? Much of the wording is quite vague, and so we can ask whether there is really any meaningful common understanding of such things as 'a just economic order'. Presumably all would endorse this. There is, however, a great gulf between the democracy and enlightened and benevolent capitalism that many contemporary Western Christians may endorse, and other systems. For instance, Islamic banking and social thinking would be deeply critical of the capitalist system and much else. Likewise 'for many traditional Hindus, the question of dharma in relation to social position (*varna*) and caste (*jati*) mean that a just social order may not mean freedom and equality in the modern Western sense'.[13] Others have also questioned the notion of individuality that seems built into various declarations of Global Ethics.

All the directives were contentious in discussions at the Parliament, especially the fourth on equal partnership between men and women. Questions may be raised about what is compatible or incompatible with this, for instance: the Vatican's stance on contraception and abortion; the different religious duties for men and women in Islam (attendance at the mosque for Friday prayers is not considered obligatory for women, which must be seen in the context of the Qu'ran's endorsement of a full spiritual equality between men and women); some forms of Judaism divide men's and women's spheres as, respectively, public space and private space (that is, the home). The first directive on non-violence also raises issues between those who would endorse an absolute pacifist position (Jains and some Buddhists) and those who enjoin self-defence as valid, even religiously mandated (some Muslims and Khalsa Sikhs). It is not clear that endorsing a universal Global Ethic is as easy as is sometimes assumed.[14]

A Western liberal agenda? This concern has been raised by many, and some see it as its greatest weakness. Recognizing that advocates of

---

13 Hedges, 'Concerns', p. 158.

14 Knitter (*One Earth*, Chapter 6), for instance, sees concern for the world as being a linking factor, but this would involve certain readings of certain texts within certain traditions in ways not all within those traditions would endorse.

a Global Ethic are not Western cultural–ethical imperialists, and that Küng in particular consulted widely on a global scale, it is still perceived by many as a Western document, or at least a Western-inspired/shaped document. As a Global Ethic is often seen as associated with a pluralist stance, it is perhaps interesting to observe that John Hick exercises some caution over the project. Indeed, it is worth quoting at some length his response as a Protestant to Swidler's proposals:

> The difficulty in offering a distinctively Christian comment . . . is that it is already . . . a Christian document. For since the European 'Enlightenment' of the eighteenth century Western Christianity has been increasingly suffused with the individualistic, democratic, liberal, historically-minded, science-oriented outlook of the Enlightenment, an outlook that constitutes what can comprehensively be called the ethos of 'modernity.' Indeed Christianity . . . is identified in the minds of many . . . with these liberal ideals of modernity . . . For . . . secular modernity has transformed the outlook of most of the Christian world . . .[15]

While Hick has rightly noted that the fact that it originates in the West does not mean it can be dismissed as 'Western', the fact that he has also called for a range of responses originating from every religious culture suggests that this problem still remains an issue. Four issues can arise:[16]

First, why should others want to respond to a Western document?

Second, even if they do other cultures may find their responses subsumed in a dominant Western discourse.

---

15 Hick, John (1999), 'Towards a Universal Declaration of a Global Ethic: A Christian Comment', in Swidler, Leonard (ed.), *For All Life*, Ashland: White Cloud Press (this paper may also be found at, http://astro.temple.edu/~dialogue/Center/hick.htm), pp. 100–1. For Hick's views on the Global Ethic generally see Hick, John (2007), 'Is there a Global Ethic?', lecture at the Centre for the Study of Global Ethics, University of Birmingham, UK, February 2007, http://www.johnhick.org.uk/ethic.pdf, accessed 27 March 2008.

16 Hedges, 'Concerns', pp. 160–1.

Third, should we even be proposing a Global Ethic now? Are we not presenting localized discourses to be brought into conversation?

Fourth, should we be seeking a Global Ethic at all? May we not be better off with a number of localized and contextual ethics which can dialogue and relate with one another?

As we have seen there are definite power relations built into the current dynamic of dialogue and religious discourse (see, especially, Chapters 2 and 3), and the assumption that somehow dialogue, especially within this context, should or must lead to a single unified answer may not allow us to 'celebrate religious diversity as something really precious'.[17] As R. S. Sugirtharajah, a Sri Lankan post-colonial theologian working in the UK, has pointed out, Third World concerns get 'smoothed out' in 'First World' contexts, which relates to what we have said of the need for realizing that we are all doing contextual theology, which requires a repositioning of assumptions and controlling narratives (see Chapter 1).[18]

Are the faiths monolithic? In relation to our earlier discussions around the nature of 'religion' this is pertinent (see Chapters 2 and 5). Most of the examples set forward to discuss this area make neat characterizations of what is *the* 'Christian', 'Islamic', 'Hindu', 'Buddhist', etc. ethical position. This certainly tends to both promote an elite reading from the educated and powerful figures who are seen to 'represent' their traditions, as well as effacing little traditions and diversity. The most nuanced positions do little more than distinguish denominationally. Also, in relation to my first point, it serves to distance those who don't fit within this picture, so followers of 'true religion' may be seen as those who fit the ethical criteria laid down, and others can be branded as extremists or not following their religion: 'Such a reading, of "proper" and "improper" traditions, simply serves to "other" the

---

17 Schmidt-Leukel, Perry, 2005, 'Tolerance and appreciation', *Current Dialogue* 46, available at, www.wcc-coe.org/wcc/what/interreligious/cd46-05.html, accessed 3 June 2010.

18 Sugirtharajah, R. S., 2003, *Postcolonial Reconfigurations: An Alternative Way of Reading the Bible and Doing Theology*, London: SCM, p. 162.

Other.'[19] Such concerns were seen voiced by Russell McCutcheon in relation to Interreligious Dialogue, and here it can be seen relating to what he calls:

the 'no cost Other,' whose concerns we can easily take on board, and whose wants and needs are 'of such obviously universal significance that the inevitable distance between some posited "us" and "them" can be overlooked' (McCutcheon 2006: 11). But what, he asks, of those Others who do not meet our requirements for 'civility' and 'decency,' and who 'despite holding the sort of "deep beliefs" that we are so often told we ought to respect, happen to hold the wrong set of deep beliefs' (McCutcheon 2006: 22). McCutcheon's answer is that 'we withhold the classifications "religion," "faithful," and "spiritual,"' while 'they can be understood as deviants . . . or portrayed . . . as enemies' (*ibid.*).[20]

Certainly the Global Ethic project needs to attend to the way it ignores diversities of views, and can sideline those who do not fit its basic premises. One way that Knitter proposes to get beyond this, is the common experience of suffering, which relates to our final point.[21]

Can we hear the voice of the excluded? It has been argued that many of the voices we must most urgently hear and attend to are those which are hardest to hear. As such, in expressing a Global Ethic we tend to see privileged elites setting out what is good and just for the less privileged. This is a double-edged sword, because while it is very easy to dismiss

19 See Hedges, 'Concerns', pp. 162-3. A similar concern was voiced by a colleague of mine, Dr Anna King, at a recent interfaith event we both attended, where we challenged one speaker on the way certain strands of religion were judged to be inauthentic, or not representative of what that religion actually teaches at its true core.

20 Hedges, 'Concerns', p. 162, citing McCutcheon, Russell, 2006, 'The Costs of Discipleship: On the Limits of the Humanistic Study of Religion', lecture delivered at the University of Toronto, http://www.as.ua.edu/rel/pdf/mccutchdiscipleship. pdf, accessed 27 March 2008.

21 Knitter, *One Earth*, pp. 56-7.

this as patronizing, it must also be recognized that there is a legitimate concern in seeking to protect the rights of those who lack voice and power. However, the Global Ethic needs to be aware that it walks a fine line here.

Do we want a global ethic?

While we must be deeply sympathetic to the ideal that all religions can work together in the pursuit of human justice, the alleviation of poverty, ecological destruction and other issues, I believe we are right to remain unconvinced that, at least as presently formulated, the Global Ethic is the answer. Certainly, Alan Race is right in suggesting that the problems should sound a warning rather than stopping ethical dialogue; however, we may need to rethink how we advance this area of thought.[22] One major problem is that it often seems to be assumed that we more or less have *the* Global Ethic, and that all it may need is a little bit of local colour, a notion criticized by Fu Shan Zhao.[23] Zhao argues that much more dialogue is needed for anything 'meaningful and fruitful' to be achieved.[24] In the light of such concerns, we may suggest that the Global Ethic documents

---

22 In response to the criticisms I have raised Race offers what is probably the best defence of the current set-up of the Global Ethic (Race, 'Interfaith', pp. 163ff.).

23 Zhao, Fu Shan, 1999, 'For Dialogue on a Global Ethic: A Confucian/Taoist View', in Swidler, (ed.), *For*. I have argued that Swidler is mistaken in seeing Zhao's position as substantively the same as his, failing to see his radical critique (Hedges, 'Interfaith', pp. 121–2; on this see also p. 123, especially the references to Widdows, Heather, 2007, 'Is Global Ethics Moral Neo-colonialism? An Investigation of the Issue in the Context of Bioethics', *Bioethics* 21.6, pp. 305–15, and Katongole, Emmanuel, 2000, 'Postmodern Illusions and the Challenges of African Theology: The Ecclesial Tactics of Resistance', *Modern Theology* 16.2, pp. 237–254.

24 Zhao, 'Dialogue', p. 153; see also Hick, 'Is There'. I believe that Hick has moved from a position that more closely mirrored that of Küng and Swidler in his earlier work (Hick, 'Towards') to one that more closely matches my own in his latest thought in the area: 'a global ethic remains to be uncovered, and that to do this requires world-wide consultation going beyond the present Western versions' (Hick, 'Is There', p. 16).

may be re-envisaged as 'an ethic to the globe' in which instead of being seen as bases for a global ethic, we understand them as the local presentations of how we want to act ethically in global terms.[25] That is to say, understand them as Western Christian documents for an idealized way for us to behave – certainly it is clear that the Western 'Christian' world hardly lives up to these ideals! They may also be seen, therefore, as the initiation of a debate about global ethical thinking, inviting others to respond. At present, they act too much as a template.[26]

Challenging our ethical norms

To truly allow global ethical thinking to reflect the differences between cultures, we can argue that the following three principles are useful:

1. A respect and acknowledgement of diversity, not as something negative, but as the very centre point from which we can grow and develop.
2. A belief that no single answer will do justice to the diversity of positions that we find expressed in the many and varied faith systems around the world.
3. A desire to respect differences and live in encounter with the views of those who may be very different, and even challenging and disturbing to our own.[27]

Accepting and learning from difference may involve some difficult revisualizations and reworkings of our ideas.[28] For instance, as Western 'liberals', we may be uncomfortable with the treatment of women in certain parts of, for instance, the Middle East and Central Asia (the Islamic world?), such as enforced veiling and the lack of access to education and other 'rights'. However, it may be better that we accept this

25 I develop this argument more fully in Hedges, 'Interfaith'.
26 See Hedges, 'Interfaith', pp. 120–6.
27 Hedges, 'Interfaith', p. 125.
28 What follows is an example used in Hedges, 'Interfaith', p. 124.

with tolerance, although engaging dialogically, and posing alternatives, with those who hold these views, instead of making demands that they change their customs and culture because it offends our sensibilities, or telling the Other that their ways do not match a Global Ethic and its demands of 'equal rights' – which, as we have noted, they may believe they already meet in their own terms. Perhaps there are things we can learn. For instance, the whole culture of veiling has been lambasted by Western (and Islamic) feminists; however, an increasing number of intelligent and educated Muslim women around the world are now choosing to take the veil. For many, it is a statement of faith, and morality, against the permissiveness of 'Western' society and values. It is also, for some, a way to be treated as a person – that people will react to the mind and intellect, rather than simply physical appearance. There are, then, positive virtues in the practice, which twenty, or even ten, years ago may have passed unnoticed.[29]

Our ideals of Western individualism and openness are seen by many others as instances of the moral decay and the decadence and debauchery of much Western 'civilization'. Indeed, sometimes it is hard not to extol the virtues of social cohesion and collective and personal responsibility found in certain less 'open' and 'free' systems and cultures. Certainly, it may well be the case that many religious values conflict with the norms of Western cultures, and we should, of course, note that this would include a Christian critique too.[30]

Our desire to found global ethical thinking upon a variety of systems should not lead us to relativism, and we should certainly be aware of Twiss' observation that the suffering and poor of the world desire

---

29 See Geaves, Ron (2005), *Aspects of Islam*, Washington, DC: Georgetown University Press, p. 232, and Dwyer, Claire (1999), 'Veiled Meanings: Young British Muslim Women and the Negotiations of Differences', *Gender, Place and Culture*, 6.1, pp. 5–26.

30 I have argued this in Hedges, Paul, 2008, 'Negotiating a Possible Basis for Human Rights Discourse between the Western (Christian), Islamic and Chinese (Confucian) Contexts', paper delivered at the 1st International Winchester Interfaith Conference on 'Interfaith Dialogue in Modernity and Post-modernity', Winchester University, UK.

a Global Ethic or common set of Human Rights and it is oppressors who would welcome an ethic that respects their own 'cultural norms'.[31] We have discussed the 'excluded' above, and in relation to this I would fully endorse Knitter's claim that we should privilege sufferers in these issues.[32] Certainly, we do not wish to give succour to Third World dictators or First World polluters! Knitter has suggested that 'the most effective way to carry on a correlational dialogue among religions is to make it a globally responsible dialogue', which will include 'suffering persons and the suffering Earth'.[33] While I concur fully with his intention, my suggestion is that we move the basis of our thinking, which does not mean no longer asking challenging questions and voicing our moral outrage, but, while doing this, to also take seriously the questions that challenge us and also listening to the voices of moral outrage directed towards us.[34] This, I believe, may lead us to realign some of our premises which have fallen too smoothly into place.

Human Rights, religious wrongs: some tentative suggestions

I will end this with some observations on how hearing other voices will lead us to question our own assumptions and basic standpoints. Some of this may seem controversial or shocking, but until we are able to be radically open enough to let our fundamental values be challenged we have not truly engaged in the moves towards mutual fulfilment (see Chapter 6). With our focus on ethical issues, let us look at Human Rights. This may seem a simple and straightforward point of agreement, but it is not: some Others (non-Western, non-elite) may need 'protection' against these 'rights'. Sometimes the neoliberal interests that promote

---

31 Twiss, Sumner B. (2000), 'Religion and Human Rights: A Comparative Perspective', in Twiss, Sumner B. and Grelle, Bruce (eds), *Explorations in Global Ethics: Comparative Religious Ethics and Interreligious Dialogue*, Boulder: Westview, pp. 157–9.

32 Knitter, *One Earth*, pp. 87–93.

33 Knitter, *One Earth*, p. 17.

34 See Boff, Leonardo, *Global Civilization: Challenges to Society and Christianity*, trans. Alexandre Guilherme, London: Equinox, pp. 48–51.

Human Rights see free trade as having priority over moral or humanitarian concerns, arguing that free trade will inevitably improve conditions in countries where these are seen as weak.[35] However, transnational corporations (TNCs) move their workforces around the world seeking those countries who will offer the lowest overheads, that is, the minimum wages and other benefits[36] and, as such, the globalization of Human Rights goes hand in hand with economic exploitation. Instances of violations of Human Rights stemming from TNCs and so-called 'free trade' abound.[37] In such instances, it is clear that the notion of 'rights', my 'right' to cheap food, clothes, a car, foreign holidays, etc. are part of the problem.[38] I am not urging that we abandon the concept of Human Rights or Global Ethics, but we must realize that we have only provisional and not idealized systems and representations of what we would wish these to be. Moreover, in practice they can be employed in ways which are both positive and negative.

In relation to these issues, how do the reflections on the theology of religions and interreligious dialogue outlined here help? At the bottom line, it must be seen that we should not seek either unity, a claim that all religio-cultural systems have the same ethical standpoint, nor promote 'difference' which leads either to ethical colonialism or relativism (the post-liberal particularist stance appears utterly impractical in such a situation). Rather, by embracing a 'radical openness' we may be ready to understand the situation we and others find, which may involve a critique of our own ethical norms, even a critique of the way we, in the Western world, frame a Human Rights or Global Ethics discourse; but this is not to deride their value, or to say that we should, or cannot, challenge others on ethical imperatives. We should be aware that while the stance of radical openness I have endorsed may seem linked to what many may see as

---

35 Evans, Tony, 2005, *The Politics of Human Rights*, 2nd edn, London and Ann Arbor, MI: Pluto Press, p. 77.

36 Evans, *Politics*, p. 88.

37 Evans, *Politics*, 90–9.

38 These ideas are explored in Hedges, 'Negotiating', which suggests that a religious critique of Human Rights may even be called for. I hope to explore the issues around this further in future papers and publications.

a liberal agenda in various ways, it is not simply a call for those often seen as more 'conservative' to change and be challenged by the Other, but for all of us to recognize where we must be challenged. Whether theologically, ethically, politically or socially a radical openness to the Other will involve a questioning of our standpoints.

Moreover, while I have stressed some problems with seeking to find common ethical ground we must hold the tension between difference and unity. In this regard, to focus on the question of Human Rights we may say the following. Having developed in a Western cultural context, the notion of Human Rights has a basis in a Christian tradition (with Jewish and Greek elements), but this does not, however, mean we must believe it is the only system that expresses these ideas. It has been convincingly argued that the African, Confucian and other religious cultures, in many practical ways, are alive to concerns related to what we in the West would term 'Human Rights'.[39] I would argue that where commonality can be found is in the notion of 'human dignity'.[40] This does not entail us finding a single common denominator, rather finding common ground upon which our different systems can agree and work in harmony. Certainly there will be many disagreements in the particulars, but those are issues to be worked out in context. It goes beyond the scope of this chapter to try and work out the details of this in specific contexts. However, we

---

39 See: Zhao, 'For Dialogue'; Liu, Shu-Hsien, 1999, 'Reflections on Approaches to Universal Ethics from a Contemporary Neo-Confucian Perspective', in Swidler, Leonard (ed.), *For All Life*, Ashland: White Cloud Press; Nkulu, Mutombo, 1999, 'The African Charter on Human and People's Rights: An African Contribution to the Project of Global Ethic', in Swidler (ed.), *For All Life* (this paper may also be found at http://astro.temple.edu/~dialogue/Center/mutombo.htm); Mitra, Kana, 1999, 'A Hindu Dialogue on a Global Ethic', in Swidler (ed.), *For All Life*; Shaffer, Ingrid, 1999, 'Philosophical and Religious Foundations of a Global Ethic' (available at, http://astro.temple.edu/~dialogue/Center/shafer.htm, accessed 15 January 2001).

40 Hedges, 'Negotiating'. This paper specifically focused on the Confucian and Islamic traditions, but I believe it is equally applicable to at least some other traditions (including at least Christian and Buddhist). Moreover, I hope this will also represent a variety of positions within each tradition, rather than presenting each as a monolith with one voice.

may note two particular ideas that Knitter, in dialogue with others, has brought into this question which are pertinent to our concerns. First, as Knitter argues, citing David Tracy, responsibility is inherent in the religious conversation in this area.[41] I believe this accords with what I have just suggested is the place of human dignity. Second, making use of the thought of Michael Amaladoss, Knitter observes that this area will take us beyond those things seen as explicitly 'religious'.[42] As argued previously (Chapter 2) if the 'religious' realm is, in many ways, indistinguishable from the 'secular' realm (recognizing the provisionality of these terms, and the way borders are very much culturally and tradition specific and, indeed, in many contexts make no coherent sense as understood in terms of the modern Western connotations) we should expect interreligious dialogue and the theology of religions not simply to lead us, in the creation of identity, to some cosy spiritual home at some idealized level, but to be inherently drawn into the liberative praxis of religion at social, political and ethical levels.

Conclusions

These final reflections on global religious ethics are only some brief investigations and can do little more than hint at lines of enquiry. Nevertheless, we may hope they would indicate why it is important that we resolve the impasse in Christian thinking in relation to interreligious encounter. A more adequate (dare we say 'correct'?) way of visually interreligious relations, I believe, will allow us not just to have the radical openness to religious Others that we need to understand and redirect ourselves and our theology, but it also allows us to address ethical, social and political issues as well (which we must understand are not divorced from the

---

41 Knitter, *One Earth*, p. 56, citing Tracy, David, 1987, *Plurality and Ambiguity: Hermeneutics, Religion, Hope*, New York: Harper and Row, p. 91.

42 Knitter, *One Earth*, pp. 138–9, citing, Amaladoss, Michael, 1992, 'Liberation as an Interreligious Project', in Wilfred, Felix (ed.), *Leave the Temple: Indian Paths to Human Liberation*, Maryknoll, NY: Orbis, pp. 159–74, p. 166.

religious realm). As such, I would suggest that the theology of religions is not an obscure area for male, theoretical, Western academics to discuss issues of salvation, rather a clarification of it is an integral part of what we must do as global beings, at least speaking from within the Christian tradition. Yet, such clarification towards the radical openness I believe our tradition entails, does not give us easy answers. We cannot move glibly or easily into a mutual fulfilment of ethical concepts based around certain things we already, more or less, agree on – this I believe is the current failure of many attempts to work towards a Global Ethic. Rather, we need to be radically challenged in our religious and ethical certainties and open to other voices, positions and worldviews. As such, I do not pretend to end with answers, rather with challenges for the road ahead which, I hope, will unbalance and unsettle us all who too easily live in comfortable religious, ethical and cultural houses.

Further Reading

Readings that will explore the issues and ideas found in each chapter are given here. In some cases, the same work will be found as suggested reading for several chapters, which tends to indicate the significance of it. The readings vary from those which explore a particular point of view, to those which provide major background to the ideas of that chapter. As such, they are not given because they endorse similar ideas to those I expound within this text, but are intended as a guide to exploring the themes found within each chapter further.

Chapter 1

Clooney, Francis, 2010, *Comparative Theology: Meaning and Practice*, Chichester: Wiley-Blackwell.

Fletcher, Jeannine Hill, 2008, 'Religious Pluralism in an Era of Globalization: The Making of Modern Religious Identity', *Theological Studies* 69, pp. 394–411.

Hedges, Paul and Race, Alan (eds), 2008, *SCM Core Text Christian Approaches to Other Faiths*, London: SCM.

Jeanrond, Werner G., 2002, 'Belonging or Identity? Christian Faith in a Multi-Religious World', in Cornille, Catherine (ed.), *Many Mansions? Christian Identity and Multiple Religious Belonging*, Maryknoll, NY: Orbis, pp. 106–20.

Küster, Volker, 2005, 'The Project of an Intercultural Theology', *Swedish Missiological Themes* 93:3, pp. 417–32.

Kwok, Pui-lan, 2007, 'Theology and Social Theory', in Kwok, Pui-lan, Rieger, Joerg and Compier, Don H. (eds), *Empire and the Christian Tradition: New Readings of Classical Theologians*, Minneapolis, MN: Fortress Press, pp. 15–29.

Panikkar, Raimon, 2002, 'On Christian Identity: Who is a Christian?', in Cornille, Catherine (ed.), *Many Mansions? Multiple Religious Belonging and Christian Identity*, Maryknoll, NY: Orbis, pp. 121–44.

Schmidt-Leukel, Perry, 2009, *Transformation by Integration: How Inter-faith Encounter Changes Christianity*, London: SCM.

Schreiter, Robert J., 2004, *The New Catholicity: Theology between the Global and the Local*, Maryknoll, NY: Orbis.

Woodhead, Linda, 2004, *An Introduction to Christianity*, Cambridge: Cambridge University Press.

Chapter 2

Ariarajah, Wesley S., 2002, 'Power, Politics, and Plurality: The Struggles of the World Council of Churches to Deal with Religious Plurality', in Knitter, Paul F. (ed.), *The Myth of Religious Supremacy*, Maryknoll, NY: Orbis, pp. 76–93.

Clarke, J. J., 1997, *Oriental Enlightenment: The Encounter between Asian and Western Thought*, London: Routledge.

Cornille, Catherine (ed.), 2002, *Many Mansions? Christian Identity and Multiple Religious Belonging*, Maryknoll, NY: Orbis.

Fitzgerald, Timothy, 2007, *Discourse on Civility and Barbarity: A Critical History of Religion and Related Categories*, Oxford: Oxford University Press.

Hedges, Paul, 2006, 'Defining Religion', Part I, *Interreligious Insight* 4:3, pp. 9–15; 'Defining Religion: A Religious Orientation Typology', Part II, *Interreligious Insight* 4:4, pp. 34–42.

Hedges, Paul, 2010, 'Can We Still Teach "Religions"? Towards an Understanding of Religion as Culture and Orientation in Contemporary Pedagogy and Metatheory', in Durka, G, Gearon, L., de Souza, M., Engebretson, K. (eds), *International Handbook for Inter-Religious Education*, New York: Springer Academic Publishers.

Kwok, Pui-lan, 2005, *Postcolonial Imagination and Feminist Theology*, London: SCM.

Masuzawa, Tomoko, 2005, *The Invention of World Religions, Or, How European Universalism was Preserved in the Language of Pluralism*, Chicago, IL: University of Chicago Press.

Race, Alan, 2008, 'Interfaith Dialogue: Religious Accountability between Strangeness and Resonance', in Hedges, Paul and Race, Alan (eds),

SCM Core Text Christian Approaches to Other Faiths, London: SCM, pp. 155-72.

Chapter 3

Berling, Judith, 1997, *A Pilgrim in Chinese Culture: Negotiating Religious Diversity*, Eugene, OR: Wipf and Stock.

Cheetham, David, 2003, *John Hick: A Critical Introduction and Reflection*, Aldershot: Ashgate.

Eck, Diana, 1993, *Encountering God: A Spiritual Journey from Bozeman to Banaras*, Boston: Beacon Press.

Griffin, David Ray, 2005, 'Religious Pluralism: Generic, Identist, Deep', in Griffin, David Ray (ed.), *Deep Religious Pluralism*, Louisville, KY: Westminster John Knox Press, pp. 3-38.

Hick, John, 1989, *An Interpretation of Religion: Human Responses to the Transcendent*, Basingstoke: Macmillan.

Knitter, Paul F., 2005, 'Is the Pluralist Model a Western Imposition? A Response in Five Voices', in Knitter, Paul F., *The Myth of Religious Superiority: A Multifaith Exploration*, Maryknoll, NY: Orbis, pp. 28-42.

Phan, Peter, 2004, *Being Religious Interreligiously: Asian Perspectives on Interfaith Dialogue*, Maryknoll, NY: Orbis.

Schmidt-Leukel, Perry, 2008, 'Pluralisms: How to Approach Religious Diversity Theologically', in Hedges, Paul and Race, Alan (eds), *SCM Core Text Christian Approaches to Other Faiths*, London: SCM, pp. 85-110.

Schmidt-Leukel, Perry, 2009, *Transformation by Integration: How Inter-faith Encounter Changes Christianity*, London: SCM.

Schmidt-Leukel, Perry (ed.), 2009, 'Pluralisms', in Hedges, Paul and Race, Alan (eds), *SCM Reader Christian Approaches to Other Faiths*, London: SCM, pp. 41-58.

Chapter 4

D'Costa, Gavin, 2000, *The Meeting of Religions and the Trinity*, London: Continuum.

DiNoia, J. A., 1992, *The Diversity of Religions: A Christian Perspective*, Washington, DC: The Catholic University of America Press.

Griffiths, Paul J., 2001, *Problems of Religious Diversity*, Oxford: Blackwell.

Hedges, Paul, 2002, 'The Inter-Relationships of Religions: some critical reflections on the concept of particularity', *World Faiths Encounter* 32, pp. 3ff., 3–13.

Hedges, P., 2008, 'Particularities: tradition-specific post-modern perspectives', in Hedges, Paul and Race, Alan (eds), *SCM Core Text Christian Approaches to Other Faiths*, London: SCM, pp. 112–35.

Hedges, Paul, 2009, 'Particularities', in Hedges, Paul and Race, Alan (eds), *SCM Reader Christian Approaches to Other Faiths*, London: SCM, pp. 61–70.

Lindbeck, George, 1984, *The Nature of Doctrine: The Church in a Postmodern Age*, Philadelphia: Westminster Press.

McGrath, A., 1996, 'A Particularist View: A Post-Enlightenment Approach', in Okholm, D. L. and Phillips, T. R. (eds), *Four Views on Salvation in a Pluralistic World*, Grand Rapids: Zondervan, 151–80.

Chapter 5

Chung, Hyun Kyung, 1990, *Struggle to Be the Sun Again: Introducing Asian Women's Theology*, Maryknoll, NY: Orbis Books.

Egnell, Helene, 2006, *Other Voices: A Study of Christian Feminist Approaches to Religious Plurality East and West*, Uppsala: Studia Missionalia Svecana.

Fletcher, Jeannine Hill, 2003, 'Shifting Identity: The Contribution of Feminist Thought to Theologies of Religious Pluralism', *Journal of Feminist Studies in Religion* 19, pp. 5–24.

Fletcher, Jeannine Hill, 2008, 'Feminisms: Syncretism, Symbiosis, Synergetic Dance', in Hedges, Paul and Race, Alan (eds), *SCM Core Text Christian Approaches to Other Faiths*, London: SCM, pp. 136–54.

Fletcher, Jeannine Hill, 2009, 'Feminisms', in Hedges, Paul and Race, Alan (eds), *SCM Reader Christian Approaches to Other Faiths*, London: SCM, pp. 71–85.

King, Ursula, 1998, 'Feminism: the missing dimension in the dialogue of religions', in May, John D'Arcy (ed.), *Pluralism and the Religions: The Theological and Political Dimensions*, London: Cassell, pp. 40–55.

McCarthy, Kate, 1996, 'Women's Experience as a Hermeneutical Key to a Christian Theology of Religions', *Studies in Interreligious Dialogue* 6.2, pp. 163–73, p. 165 (this is reprinted in Fletcher, Jeannine Hill, 2009,

'Feminisms', in Hedges, Paul and Race, Alan (eds), *SCM Reader Christian Approaches to Other Faiths*, London: SCM, pp. 71–85, pp. 75–84.

O'Neill, Maura, 2007, *Mending a Torn World: Women in Interreligious dialogue*, Maryknoll, NY: Orbis.

Suchocki, Marjorie H., 1988, 'In Search of Justice: Religious Pluralism from a Feminist Perspective', in Hick, John and Knitter, Paul F. (eds), *The Myth of Christian Uniqueness*, London: SCM, pp. 149–61.

Chapter 6

Aleaz, K. P., 2005, 'Pluralism Calls for Pluralistic Inclusivism: An Indian Christian Experience', in Knitter, Paul F. (ed.), *The Myth of Religious Superiority: A Multifaith Exploration*, Maryknoll, NY: Orbis, pp. 162–75.

Chung, Hyun Kyung, 1997, 'Seeking the Religious Roots of Pluralism', *Journal of Ecumenical Studies* 34:3, pp. 400–1, reprinted in Fletcher, Jeannine Hill, 2009, 'Feminisms', in Hedges, Paul and Race, Alan (eds), *SCM Reader Christian Approaches to Other Faiths*, London: SCM, pp. 72–5.

Fletcher, Jeannine Hill, 2008, 'Feminisms: Syncretism, Symbiosis, Synergetic Dance', in Hedges, Paul and Race, Alan (eds), *SCM Core Text Christian Approaches to Other Faiths*, London: SCM, pp. 136–54.

Keenan, John P., 2009, *Grounding Our Faith in a Pluralist World – with a little help from Nāgārjuna*, Eugene, OR: Wipf and Stock.

Oduyoye, Mercy Amba, 2003, 'African Culture and the Gospel: Inculturation from an African Woman's Perspective', in Oduyoye, Mercy Amba and Vroom, Hendrik (eds), *One Gospel – Many Cultures: Case Studies and Reflections on Cross-Cultural Theology*, Amsterdam: Rodopi, pp. 39–62.

Pieris, Aloysius, 1996, *Fire and Water: Basic Issues in Asian Buddhism and Christianity*, Maryknoll, NY: Orbis.

Schmidt-Leukel, Perry, 2009, *Transformation by Integration: How Inter-faith Encounter Changes Christianity*, London: SCM.

WCC website: 2006, 'Religious plurality and Christian self-understanding', available at http://www.oikoumene.org/fileadmin/files/wccassembly/documents/english/pb-14-religiousplurality.pdf, accessed 10 September 2009.

Williams, Rowan, 2006, 'Christian Identity and Religious Plurality', Plenary Session Paper from the World Council of Churches Assembly, Porto

Alegre, available at http://www.oikoumene.org/en/resources/documents/ assembly/porto-alegre-2006/2-plenary-presentations/christian-identity-religious-plurality/rowan-williams-presentation.html, accessed 4 August 2009.

Chapter 7

Hedges, Paul, 2008, 'Are Interfaith Dialogue and a Global Ethic Compatible? A Call for an Ethic to the Globe', *The Journal for Faith, Spirituality and Social Change* 1:2, pp. 109–32.

Hedges, Paul, 2008, 'Concerns about the Global Ethic: A Sympathetic Critique and Suggestions for a New Direction', *Studies in Interreligious Dialogue* 18:1 (Fall), pp. 153–68.

Hick, John (2007), 'Is there a Global Ethic?', lecture at the Centre for the Study of Global Ethics, University of Birmingham, UK, February 2007, http:// www.johnhick.org.uk/ethic.pdf, accessed 27 March 2008.

Katongole, Emmanuel, 2000, 'Postmodern Illusions and the Challenges of African Theology: The Ecclesial Tactics of Resistance', *Modern Theology* 16.2, pp. 237–54.

Knitter, Paul F., 1995, *One Earth, Many Religions: Multifaith Dialogue and Global Responsibility*, Maryknoll, NY: Orbis.

Küng, Hans, 1993, 'Declaration Toward a Global Ethic', in Küng, Hans and Kuschel, Karl-Josef (eds), *A Global Ethic: The Declaration of the Parliament of the World's Religions*, London: SCM Press, pp. 23–4.

Santos, Boaventura de Sousa, 1999, 'Towards a Multicultural Conception of Human Rights', in Featherstone, Mike and Lash, Scott (eds), *Spaces of Culture: City, Nation, World*, London: Sage Publications Ltd, pp. 214–29.

Swidler, Leonard (ed.), 1999, *For All Life*, Ashland: White Cloud Press.

Twiss, Sumner, 1998, 'A Constructive Framework for Discussing Confucianism and Human Rights', in Tu, Weiming and Bary, Wm. Theodore de (eds), *Confucianism and Human Rights*, New York: Columbia University Press, pp. 27–53.

Index of Biblical References

Index

Note: references to words, names and terms in this index do not necessarily denote a reference to that precise term, that is, references to mission cover missionaries, missiology, etc.